The
EARTH
KEEPER

Undeveloping the Future

*The Extraordinary Story of an Earth Conqueror Turned
Preservationist Who Uncovers Our True Nature and
Reveals the Creative Power of the Universe*

ADAM C. HALL

Foreword by Alberto Villoldo, Ph.D.

Agape Media International
Los Angeles, California

Agape Media International

Published by
Agape Media International, LLC
5700 Buckingham Parkway
Culver City, California 90230
310.258.4401
www.agapeme.com

HAY
HOUSE

Distributed by Hay House, Inc.
P.O. Box 5100, Carlsbad, CA 92018-5100
(760)-431-7695 or (800)-654-5126

Hay House USA: *www.hayhouse.com*®
Hay House UK: *www.hayhouse.co.uk*
Hay House Australia: *www.hayhouse.com.au*
Hay House South Africa: *www.hayhouse.co.za*
Hay House India: *www.hayhouse.co.in*

Book Credits
Executive In Charge Of Publication: Stephen Powers
Editor: Fu Ding Cheng
Cover and Interior Design by Frame25 Productions
Author Photograph by Lizanne Judge
Cover Photograph by andreiuc88 c/o Shutterstock.com
Logo and Website Design by Ray Campbell and Ben Guevera
Creative Advisor: Laurel Arica
Representation: William Gladstone

© 2013 Adam C. Hall

The author of this book does not dispense medical advice or prescribe the use of any technique as a form of treatment for physical, emotional, or medical problems, without the advice of a physician, either directly or indirectly. The intent of the author is only to offer information of a general nature to help you in your quest for emotional and spiri-tual well-being. In the event you use any of the information in this book for yourself, which is your constitutional right, the author and the publisher assume no responsibil-ity for your actions.

UnDevelopment™ is a registered trademark of Chaska Holdings, Inc.

Printed in USA on recycled paper.

Hardcover ISBN: 978-1-4019-42526
Digital ISBN: 978-1-4019-4253-3

Library of Congress Cataloging-In Publication Data available upon request

I am responsible for what I see
I choose the feelings I experience, and I decide
Upon the goal I would achieve
And everything that seems to happen to me
I ask for, and receive as I have asked

I have done this thing, and it is this that I shall undo.

—A Course in Miracles

To my beloved mother Marian
To my Kaliana Mitra Lizanne
To our Great Mother Earth GAIA

Together you have shown me the way home
Thank you for the guidance, love, and wisdom
Your gifts reflect the divinity of the one heart of love

—Adam

ACKNOWLEDGMENTS

My life has been blessed with the following great Collaborators, the "cast" in my play called life. Each of them shared their gifts. Some still do. Each of them has made a difference. Each of them touched my life. All of them are brilliant, magnificent, and glorious beings. In deep gratitude and love.

B. Gladstone, agent.
"I am doing you a favor."

S. Powers, publisher.
"Earth Day 2013 will be your day."

FD. Cheng, editor.
"Show it, feel it, live it!"

J. Rasmussen, shaman.
"You are the one you've been waiting for."

M. Burns, friend.
"Let me crunch the numbers."

M. L. Hall, daughter.
"I love you to infinity and beyond."

S. E. Hall, daughter.
"Forever your little girl...truly."

M. M. Hall, daughter.
"We want you to come home."

L. Hall, granddaughter.
"Gage."

G. Darling, ex-wife.
"What are you, the Dalai Lama?"

S. Ritchie, friend.
"I'm Switzerland."

A. Brown, friend.
"You will tap the secrets of the universe."

B. Morris, friend.
"You're a brother to me."

S. Smooke, friend.
"Come on, Hall, I got to get to work."

B. May, friend.
"I love you."

D. Mapes, friend.
"Enjoy the playground, earth brother."

L. Vincent, teacher.
"Believe, believe, and believe."

S. Darling, ex-father-in-law.
"Adam, you're a brave man."

R. Fuller, teacher.
"Lift your head about the cacophony of social distortion."

Ben Hall, brother.
"Can you feel the butterfly."

Jenny Hall, sister.
"Get out, you can walk home."

Peter Hall, brother.
"What should I do?"

Lem Hall, father.
"You are all Golden!"

Phyllis Siebert, grandmother.
"God loves you."

L. Birkbeck, astrologer.
"All true leaders know what they are following!"

L. McClosky.
"Being human is often so difficult and so extraordinary."

CONTENTS

FOREWORD

By Alberto Villoldo, Ph.D.

"Only the one who dies truly lives."[1]

At the heart of every esoteric teaching is a potent secret that has been kept from all but the shamans, priests and high initiates—in part, to prevent its catastrophic misuse. This secret, hidden from the masses for millennia, is that the Creative Power of the Universe is hidden within each one of us. When we discover this power and use it responsibly, each of us can dream into existence the fulfillment of our greatest destiny.

In the last few years, the secret of our innate power has become part of popular culture—as witnessed by such now-familiar adages as, "We create our own reality" or "Ask and it is given." Many people try to apply these truths to get what they want from life—with varying degrees of success.

Few understand that the deepest nature of this secret is that we each have to master ourselves for any of its outer magic to really lift us to a place of lasting happiness. One who did learn this essential key—to a profound degree—is the author of this book, a man who achieved the American Dream in all its glory and then woke up to the nightmare of his own life condition.

It is thus a great pleasure for me to write the foreword to this memoir of awakening and transformation by a man who has been both my

---

1 Anand Mehrotra, Yogi, Quoted by David Ottenheimer, flyingpenguin.com

student and my friend—Adam C. Hall. At the time our paths first crossed in 2005, Adam was already well along in his journey through a life-changing metamorphosis that would ultimately alter his mind-set from Earth Conqueror to Earth Keeper.

To come this far, Adam had to come to terms with the misery that was at the center of his very privileged and comfortable life. He had been compelled by circumstances to recognize and release many of the conventional delusions that were draining the joy from his existence. And he had endured the loss of all that he treasured most. It was only then that Adam was finally able to open to discover the priceless treasure that is a living presence within every human heart.

When we first met, this very palpable presence had become the guiding force in Adam's life. Still, he had not yet found his highest destiny—the Calling of his Soul for service to the greater community of life.

A Time Like None Other

What makes Adam's story so compelling is not only the skill with which it is told, or the details of his many daring (and often amusing) adventures—or even his willingness to bare his naked psyche to the judgment of his readers. The biggest reason why his story is so important is that it serves as a perfect mirror for our times.

We have entered an era like none other in history. The economy of the Western world and the ecology of the entire planet are threatened with the possibility of imminent collapse. But of even greater significance than these dire circumstances is the dramatic shift occurring within human consciousness—which gives rise to what we think of as Reality.

The ancient prophecies of the Hopi, Maya, and Inka (among others) all point to this moment—2012 and beyond—as the time when we step from one reality to the next. According to these prophecies, humanity will soon undergo a rapid evolution—within a single generation—that will affect all future generations. And evolve we must if we are to remain a viable species on a healthy planet.

The Father at War with the Mother

The precarious position that we find ourselves in is the culmination of an ancient conflict between two contrasting worldviews. One view is that of the conquistador who feels entitled to rule over the Earth; to plunder the planet's resources; to decimate human, animal, and plant populations at will; and to violate others with impunity in order to gain control over their minds and their property. This worldview derives from the belief in an angry, jealous and punishing masculine god who looks with favor upon those who "smite their enemy" in His name.

The other worldview belongs to a much older tradition: In nature-centric cultures around the world, it is the Great Mother who is recognized as the source of all life. And rather than being distant from—and demanding of—Her creation, She indwells and nurtures us all through endless cycles of life, death, and rebirth. In this view, it is the role of us humans to maintain harmony and balance within the Gaia's all-providing Garden.

History is essentially the story of those who conquered those who lived with an awareness of their place in the greater tapestry of life. It is the lack of this awareness of our oneness with—and responsibility toward—the whole of Creation that has brought us to the brink of extinction. But it is the very pressure of the extreme crises we now are facing that is adding impetus and urgency to the anticipated birth of a new, more illumined human.

Ancient Practices for Averting Contemporary Crises

Of the many people who come to work with me, Adam was among those who have had to travel the greatest distance in their own psyches to find their inner wisdom. This is because I am privileged to teach a very ancient indigenous wisdom that has the power to radically alter lives.

These teachings, which derive from a culture that honors the sacred feminine, were hidden for centuries from the European conquistadors and from the punishing religions that would sooner torture a person to death than allow him or her to practice beliefs that were not sanctioned by the Church. Such was their fear of the creative power of the Universe and of their need to control it by force if not by religious "conversion" in order to promote docility among those whose lands they had occupied.

How I came to acquire this knowledge is another story altogether—which I relate in my own books. But to summarize it quickly here, I am a medical anthropologist who had intended to study the healing practices of the high mountain shamans in the Americas. But in the course of this pursuit, I met a university professor, don Antonio, whose life was far richer than I could possibly have imagined.

Don Antonio was among the last of the Laika, an ancient society of high shaman priests who have lived in the Andes and the Amazon since time immemorial. Over the 25 years that don Antonio mentored me, I learned the wisdom teachings of his ancient lineage of EarthKeepers and became an initiate and practitioner of these sacred teachings. What Adam was seeking when he chose to journey with me to the Amazon and the high peaks of the Andean mountains were the keys that would grant him greater access to his own authentic Self and to the unlimited powers of creation that reside within us all—through which we can manifest our higher vision of reality. This is what I share with my students. The Laika call it *The Four Insights.*

Dog Eat Dog

Before his transformation was upon him, Adam was fully entrenched in the quality of consciousness that lays waste to the world. His way of manifesting his dreams was to pursue wealth and fortune relentlessly, without concern for the repercussions of his actions in other people's lives. It took a sudden wake-up call for him to finally recognize what his choices were doing to his *own* life—and then to care about their impact on others and the planet.

Adam believed in Survival of the Fittest and was determined to be among the "winners" in life—no matter how many losers he created in his wake. He behaved like a "millionaire jerk," as he describes it, because at the time greed seemed to his rational mind like the only practical way to operate.

Adam viewed his lavish lifestyle as validation of his predatory philosophy. But though he lived with his beautiful wife and three lovely daughters in a palatial home overlooking the ocean in Malibu, California—and experienced every comfort that wealth can buy—he was restless, angry, drinking too much, and a total stranger to himself. It took time for him to recognize that the ultimate source of health, wealth, and happiness is not our purchased possessions but our Self-possession.

Going for Broke

In *EarthKeeper*, Adam intimately shares how he discovered this truth and then applied it to every area of his life. He went from being a major real estate investor and developer, family man, and recreational golfer to being broke, alone and essentially homeless. But the powerful awareness that had led him to walk away from the life he'd worked so hard to create continued to compel him inward and onward in a quest for liberation from the enormous pain at the core of his being.

Power stalked him in a big way. Spurred on by a series of synchronistic encounters with angels (human and otherwise), along with teachers and guides in a multitude of forms, Adam imbibed books of spiritual insights and guidance, took yoga classes, began meditating regularly, saw various types of unorthodox healers, and exerted himself in a multitude of ways that had once seemed completely alien and ludicrous to him.

Repeatedly, he challenged and confronted his limitations and fears, enduring hardships and humiliations as he unwound the layers of defenses that had caused him to become callous, cold-hearted, driven, and frantic. His relentless pursuit of meaning gave him no rest till he found it.

Dying to Be Happy

In a very real sense, Adam had to die to a way of life that many are dying to live and that some would even kill for. He examined the values and worldview that formed the basis for his outwardly comfortable life and found them essentially empty of merit. He mapped his history and delved into his psyche to discover the source of the guilt and sorrow that were driving him to ruin—and to find a greater purpose for his life.

Adam literally stripped himself down to the basics to separate authentic truth from his fictitious identity. The more honest he was with himself, the more willing he became to take responsibility for the pain and suffering he experienced personally and which he'd inflicted on others. Over time, he became forgiving of himself and others where previously he would have projected only anger, blame, and criticism.

At the same time that he was facing his inner demons, Adam was also pursuing physical and spiritual adventures as another way to meet and test his Self. That's what gives his story the flavor of an Indiana Jones saga—although Adam was searching for a far more elusive and even more valuable prize. The first rewards for his efforts were simple, basic, and life changing: He became humble, grateful, compassionate, accepting, and relaxed more and more of the time. He was finally at home with himself.

Bridging the Gap

But how was a former "predator" going to turn all this "peace and love" into a rewarding, income-earning form of service in the world? What was a man with a quarter century of experience in real estate investment and development going to do for a living—now that he'd become a dedicated EarthKeeper and sworn to protect wild nature and humanity itself?

Through his entrepreneurial eyes, Adam had assessed the value of land by all the ways it could be used to maximize profits for investors. But after his journeys in the Amazon—where the intricate interrelationship of all life is so exquisitely evident—he could not close his eyes to the priceless beauty of the untouched wilderness and the land in general.

He now understood that Nature, in its pristine state, is our only direct connection with Reality. It is only in natural settings—unaltered by human ingenuity and disregard—that we can witness universal life principles at work on Earth. Without this reference point to natural life, we are lost in an increasingly dysfunctional "busy" world of our own unenlightened invention.

Adam recognized the urgent need to preserve what is left of our wild spaces to protect our sanity as well as to produce clean air, and to inspire a sense of the sacred outside our fabricated places of worship. It was these profound realizations that turned this once cutthroat real estate man into an ardent, entrepreneurial conservationist. Instead of development of the land, his mantra became undevelopment.

The ingenious, synergistic plan that occurred to him for reconciling entrepreneurship with conservation may seem both surprising and obvious to you once you read it. But it's important to note that in order to develop a strategy that makes allies of developers and conservationists—while at the same time benefitting the forgotten people in small towns and inner cities across the nation—Adam literally had to bridge the divide in his own consciousness that had made him feel so separate from and antagonistic toward almost everyone else in the world.

Hero's Journey

As Adam demonstrates in *EarthKeeper*, we each have it within us to become the leading transformational figure in our own lives. Every one of us has a greater destiny to which we can awaken.

His awakening required that he leave behind his version of the American Dream. Gradually he awoke to a reality that far surpassed his earlier capacity to imagine what the Good Life looks and feels like. The man he was before undertaking his journey through death-and-rebirth could never have found—let alone entered—the beautiful world in which he now resides and thrives.

Now it is vital to the future of life on Earth—as well as to our individual well-being—for more of us to discover that the source of our power, prosperity, and happiness is not outside ourselves. There's no time anymore to make a career out of healing old wounds and moving beyond outdated paradigms.

Something far more dramatic is required of us now. We are meant to use the infusion of Universal wisdom to see through the fantasies of our identities and to pierce the illusion of lack and dependency that has fueled our dysfunctional behaviors.

Fortunately, many people have undertaken this transformational journey during the last several decades. There are many guides and resources to assist those who are now stepping onto the path. This book is such a guide, and a brilliant one. Still, it requires a Herculean effort to embark on this journey, and not simply to entertain it as a possibility.

Reweaving the Fabric of Reality

We are gods-in-the-making walking through this illusion that we call Reality—in forgetfulness of our true nature and origins. All around us, the world functions in accordance with our collective expectations, for we are dreaming it into existence. Yet, as with the dreams we enter into when we fall asleep at night, we are usually not aware that they are a product of our own imaginations until we awaken to a larger reality.

Now, there is a Great Awakening to an even larger reality occurring in people all over the world. More and more of us are becoming aware of the fact that we participate with the Divine in the co-creation of our universe and that all of Life is be honored and valued.

None of us knows what the coming years will bring to us individually or as a planet. Expectations range from the long-anticipated cataclysm that ends humanity forever—to the dawn of a new golden age. Whatever awaits us, it is safe to predict that those who have done the inner work to bring forth the best in themselves will be able to meet the upcoming challenges and opportunities with wisdom, equanimity—and grace.

The Earthkeepers of indigenous cultures believe that this is the time we have been waiting for to dream a new world into being, personally and collectively. And to wake up from the nightmare of history.

Dream boldly!

Alberto Villoldo
November, 2012
Founder of The Four Winds Society
Author of *Shaman, Healer, Sage* and *The Four Insights*

AN INVITATION FROM THE AUTHOR

I invite you on a journey that is both vast in nature and yet as personal as your inner feelings. The EarthKeeper shares my quest to emancipate myself from the life I created. Through lived experiences I was able to connect deeply with nature. It was in nature that I discovered her gifts. These gifts are available to all and have the capacity to instantaneously change a life of pain and suffering to a life of joy. I had enslaved myself to a self-serving way of life. In order to liberate my soul, I set the intention to cultivate a better future, a future that nourishes peace, love, and freedom as the essential pillars of life. I had to redefine what real wealth meant. In order to accomplish this feat, I decided to undevelop my past. Paradoxically, I had to die to live. Why did I do it? Because I am worth it! And what good would I be to my family, friends, and planet if I did not claim my destiny?

As you read the book, I would encourage you to take the time to reflect on your own journey. Take notes, in particular when a feeling arises. See if you can recall key moments in your life(s) that influenced the direction you were heading. Please note that just because I or anyone else says it's so, it does not mean it's so. Only you can decide what serves your best interest. I do not endorse nor recommend any experiences that are shared in the book. I only encourage the reader to create his or her own. Certain names have been changed.

The story central to this memoir started in my early forties when I was speeding down the Pacific Coast Highway in California with cell phone in hand. Though it was the crack of dawn, I was already at work, and about to close a very big business deal, when a stray dog appeared on the road. With a SCREECH, I barely missed hitting it, and pulled over to the side of the road, shaken. As owner of a commercial real estate company, I was as ruthless as I was successful, since I was convinced that it was better to be predator than prey. Life was "grand" with all the trappings of the American Dream—Country Club, a new custom 6000-square-foot home in Malibu, a beautiful wife, three lovely daughters, and money in the bank. But thanks to that stray dog, it all began to unravel, leaving me naked with the questions, *Who am I? What's my life really about?*

Once I could stop long enough to ask such questions, I noticed that I had been popping Tums for my perennial stomachaches, that I blocked serious issues with my wife by becoming a workaholic, and I flared up in rage at friends and foes alike because of an unbridled temper. I was not a nice man, but a millionaire jerk who, in spite of the trappings, was secretly discontented with life. However, I was also totally lost as to what I should do about it.

As fate would have it, a psychic working a chic holiday party planted a word in my head that would not go away: *separation*. That word was like one pure seed planted in a garden choking with weeds, dying flowers, and muck all so overgrown and entangled that it made me feel suffocated.

However, finally, I *did* notice, and soon enough, I knew I should take a break to reassess everything in my life. *Is this what a mid-life crisis is supposed to be?* I wondered. In any case, I sensed with trepidation that I was due for big changes. With great enthusiasm, mixed with fear and guilt, I told my yearnings for reassessment to my wife, who withered me with a look, "What's your problem? We've got the perfect life." Devastated, I was on my own, determined to end my anxieties, insomnia, and cutthroat manners. *There must be another way to live*, I kept repeating to myself.

So began a profound journey of self-discovery that cost me my family, my business, and my old identity. Nothing was untouchable. Once begun, I knew I wanted to go "all the way," though I was not clear as to what that meant at the time. Quickly, I realized that I had been separated from my spiritual source, and threw myself into reading—*The Sacred Path Workbook* by Jamie Sams, *A Course in Miracles, The Power of Now* by Eckhart Tolle. From this, I became inspired to embark on something I had never heard of before, a Vision Quest. This I did in the Navajo

Nation in Arizona, which in turn forced me to take responsibility for my own inner demons—oh, how I could see my own pride, arrogance, and self-importance. To face this required courage and an open mind with no assumptions, which in turn opened me to the power of forgiveness and a much greater worldview than my ego-driven concepts could contain.

Shortly thereafter, travels to Thailand and Cambodia further opened my heart to compassion, and then "power journeys" in Peru gave me direct experiences of transcendent realities. Almost by magic, one thing led to another, transforming me all along the way. What a great adventure it has been!

After years on this quest working with therapist, teachers, shamans, psychics, and mystics, I feel that my garden, so to speak, has finally been cleared of all the old and dying weeds, and planted anew. Still, I remain ever vigilant to keep it pristine and beautiful, which fills me with harmony and gratitude knowing that my new plantings embody lasting values that will gain strength year by year.

With this gratitude, I became inspired with a new mission in life—to utilize my experience as a real estate investor and developer, and give back to the world by gathering together groups dedicated to acquiring large tracts of pristine land slated for development, and *not* develop them. Instead, we would ensure that they forever remain in their natural, undeveloped state for future generations. Thus, I have found a new calling as one who honors, preserves, and cultivates our precious land for future generations, what indigenous cultures call an "EarthKeeper."

This manuscript first began as a healing device by helping me to organize my thoughts and gain clarity of the new life I so longed to create. By jotting down notes, fragments, and desires, I found great healing to see my fears, anger, and dreams written out so openly in black and white. Then, later, when I began to tell my revelations to friends, they often remarked on the courage it takes to be so vulnerable. However, they could also see how transformed I had become because of this self-examination. Inadvertently, many felt inspired to examine their own lives. "How's *your* garden?" my stories seemed to say to them.

Once I could see the broader benefits of my adventures, I felt it worthy to share them with a broader public, and so it developed into the book you have in your hand. I see it as another example of the noble quest that resides in all of us, the awakening to our destiny. As you read, may light fill your paths and turn tangled plots into fragrant gardens. We are the ones that we have been waiting for! The legacy of our new humanity calls upon each of us now. We are all Earthkeepers! We all have a destiny!

Our moment has come to claim our Legacy. Please join me.

Blessings, Peace, and Love,

AdC/Hall

1

THE PERFECT LIFE

On the Road

It was a typical morning in Malibu, California, crisp, bright, and fresh. At the crack of dawn, I was already gliding along curvy Pacific Coast Highway headed for work. Punching a number on my cell, I barely noticed the sandy bluff, palm trees, and cliff-side houses whipping by in a blur. My thoughts were totally focused on an important conference call to New York. It was do or die on the funding for a jumbo loan on a nursing home.

Time is money, so starting at six a.m. gave me an edge in the vicious game of real estate development and investment banking. Ringing in my ears, I could always hear the advice of my mentor, a leader in the industry, the president of one of the largest mortgage companies in the U.S.

"Whether you are a lion or gazelle, as soon as the sun rises, run like hell. Eat or be eaten!"

And that was exactly what I was doing, but I wasn't going to merely survive, I was going to prosper. Triumph! I was a panther who hit the ground running at the crack of dawn, squeezed every second from a twelve hour day, and remained ever-vigilant to pounce on a deal.

Zipping along full throttle, I felt like a predator cornering my prey, a $9,000,000 deal that will yield me $90 grand for a few phone calls! I chuckled to myself. This is the life, but you've got to have the courage and the know-how.

Finally, a voice on the other end announced the lawyer for this deal. After a few remarks, I was on hold again as the other parties got on the line. My stomach growled. Forcing myself to be patient, I punched a button to switch over to speaker-phone. When everyone was on, and introductions were made, I listened intently as they reviewed the major points of the deal and began hammering out the details.

Then I noticed in the glistening Pacific, a pod of dolphins jumping in perfect unison, their skin shining like glossy enamel. How magical! It triggered a memory, a weekend barbecue with friends and family where in the midst of the turquoise pool, one of my daughters—the center of my universe—was riding a sleek inflatable porpoise in utter glee. But immediately, I caught myself in my indulgence, and pushed the memory away. "Oh no, you don't," I reprimanded myself. "Don't ever relax!"

After all, I had it all, the "perfect life" of the American Dream. A Technicolor dream-house with terra-cotta tiles decorating a 6,000-square-foot Spanish Hacienda with bathrooms decked out in imported Italian marble. All this complemented by my sultry black Range Rover so I could cruise along my neighborhood of wide beaches by a cerulean sea. But all this depended on staying focused. I could never let myself relax and get distracted by beauty, money, prestige, or drink. That would make me soft, make me lose my edge, make me prey!

Suddenly, right before me, a lumbering white van! "I'm going to hit it!" A wave of terror coursed through my body. I jammed on the brakes, swerved to the right, and, fishtailing, headed straight for a dog ambling across the road.

Time stood still as I caught its expression, mesmerized, motionless! Swerving again, I barely missed the dog, and desperately regained control and instinctively slowed down to a crawl to regain balance. Breathing deeply with heart pounding, I was so relieved—I missed the dog! I forced myself to take more deep breaths to calm down, only to hear rude honking from the car behind.

"Asshole!" I yelled instinctively, as he pumped his gas and sped past in a blur.

"What was that, Adam, you say something?" a voice on the speaker-phone asked.

"I…uh…"

"You okay…with everything?" the voice continued, "After all, it's what we'd already talked about."

"I just, I almost hit a dog," I blurted out.

"What? A dog?" he snickers. "Let's get back to what's important here."

"Uh, absolutely. Let's get back to it."

"So, do we have a deal?"

"I'll have to go over it with my partner."

"He's already agreed."

"Uh, then let me run it by my lawyer."

"Your partner is your lawyer."

I remained quiet. After staring at death on the highway, this negotiation seemed so irrelevant. "How long do I have?"

"Two hours, or the deal is off the table."

"Two hours? You'll hear from us," and snapped the phone shut. "The old 'Bait and Switch Game,'" I muttered to myself. I was getting sick and tired of people who don't do what they say. Though millions were at stake, I was feeling nothing but disgust with the whole deal.

Pausing at a light, I gazed out at the ocean, that vast expanse that could make anyone feel calm, but I couldn't relax. The gnawing in my abdomen began to burn. I rationalized that it was all part of the price I had to pay to maintain my lifestyle. As long as I continued to bring in money, all was well. Or was it?

In the Office

At work, everyone gave me a lot of space. I was in a sour mood, and as the boss, I felt entitled to get exactly what I wanted. Last week, my personal assistant quit on me just because she couldn't take the heat required for big success. After a little misunderstanding, I had berated her, "Six months on the job, and you're still wasting my time. Why don't you go back to night school?" So she left. "Good riddance to bad garbage," I thought to myself, but now I had to survive with the help of temps who didn't know how to do anything but keep their distance.

All I cared about was riding the wave during this boom time in real estate. Deals grew more lucrative and multiplied with little effort, and my life had never been better. In the last month and a half, I made as much as $60,000 for a total of four hours work! Easy big money, that's how I liked it.

And so it went. At home, the buzzing at 5:30 a.m. was seldom heard as I routinely beat the alarm, jumping out of bed and into the shower before the crack of dawn. Many times, I was already awake from a restless night tossing and turning. If my insomnia were not because of one deal or another, it would've been from agonizing about the kids or an argument with my wife, Gigi. In any case, rested or not, I forced myself to get a jump on the world. I was not about to be eaten alive in the vicious world of commercial real estate. Thank God for the roll of Tums by my bed for my increasingly sensitive stomach. I should have these rolls everywhere, I was beginning to think.

But deep down, something was amiss. But what? All I knew was that "something" was chipping away at my "perfect world." Slowly, unnoticeably, my showers were getting longer, from five to ten minutes. Five extra minutes for the enemy to get a jump on me. Still, the hot showers helped me calm down and shake off the drinks from the night before. Whether from age, stress, or whatever, it seemed that it was taking me longer to get my body and mind going. I'd arrive at the office at 6:30 a.m.—a whole hour later—and I didn't care! Something, indeed, was amiss, but I soldiered on.

Eat or Be Eaten

One day, I felt a twinge of an old excitement, and put on my favorite black suit and a crisp white shirt, topped off with a cool tie from Barneys New York. In the mirror, I looked and felt powerful. It was my power suit, saved for special days when I was to close a deal, and today was going to be big. I knew from early days in business how important it was to dress the part. Image was not everything, but it sure was close.

I cruised down Pacific Coast Highway before daybreak. Things were going to be good if I could drive the 18 miles to my office in Brentwood without hitting a red light. Even five minutes later could bring out more traffic and make all the difference in the world.

Sailing along at a lively clip, I got caught behind two slowpokes driving side-by-side, taking both lanes. "Damn tandem riders," I muttered to myself. "Don't you know that some of us have to get to work?" I shouted to no one in particular. I flashed them with my high beam. They didn't care. *Must work for the government*, I thought. I flashed them again. Still, they puttered along, throwing me off my rhythm. I leaned on my goddamn horn and didn't let up until I saw some action. Finally, the guy in the Volkswagen pulled over, and I punched by these two losers.

Sure enough, that small delay caused me to hit a red light. Fuming, I watched as the two slowpokes pulled up beside me at the signal. My body tightened up, and I was not even ten minutes out of my driveway.

Pulling up into the parking garage of my office, I wound around and around with tires screeching as I descended into the bowels of the building, trying to make up for lost time. Being five minutes behind the targeted arrival time, I practically ran over a lady who was forced to flee in terror. *What am I doing? Isn't practically hitting a dog bad enough?* I demanded of myself, but the thought disappeared as fast as it came.

Finally, in my large corner office, I felt a rush of adrenaline. The old charge of excitement like a jaguar zeroing on its prey, that was me. Today, I was going to close the biggest deal of my career. $130 million at stake! A hotel portfolio. Immediately, I punched in the numbers to the lender in New York.

"Hello, Mark, it's Adam Hall. How are we looking on the Nash portfolio closing?"

"Not good, Adam," he answered nonchalantly, "we've run into a little snag."

"Snag? Don't give me that bullshit! We've been at this for months, and now you guys come up with some lame excuse to not close this deal!"

"Adam, calm down. I didn't even say what the snag is."

"Okay," I said, "so what's the problem?"

"A small title issue. Should be worked out in a day or two. The only problem is that your clients' interest rate lock expires today. The rate will be a tenth of a percent higher."

"You're kidding me!" I exploded. "Get your boss on the phone right now!"

"Okay, Adam. I'm going to put you on hold to see if I can get him on the line."

I stared at the clock on my desk. The seconds ticked away. After a whole minute on hold, my heart began racing with the horrible thought that I could lose this deal. Just then, my sales manager, Jim, walked in staring at me weirdly.

"What's going on?" he inquired delicately. "Your face is all red."

"I'm on hold with New York on the Nash portfolio, and those whores on 'Obstacle Street' are trying to jack up the rate on the loan."

Mark's voice on the phone suddenly cut back in, "We may be whores, Adam, but we're the ones who are going to put a lot of cash in your pocket, so get a grip! I spoke with my boss and we're going to hold the rate and get this closed tomorrow."

"Great!" I replied, relieved. "Sorry about losing it, but I am sick and tired of seeing my clients get jerked around. I'll give you a ring in the morning."

Hanging up, I confronted my sales manger with another problem. "So, Jim, how are the sales guys doing? Do they have any interest in the proposal to take ownership in the company?"

"Don't think so. They seem happy just the way things are."

"I'm not surprised," I answered cynically. "They're fat and happy while I'm flipping the bills to cover all the operational cost."

I sat down, suddenly feeling weary. "You know, Jim, running a business really sucks at times. It's always about what *they* want. Who was that asshole in that movie '*Obstacle Street*' that said 'Greed is good'?"

"That was Gordon Gecko," Jim replied evenly. "And the movie was called '*Wall Street*.'"

"Well, that greedy bastard was right to a point. Greed is good as long as we're on the winning side of the deal. Where there are winners, there are losers, and it's most certainly not going to be us! Or at least, I should say, *me*." A moment of gross egotism leaked out. I glanced at Jim, but could see no reaction.

"So, Jim, see what you can do to get the guys on board. Dealing with all this shit is making my stomach turn. I'll be around for a bit, but after that I am going to head up to the club. Got to get some relief from this insanity." Jim nodded obediently, and quietly left.

I popped a few Tums in my mouth and stared out blindly through my big picture window, feeling frustrated. The sales guys were not on board, and the goddamn Nash deal was still not closed. What a dismal morning; I needed escape. My door cracked open. My assistant, Stephanie, gingerly poked her head in to see if it was safe to enter.

"Hi, Adam, here is your mail. Would you like a cup of tea?"

"You crazy! No!" I shouted. "Can't you see I'm so hot I can barely breathe?" My rage froze her in her tracks as I ripped off my precious tie from Barneys, and threw it on the floor. After a moment, I noticed she was still there waiting, "Look, sorry for the outburst, but I'm having a rough day. Could you please close my door?"

I took a moment to calm down, and began going through a stack of bills. Every day, new bills would appear from God knows where, and before I knew it, I'd be all worked up again. Finally, I worked my way to the last piece of mail, a letter. To my shock, it was addressed to "*Mr. A Hole.*" I stared in utter disbelief. What kind of sick joke was this?! Opening the letter, I found that it was a sincere "Thank You" from a Korean client expressing appreciation for a deal we had done recently. I had to admit that from "A. Hall" to "A Hole" is understandable if you're Korean, and yet, deep down, I sensed a perverse truth to it all.

Having had enough of the office for the day, I left early to get a quick bite at my favorite dive of a restaurant on the way to the Club. I found a parking space right in front, and thought that at least one good thing happened today. While waiting in line to order, my stomach began to growl and churn. I got lost staring at the rotisserie chicken going round and round with its juices dripping through open flames onto red–hot coals. "That's me," I thought to myself, "I'm that chicken, turning in the fires of a cut-throat business with my life juices being roasted out of me."

A sharp pain suddenly burned my side as the counter clerk caught my attention.

"Hello, hello, hello, is anybody there? Sir, can I take your order?"

I hesitated for a second, "No, I'm not really that hungry, after all, but thanks anyway." Holding my aching stomach, I sauntered out.

Escape in the Country Club

Back in my car, I floored it on to Sunset Blvd. I could not wait to get to my one and only sanctuary, the Club. When I saw the west gate into the Country Club, I took a deep breath with a sigh of relief. Going through those grand gates, I felt as if I was driving into a refuge from the insane pressures of life. Thank God for golf, where troubles and woes miraculously evaporate.

"Hello, Mr. Hall, it's nice to see you again," the parking lot attendant said with a warm smile.

"Hi Doug, how are you doing?" I said with a soft smile.

Somehow the club made me human again. With my spirits lifting by the second, I put on my golf shoes and headed straight to the bar for a Myers's Rum and O.J. My group—friends I've met at the club who matched my ability to golf, gamble, and drink—was next to tee off, so I walked directly over to the first hole. Perfect timing.

The Country Club was a world unto its own. Yes, it was in the midst of a major urban city, but being nestled in the foothills surrounded by lush vegetation, I could see why the stars from Hollywood and powerful business leaders would choose to build their mansions here. The fairways of the Club were walked by the likes of Dean Martin and Bing Crosby in the old days, Pete Sampras and Tom Cruise in our times…and me.

As I walked down the fairway, the gentle breeze blowing through my hair and the smell of freshly cut grass and pine all collaborated to rejuvenate me in minutes. When my tee shot went down the middle, straight and true, I was home. By the time we reached the 15th hole, my team was up by three strokes, and I had rediscovered what being alive is all about.

Just then a deer and its baby doe sprang out from a nearby shrub. For endless moments, I stared eye-to-eye with the mother. Time slowed as I felt a profound stillness. Her look was so pure, innocent, and…sacred. But something distracted me from this reverie.

"Uh, earth to Adam, earth to Adam," a voice cut in, "it's your turn to putt."

Jolted back to reality, "Sorry guys, but look!" I pointed, "That deer over there, and her baby, so magical!" They all turned to look, and saw what I was seeing—nothing. The deer must've jumped off and disappeared.

"Starting to see things, Adam?" one of my buddies joked. "Want us to wait so you can also go hug a tree?" They all laughed.

"This putt's going to go in the hole to close you jokers out," I replied, feeling ever so confident. Carefully, I sized up the turf for a twenty-foot putt to win a hundred bucks for my team. "Get your cash ready." After a few moments of dead silence, I hit the ball as everyone watched the ball roll down the green, curving a little to the left at the last moment to fall perfectly into the hole, "Plop."

At the 19th hole, full of laughs and cocktails, the last thing I wanted to do was to go back home into the madness of life. I ordered another drink, braced myself, and dialed my wife to tell her I'd be late. As soon as we connected, a toxic cloud seemed to come through the phone and wash over me.

"Adam, you're spending more time at the club than with your own kids and me, so why don't you just come out and say it, you don't like us anymore."

"Of course I do, honey, but I'm here working out things to take care of business," I lied. "You know all the details required to close a deal. Besides, I'm sick and tired of all our fighting, especially in front of the kids."

"Yeah, whatever."

"Look, I got to go. See you when I…."

Dial tone. She had hung up without saying goodbye. It left me with a bitter taste of guilt. What a genius she has for doing that. Even though we had recently returned from a vacation in Hawaii, I felt ready for another getaway.

But this feeling of a getaway was different. It wasn't just another escape, another indulgence (which I was an expert at), but rather like a *calling* coming from another place I couldn't put my finger on. A bubbling up of *another way to be.* It made my life seem forced, unnatural—everything that deer was not. Deep down, I had the inkling that this "calling" cannot—will not—be suppressed by work or drink, but who has time to explore abstract feelings when there was so much to do in the real world.

Social Life

Parties had become a convenient excuse for my wife Gigi and I to drink and talk about our "perfect life" with other affluent Malibu couples. Gigi loved to gossip with some close friends, mothers of our kids' playmates, while I hung out with a sprinkling of golf buddies and business entrepreneurs.

"Did I tell you," one woman whispered to a tight group leaning in to catch the latest in juicy gossip, "…about my neighbor? He tried to commit suicide, but botched it so completely, he missed himself and left a bullet in his maid!" Everybody broke out laughing. "And now, he's in rehab. And the maid—an illegal immigrant of course—might get deported." More snickering and chuckling.

I had to go outside. All this gossip over sordid scandals—not to mention endless small talk about expensive and trendy purchases, judicious name-dropping, catty remarks—was not my thing. It made me sick to hear them with so much judgment as they entertained themselves with the suffering and misfortune of others. *What happened to compassion?* I asked myself. But that thought passed quickly, and within minutes, I found myself dying to know what happened next with that neighbor. What sweet irony! It would take me a few years to realize that *I* was as judgmental about them as they were about others, and that I was guilty of the very thing I was accusing them of.

In the midst of discussing the stock market with a couple of business associates, I noticed in a far corner of the room a strange scene made more alluring by candlelight. Behind a makeshift table setup, a vivacious gypsy woman was holding up her hand in deep concentration before another partygoer. Finally, with a smile, she spoke a few remarks to that partygoer, who thanked her profusely, dropped a bill into a tip jar, and dashed across the room to tell her friends what had just transpired. A palm-reader for the party's entertainment, I surmised.

I stared at the woman, a soothsayer named Klarissa, who had flamboyant red hair, frosty nail polish, and dark eye shadow. Catching my eye, she smiled and motioned for me to come over. I remained motionless for a few moments, deciding. Then, as if an invisible force pushed me in her direction, I moved over to her as she motioned for me to sit down.

"Would you like a reading?"

"Sure, why not?" I replied hesitantly.

"Okay, let's see what's in your future. Unless...." She stopped, looking me over.

"Unless *what*?"

"...you'd rather not know."

Beneath her heavy make-up, I met her gaze. Was I being challenged? Warned? "Relax," she continued, and motioned to see my right hand. Taking it gently, she turned it over, and became serious as she began to trace invisible lines with her fingertip. Suddenly, she seemed distracted and stopped.

"Relax. Don't be so nervous," she laughed.

"I, uh…I'm doing my best here," I replied, feeling unusually uncomfortable.

She refocused her attention on the lines in my palm. Now and then, she nodded to herself, and finally spoke, "Life is a journey and you've just begun." To prove her point, she ran her finger over one of my lines on my hand.

"Just *begun*?"

Unwittingly, my hand began to tremble, but she held it firmly, checked me out with a glance, and resumed her analysis. Her eyes narrowed, became serious again, and after another long moment, she nodded to herself and uttered a single word.

"Separation."

"What?" I stammered. I felt struck by a ballpeen hammer.

Sadly, she looked at me, sorry for what she had seen, but continued, "Major separation in the past. And once again, in the present. It's all happening now."

I forced myself to turn away from her. Looking around the party, I found a group at the far corner of the room where Gigi was blithely chatting away with a drink in hand.

"This separation," Klarissa continued, as if she could read my every thought, "is not necessarily about your wife."

"Then who?" I asked, trying to act calm.

"It's much more than just your wife. It's a total separation from the life you've been living."

Abruptly, I pulled my hand away. I was sweating and trembling, and I slowly got up to my feet. I had to get out of there. Smiling knowingly, she offered me her business card.

"For when the journey gets rough. To help you reach the Promised Land."

"What are you talking about?" I blurted out. Staring at her, I ignored the business card she was holding out. "It's already begun," she said, "questioning the life you've been leading."

A wave of anxiety went through my body as cold sweat rolled down my armpits. How dare she speak so nonchalantly about things that could upset my entire life! She doesn't know me!

"It's about your soul," she smiled, still holding out her card, "so have courage. Enjoy the journey, and if I can be of help…" Her warm tone and sincerity finally won over my apprehensions, and I took her card.

Suddenly, I noticed a couple of other women standing behind me patiently waiting their turn. I placed a twenty-dollar bill in her jar, and walked off to rejoin my wife. Gazing at me intently, she asked how the reading went, but I scoffed and dismissed it as gibberish. No way could I reveal my apprehensions by discussing with Gigi what I had heard.

Fortified by a few drinks, I forced the reading out of my mind, but found myself stealing glances at the other guests having their palms read. I heard somewhere that God often speaks through other people. Had God used her to communicate a message to me? I couldn't explain it, but what the gypsy woman had told me hit some nerve deep within. Drinks or not, that damn word kept creeping up to haunt me, *separation*. "But of what?" I screamed silently to myself.

At home that night, I just couldn't sleep. I ended up clambering out of bed, and took a long, aimless walk by myself around the neighborhood in the fog. The cool mist in the middle of the night was strangely comforting, and after an hour or so, I was able to return home. Gigi was sound asleep, thank God, and carefully, so as not to wake her, I climbed back into bed.

In the middle of the night, I saw myself being pulled down by an unknown force into a dark tunnel into a bottomless pit. Desperately, I struggled for survival, but the force was as powerful as it was mysterious. Despite my Herculean efforts, I was losing the battle. I *lost* the battle. I was falling, falling into a pitch-black abyss, until I abruptly woke, heart pounding. Silently lying there after my nightmare, I found myself replaying the scenario I had with that palm-reader. Over and over again, that damn word, *separation,* kept running through my mind. What did it mean? Impending disaster? How do I prepare?

Family Life

The next day, Sunday, I fully immersed myself into our children's world. How nice to watch four-year-old Morgan playing so gleefully in the sandbox. What joy to see eight-year-old Sophia riding around and around on her new bike. But the gnawing feeling in my stomach returned when I had the horrifying thought of "separation" from my precious children. Instinctively, I threw in a couple of Tums down my gullet.

The next couple of weeks, I tried to lose myself in work, but increasing tension at home sabotaged my best efforts. Desperate for peace, I pleaded successfully with Gigi into trying therapy again.

"So Adam was dead set to have a picnic with the kids," said the therapist, "and you, Gigi, insisted on going to the mall. So, where's the problem here? What did you want to do about it?" Long silence.

"Look, Gigi," I cut in, "I admit. I was being stubborn and just wanted it my way. I admit it, I'm a control freak, you know that." For a brief moment, Gigi softened, but still said nothing.

"And you, Gigi, how do you see the situation now?" repeated the therapist, trying to get Gigi to open up. But she just shook her head, shrugged, and said nothing. Dealing with intimate issues was not her strong suit. Finally, the therapist gave me a look that spoke as clear as words, "We're getting nowhere."

Driving back home, I tried to tell Gigi how frustrated I felt, but, as usual, she had the last word, "You want to go to a therapist? Then go. It's obvious that you're the one that's sick."

I felt crestfallen. I was running out of options to reconnect with Gigi, the mother of my children. Though she abhorred the meeting with the therapist, I had truly benefitted from the session. It had opened my eyes to the fact that I had a lot of work to do, and I was determined to do it.

The following weeks, every transaction at work seemed to come with unforeseen complications, and I became a workaholic. The only sense of balance I maintained for the sake of my sanity was to not work on weekends, a time reserved exclusively for my family.

Saturday, I loved watching Sophia play soccer. In those days, aside from the Club, it seemed to be the only reprieve from my troubles. At other times, I'd go shopping with my oldest, thirteen-year-old Maya. I loved being with her, but since shopping wasn't my thing, I would space out, and I knew she could sense it. I was the proverbial missing father, there, but not there.

Around the dinner table in the evening, under the gentle behavior of family dining, subtle snippets of sarcastic digs would fly all around.

"Maya," Gigi would say, "be nice and pass the vegetables to your father. He's a guest at the table, and one must always be hospitable to guests." Wincing, I threw Gigi a dirty look because the kids were right there. But they saw everything.

"Yeah, right, Dad. Where *are you* every night?"

"Hey, come on," I replied lamely, "I'm supporting you all, aren't I?"

And so it went, tensions between us increased as snide remarks turned into open yelling. One time, over something insignificant—she didn't pick up clothes at the cleaners—we flared out into a screaming match. Futilely, we tried to stifle our arguments so the children wouldn't hear, but whether in the family room or upstairs, they heard everything. We were in a pitched battle to prove the other person wrong. Within a few months, the children began taking sides and formed alliances mostly against me. How pathetic, my so-called "perfect life." It couldn't go on, but what could I do?

Having trouble sleeping, Gigi turned to retiring with one of the children, while I ended up spending long nights alone, lost in my own thoughts.

One day at the office, not getting what I wanted with some deal in escrow, I screamed into the phone at the other broker! Virulent, hot, abusive! Like a swordsman wildly slashing at everyone around, I had murderous intent at anyone who did not do my bidding, and he had not done my bidding. In the midst of this tirade, a strange thing happened. I found myself *outside of myself,* and for a brief instant, I calmly observed myself in attack mode. *Why in the name of God,* I asked myself, *was I treating people so viciously? This isn't really me. Where did I go wrong?*

A few moments later, I came back to normal reality, knowing only that something was indeed off. But what? My parents, siblings and friends all thought I had the perfect life, and on the surface, I did. I had worked hard for this lifestyle. Nothing had been handed to me. I had ridden the waves of a surging real estate market, survived all the back-stabbing competition, stayed the course, and earned the right to a financial windfall. This is what my mentor had taught me. This is what the world requires. But a silent voice kept screaming inside my head, "If you're so successful, why are you so miserable?"

After that, I had to leave work early and, feeling homeless, went to the only place I knew for sanctuary, the Country Club. I played a round of golf, but afterwards, I felt as lost and empty as ever.

On my way home, I impulsively pulled off the road and headed for the beach. Walking over the sand, I gazed out at the waves, forever building, peaking, and crashing. I thought about my life, the years of hard work and self-discipline that yielded me a fancy car, luxurious house, and elite lifestyle, everything necessary for that "perfect life." And then I sank down to my knees, keeled over, and wept, feeling that in my life, "everything was nothing."

2

SEPARATION

Therapist

"You little shit! You're nothing but a selfish brat." Innocently, I looked at my therapist, who betrayed no emotions. "Those were her exact words to me," I continued. "Around the dinner table, in front of everybody. I was only fourteen, and it really hurt."

"From your own mother," the therapist repeated with a smile. "I guess we're right in looking into your *wounded child*."

After a month of therapy sessions that went nowhere with Gigi, I decided to continue on my own, and one of the first issues we dealt with was what she called the "wounded child." I came to understand that our attitudes and behaviors began very early on during formative years when we were children, and that those patterns, for good or evil, often continued well past our leaving our parents' home.

"But what did *you* say that provoked her?" the therapist continued. "Everything comes from *something*."

"To mind your own business," I replied, sheepishly.

"That sounds a little disrespectful, don't you think? Especially to your own mother?"

"I know, I know. I was a little brat back in those days."

"So, what's going on here?" the therapist asked. "Do you see your own part in these exchanges?"

"Yeah, I do," I answered, looking down at the carpet. "I'm Aries, always had to be the center of attention. Always talked longer and louder than anybody else, interrupting all the time. Let's face it, I *was* a brat."

"So, what did your dad do about all this?"

"Well, my mom would prod him, 'C'mon, Lem, do something here. Why do I always have to be the bad cop?' And then my dad would take me to the other room, tell me not to treat my mother like that, make me apologize, and we'd carry on."

"If you can take responsibility for the consequences of your own actions," the therapist counseled, "then you wouldn't feel like such a victim. Every action has its reaction, so now you can learn to be responsible for your own acts."

Consolation?

The next day, sitting by myself by the pool nursing my usual Myers's Rum and O.J., thoughts ran through me in a stream of consciousness— Gigi is such a victim, blaming me for all her problems, but I'm a victim, too…The innocence of children should be protected, there should be a Children's Bill of Rights guaranteeing their right to express themselves… The therapist is right, so many of my problems were caused by my own bratty attitude. So what can I do to save my relationship with Gigi?

Suddenly, I had an epiphany, and sat up excited: Gigi and I could take a trip! A physical and psychological journey. We would gain new perspectives on our lives and resurrect our marriage.

The next morning, I took Gigi for a walk on the beach. The overcast weather could not dampen my spirits even though I wasn't sure what I was going to say. Gigi, huddled in a long coat, was a bit nervous. She could sense something was up, but had not a clue as to what, and as a control freak like her, I could easily understand her nervousness. But that was okay, that's why we were having this talk. Faith, I told myself, faith.

Unexpectedly, the sun broke through the clouds, golden rays illuminated the waves, and instinctively, I took that as a cue and sank to my knees before Gigi, looking right into her eyes.

"What are you doing?" she asked, embarrassed. "C'mon, get up."

"I want you to really listen to me," I began.

"I'm listening."

"First, I want to ask for your forgiveness. If I've ever hurt you..."

"Adam..." she cut in, "what's going on?"

"What would you think about us taking a journey together?"

"We just got back from Hawaii. Where do you want to go now?"

"Inside my heart."

"What?" Conscious of people all around, Gigi hissed, "Adam, will you please get up."

But I remained kneeling, "I want us to take a spiritual journey together."

"Get up!" she shouted, and walked off briskly. I rose and chased after her.

"Gigi, if we do this together, we might have a chance to salvage our marriage."

Gigi froze in her tracks, and faced me, "What are you saying, salvage our marriage?"

"I'm begging you to do this with me."

"I'm not interested in some God-forsaken spiritual mumbo jumbo."

"You don't have to answer right now. Take time and just think about it."

"Adam, please don't have a mid-life crisis on me. Micky's husband went off with a coed. Is that next?"

"You're not hearing me. You never do."

"I heard every insane word you said."

"I want us to go on a spiritual quest."

"You...on a quest? That's a joke. You're not the Dalai Lama. More like something out of Monty Python."

"I'm serious. I want to know more about my life. Why we're here..."

"Yeah!" she shouted. "Always about your life. What about *my* life?"

I hadn't thought about that, but I soldiered on.

"I want answers to…" gesturing widely, "all of it."

"There *are* no answers, she sneered. "You're not happy? Boo hoo. Wake up. You have three kids to support and a job other men would kill for. Take some pills and get on with it."

"I don't want to take pills! I don't want to be numb anymore. I want to understand! Wake up! Find lasting love and peace with you," I shouted. "I want to…be a better person."

"Really? I'd like to see that."

"Gigi, this is our chance to revive what we once had. I want to see you the way I did when we first met. We always thought we would have the perfect life together. And we still can if we want to. It's our choice. We can…"

"You're saying you don't have a great life?" she asked with a scowl. "Look where you are," she said as she swept her arm across the prime beach.

"But are you happy? Are you really happy?" I asked.

Gigi turned away and, for a long moment, remained silent and couldn't answer. I knew I had hit a chord.

"See what I mean?" I said softly. "That's why I know there's more, some other way to be. It's time we discovered…our true destinies."

"Where is this all coming from?"

"From years of living with illusions, from not being true to who I am, from losing my connection with my…soul. It's all pretense, and I don't want it anymore."

"And if I went on this journey with you?" Gigi asked.

"Great, I couldn't be happier," I replied, with my first glimmer of hope, "but only if you really want to."

Gigi considered seriously for a long while. I could practically hear her mind working, and finally she came to her conclusion.

"Adam, do whatever you have to do, but I'm not going," she spit out coldly. "Just hurry up and get it out of your system." And with that, she traipsed off, leaving me behind.

Devastated, I remained by the water's edge, sat down and stared blindly at the crashing waves. Then, I noticed that in my absent-minded doodling on the sand, I had scrawled out the letters, "s-e-p-a-r-a-t-i-o-n." I guess what that palm reader had told me was true.

To give myself some relief, I went to my old, reliable sanctuary, the Country Club. Nothing like losing yourself through a round of golf. But it wasn't the same. A friend there told me flatly, "You're not yourself,

Adam. What's going on?" I explained to him a bit about my impending separation, and he said that if he were going through a separation, he'd be here all the time. But I was well past that. What peace I was looking for could no longer be found on a golf course; I'd have to look within. So, from going once or twice a week, I found myself at the Club only once or twice a month.

Self-Questioning

For the next couple of weeks, I was plagued with doubts. Maybe Gigi was right. I did have everything, and I was just throwing it all away. Or was I just going through a mid-life crisis? Or was this a mid-life *calling*? Did I even have the luxury or resources to take a spiritual journey, whatever that really meant? What if I turned my back on everything I had, followed my hunch, and my precious quest yielded nothing?

Every morning when I stared into the mirror, I was confronted with the same questions, "Who are you? What do you have to do to figure that out?" All my instincts told me to do something drastic, and do it soon, or I might lose it all—money, prestige, family—everything I had worked so hard my whole life attaining. And if I *did* lose it all, then what? Who am I? Nothing? The void? It was a horrifying thought.

Fear sank in. I couldn't think clearly. There was no help from Gigi, because by now, we only talked out of necessity, like when picking up the kids or going to some charity event. What's more, I noticed that she had upped the ante through…the kids! As the months rolled by, she seemed to be turning the kids against me. They were joining her voice and blaming me for being absent and self-centered. This was a challenge for which I was totally unprepared.

After a while, I had to accept that we were on different paths with different destinies. She was content with the status quo and would fight to the bitter end to preserve it, and I was pulled towards changing my life towards an unknown future. No wonder she resisted my ideas. I'd be foolish to expect any support from her.

Work

Blindly, I went to work, sat in my big corner office, and stared at the walls. Work was all so meaningless, I could muster no passion for it. Still, I went through the motions: I shut down an office in Phoenix to reduce overhead, hired some fast-talking "cowboy" from Denver for some entrepreneurial scheme that failed and cost me a lot of money, and, as always, I continued to bark at my colleagues.

Scrambling through my papers, I found a big poster from optimistic days declaring my values and "Core Beliefs":

- Foster Relationships.
- Trust, Respect, and Value People.
- Honesty, Integrity, Fairness, and Ethics.

I could barely look at it; all it did was make me feel what a failure I was. My self-image was cracking and falling away like marble beneath a chisel.

An immediate concern was how to embark on my personal quest, while still keeping my family and business intact. Was that even possible? My beloved children, they were more important to me than myself, but how could I fulfill my role in their lives unless first I took care of myself? My business was slowing down. I had no heart to engender new projects, so, luckily, I could still borrow another $100,000 on my credit line to tide me over. "Another shitty encumbrance," I complained to myself. "Now the goddamn bank owns me."

As the months passed, Gigi was getting the picture that she could not stop the inevitable, that she was losing me. One evening when the kids were out, she chided me for not taking out the trash that built up into a litany of complaints until she exploded in rage, "YOU'RE RUINING EVERYTHING!" and slammed her fist down on the table. I was alarmed. She very seldom got physical.

But for some reason, I didn't react like usual. I just watched. I knew she was trying to trigger a brutal, all-consuming war, but this time, I didn't have it in me to fight. We moved to the living room, highlighted by the spacious cathedral ceiling, and I started a roaring fire. Maintaining equilibrium, I told her in a quiet voice, "Gigi, we need to take a break from one another, a trial separation. What do you think?"

"You're nuts! she blurted out. "You have it all, and now nothing is good enough for you! Take all the time you need, Adam, but get it together. I will not discuss your 'journey to nowhere' anymore." She gulped down half her glass of wine. "But don't be surprised when you find yourself begging me to take you back," she retorted, cold and steely. "Quite frankly, I think you've gone off the deep end."

"Thank you. I *am* going to take the next few months off. I'm going to reflect on just where 'nowhere' can be found," I answered with a lame attempt at a joke. "I have to say, though, I'm really disappointed you're not even willing to try."

Temptation

After this conversation with Gigi, I fled the house and drove to the Malibu Inn for a few drinks to calm my mind. Just as I was about to leave, a woman I knew walked in. Brunette, miniskirt, full (not real) boobs, and high-heel shoes, she caught my eye and sat down beside me.

Angela smiled. She knew Gigi, noticed I was alone, and quickly put the pieces together to form a picture of marital discord. I bought her a drink and asked about *her* marital problems.

"How you holding up?" I asked.

"As long as that son of a bitch is behind bars, I'm good."

"As forgiving as ever," I replied sarcastically.

"Hey, we're both here to drown our sorrows, right? What's up with Gigi?"

"She wouldn't go on a journey with me."

"Am I supposed to know what that means?"

"Have you ever thought that there has to be more to life?" I confessed.

"Adam, you're living the fucking dream. You expect the rest of us to feel sorry for you?"

"I'm not asking for that."

"Look, if you're bored with Gigi, do what every other enlightened husband does..."

"Which is?"

With two squares of colored paper, Angela folded them into a pair of snakes that she lovingly intertwined, then placed near my drink. Her look spoke of sex.

"You actually think that's a solution?" I asked.

"Probably not, but it might make you feel better, and that can't hurt."

We stared at each other. I ordered another drink to buy time to sort out my thoughts.

"Gigi doesn't have to know," she murmured. "If she finds out, maybe it'll get her jealous enough to take that journey with you after all."

"Or, maybe she'll want to take me for everything I have."

"She can only get so much, right?"

"Well, there are the kids."

"Okay, there's always that. But we won't let her find out. I certainly won't send her any details."

We drank some more, and flirted around the subject for another hour. I felt comfortable with her, and with each drink, I appreciated more her wicked sense of humor and sensuous body. Not missing anything, Angela excused herself to go to the restroom. When she came back freshened up, she shot me a challenging look, "Are you ready to do this thing?"

I hesitated. Did I really want to go through with it? I knew from people at work that affairs generally were the first step to ending a relationship. But then again, looking at her so lush and willing, I had second thoughts. Finally, I decided.

"I don't think I can do it. I'm sorry. I may be lost, but I'm not crazy." Angela smiled gamely, but I could feel her dejection, a feeling I knew too well myself.

Hurrying back home, the sight of my house threw into my face all my old problems, and I thought that I should have just gone for it. Damn, a lost opportunity. I found Gigi asleep in our youngest daughter Morgan's bed, so I took a quick shower and crawled into bed. In the morning, without a word to my wife, I left for work as fast as I could.

The Spring of Hope

From a local therapist, I started getting weekly massages. My stress levels had reached such tension that even three drinks couldn't help, so I took to getting massages.

April, a college student, did her massages to help with tuition, and actually managed to make me feel less stressed. After one session, she suggested that I stay and have a drink. I had noticed that the massage that night was a bit suggestive. Though I didn't find her especially attractive, especially dressed in nondescript sweatshirts and T-shirts, she had an inner quality, a caring that I found irresistible. One time I told her how I so treasured a cup made by my daughter, Maya, inscribed with the words, "You're the best father."

"Of course, you are," she responded. "I can tell. You are a very, very caring man." I was so touched. She made me aware how I missed loving, caring dialogues.

After a couple of margaritas, April came a bit closer and we started kissing. Slowly, we began taking one another's clothes off. Our sex was intense and passionate, and went on for weeks. Though the passion never waned, though she genuinely cared for me, we both knew it would be ill advised to continue.

A bold spirit, a psychic, a seer who was on her own journey as well, she made me feel so alive.

The last time we met, it had become clear that I was no longer in love with Gigi. April supported me in finding a way to end my marriage, and then gave me as a birthday present a thin, blue and white book, *The Man Who Tapped the Secrets of the Universe*. She explained that the secret they talk about was *found within*, and that I, too, will eventually tap those secrets.

Her gift inspired me to look more into spiritual books, and now in hindsight, I honor her as one of several key guides along the way who gave me hope at a time I needed it most. I knew, subconsciously, that this affair marked a death, a final nail in the coffin of my former life that would force me to continue ever onward and upward towards true self-fulfillment.

Separation

"Did God talk to you yet?" Gigi asked. In her sarcastic manner, she would chide me daily about the fledgling steps of my spiritual quest.

"Yeah, Dad," chimed in Maya, fourteen at the time, "Did God make you late picking up Sophia?" My heart sank. It didn't sound like the Maya I knew, so I could only conclude that Gigi was continuing to turn my own kids against me. In a way, I couldn't blame them.

Drinking more, enduring severe headaches and stomach pains, it seemed that my entire body was telling me to do something, but what? My old life was crumbling, but I haven't found my new one; I was in limbo. I could barely remember the last time Gigi had said an encouraging word to me. It was months ago, well before I almost hit that dog. How I relish the moment when she told me, "Kudos for you, Adam, for persevering to get that loan closed!" But that was another lifetime ago.

Instead, one night she accosted me while holding a piece of paper.

"What's this, Adam?"

It was a rental application that I had filled out a few days before and mistakenly left in my closet at home.

"So you went into my things in the closet, did you?" I demanded.

She turned bright red. "What's wrong with you?" she said.

"This isn't working anymore," I blurted. "Did you hear me?"

"What now, God told you to abandon your wife and kids?"

"That's not fair."

"You're telling me what's fair!"

"I'm moving out."

"Like hell you are."

"I told you, it's not working."

"Because *you* are the broken one, not working…"

"You're right!"

"What?"

"I *am* broken. Nothing's working. I need to heal myself."

"God, you're getting more insane by the day."

"I'm moving out," I repeated, because I knew it still hadn't registered with Gigi.

"Keep threatening me."

"This isn't a threat."

"Where are you going?"

"To a small place in Malibu."

Gigi walked up to me and slapped me sharply across the face, "Get out!"

"I'll pack my stuff."

"No, leave now!" she demanded, pointing to the door. "No, wait." With no warning, she yelled upstairs, "Kids, come down here. Dad has something to tell you." When they convened, she sat them down on the couch in the family room, glaring at me, "Go on, Adam. Tell them."

My heart sank; I was so unprepared. I wanted to throw up, as tears filled my eyes. Finally, I opened my mouth and stammered, "Your mom and I are going to be taking some time apart. I am moving to a place nearby. We need to figure some things out. Please know how much I love you. I am not going anywhere, but just down the road."

The kids were stunned and remained silent. Nobody moved. Everything seemed to shift into slow motion, a surreal moment I'll never forget. Even Gigi was shocked to actually hear the words. Finally, my youngest daughter, Morgan, broke the silence, "Yeah, right, Dad, you're just going on a vacation without us!"

In a blur, I got into the car. As I pulled out of the driveway, the gates could not open fast enough. *I have to get out of here!* I yelled silently to myself. Going off blindly, I began the loneliest drive of my life and found myself at the top of the hill above my house. I could not breathe. Over the expanse of the Pacific, the sun was just setting. Another perfect day, except today, I became homeless. I thought about my kids, as tears rolled down my face uncontrollably. How I'll miss my kids, I cried to myself.

Then a sobering wave of fear swept over me as I thought of how Gigi meant business when she was determined to win at any cost. Nobody ever gets the last word with her. My fears mingled with a deep sense of loss. Getting thrown out of my dream home was bad enough, and giving up my life of luxury in one of the finest parts of Malibu I could take, but the thought of not being able to see my kids felt utterly unbearable. What could I possibly do about it?

The last glimmer of sun sank into the water. *That was me,* I thought, *plunged into ever–increasing darkness.* I had very seldom cried in the last twenty years, but now, all alone in my car, tears flooded out with no restraint. In my despair, with nowhere to go, I decided to stop by my parents', and let them know what happened. I couldn't think of where else to go.

Parents

The new beach apartment I had lined up wouldn't be ready for a week, I rationalized, *so maybe I should stay with my parents? Would they even let me?* Married 56 years, they had been able to make things work for all that time. *What was their secret,* I wondered.

As I pulled into their driveway I felt a knot in my stomach. It had been twenty-four years since I drove off for UC Berkeley, and at that time, I left with bittersweet feelings because I knew it would be the last time I would ever stay here. To move back, I assumed, would be a sign of failure, especially to a family that loved adventure, that always moved forward and never looked back.

Sitting in the driveway, I contemplated all this trying to get myself together when my dad came out. At 85, how fit he looked. Tan, great health, with blue eyes, he was always compassionate and even-tempered. Though we never talked deeply about things, I always knew he cared. I rolled down my window as he came up.

"Hi, Adam, what's going on?"

"Not much, Dad. I've run into a problem, and I'm feeling a bit down at the moment."

"Come on in and let's talk about it."

I came into the house and sat on the couch when down the stairs came my mom, who, like my dad, was also tanned, stylish, and elegant. A model in her earlier years, she still looked great.

"Hi, Ad, how're you doing? Been awhile." I got up and gave her one of our cursory hugs. We weren't into open displays of affection. She looked me over and became serious, "What's going on, Adam, you don't look so well?"

Taking a deep breath I mumbled, "Gigi and I…we're separating, and she just threw me out of the house."

"I know you've been going through a lot, but you think you can work it out?" asked my dad.

"I've tried, but Gigi doesn't want to go to counseling anymore. She refuses to listen to anything I say, and when I ask her to forgive me if I did anything to hurt her, she just gets angry. What more can I do?"

"Go home and figure it out!" my mom blurted.

"I can't. She won't even let me get my things. I'm telling you, this really sucks."

We sat quietly for a moment. They caught on that the situation was serious.

"Why don't you stay with us until you get your own place?" Dad offered.

Mom shook her head, looked at Dad, and then, reluctantly, agreed.

"Thank you both, it means a lot to me. I'll take a rest, and see you for dinner."

Gingerly, I opened the door to my old room from teenage years. Dark and musty, everything looked exactly like I left it years ago, even my old high school desk. I plopped onto my same old bed and couldn't help but reflect on my life, of all the years of hard work and dedication that ended up putting me back where I had started feeling so lost. *So pathetic*, I thought to myself, *42 years of age and living back with my parents*.

Lying on the bed, I mused about how little I saw my folks nowadays, only coming when I was in need. Living less than half a mile away, I was always too wrapped up with things to visit them. Was that a continuation of being "a selfish brat" like she had on occasion described me? Emotionally cut off, I had to admit that sometimes I, too, could be a bit cold.

But then, like the therapist said, "Everything comes from *something*." For example, I noticed my mother wasn't so happy to see me. That hurt; that felt cold. All through my upbringing, she was always dishing out the orders, "Go to your room," "Don't talk back," "You can't take the car," and seldom did we have moments of physical affection. Is that where my coldness came from?

But then again, like the therapist said about taking responsibility, I had to admit how I always *did* talk back, how I *was* a little shit thinking only of myself. Was I like this with Gigi? No wonder she blew up on the beach when I told her I wanted to learn more about *my* life. *This is something that has got to change*, I promised myself.

As for my Dad, what did I get, or not get, from him to make me feel so lost? He had been in the advertising business his entire career, retiring as the West Coast Manager for *Newsweek* magazine. A gentle man with tremendous compassion for everyone, he was social, outgoing, and well liked. I never heard him swear or say anything despairing about anyone, not surprising considering he was a child of ministers. But then at home, any intimate conversations between father and son were lost when he routinely escaped into his own world of USC football games or watching golf on TV.

The good news of my upbringing was that it gave the two of us, brother Ben and I, a lot of freedom to explore the world, knowing that Mom was always there when we really needed her. Her tough love, I began to realize, came because the burden of keeping two independent teenagers in line fell onto her.

As I mused, I could see another legacy from them: the sense that life is an adventure. "Go out and explore," they constantly seemed to say. Once, as a kid, I told my Mom that I had bicycled all the way to San Rafael halfway across town. "Wow, that far? How was it?" she asked enthusiastically.

But the best example of not sitting still in the face of life's opportunities came by seeing how she led her own life. Bucking the trends, she had joined the workforce in the sixties. Always busy, she was a fashion model, then got into the clothing business, and even taught fashion design and merchandising at the highly regarded Fashion Institute. Adding to this sense of adventure, my father would take us on great vacations to Hawaii—sometimes for a month at time—or backpacking in the High Sierras. With these trips came my lifelong love of nature.

Then there was Gigi. Neither of my parents cared much for her, who they found "impolite."

"Why did you give something important to Maya and just some little toy to Morgan?" Gigi would reprimand my Mother. Sometimes, I'd try to keep the peace, "Oh, Gigi, let it go. My Mom had good intentions." But she continued to think that my Mom could do nothing right. Dad, ever gentle and considerate, was seen to be a "nice man" by Gigi.

Suspended in a state between waking and sleeping, my introspections and insights seemed especially clear until knocks on the door shook me out of my reveries.

"Hi, it's Dad. Time for dinner."

"Oh, hi, Dad, I'm not really all that hungry. Mind if I skip it?"

"No problem. See you tomorrow."

I fell back into my musings, tossed and turned until an uneasy sleep took over.

I ended up staying at my parents' for a week. They were gracious enough, but I could not wait to get out of there; I needed my own sanctuary. Klarissa's pronouncement of "separation" gained a new dimension, separation from the old life I had been living. This week with my parents made me certain that I had done the right thing to leave the old and strike out for the new. It would not be easy, but thanks to the legacy of my parents, I hoped that the sense of discovery and adventure in my genes would overcome all obstacles.

The New Apartment

The first night in my new apartment I sat on the bed and looked around my tiny space. Accustomed to a 6000-square-foot spread, I now found myself crammed into a mere 600 square feet. Sitting there wondering what to do with myself, I kept reliving a conversation I had had with Morgan.

"Are you okay, Dad?"

"Of course, sweetheart. Dad's fine."

"Are you coming home?"

"No, not right now."

"Okay, uh, Dad, I love you," and she quickly hung up. I just knew that Gigi in the background was pressuring her to stop talking because after all, "Your Dad abandoned us." With my emotions swirling and raw, and my kids receding farther and farther away, I could barely withstand my loneliness and fell on the bed praying that my kids would someday understand my need to leave.

A loud rapping! I woke up, and realized it was morning. I had slept in my clothes, and there was my father at the door who insisted on taking me out for breakfast.

At the restaurant, I sipped some tea and waited for him to come up with some precious words of wisdom. He usually knew the right thing to say in almost any situation. Calm and peaceful, he sympathized with my situation.

"Dad, I'm pretty sure I can't be with Gigi anymore."

"*Pretty sure* is not definite."

"Dad, this is all new to me, but I need space now to figure *myself* out."

"Take your time. But, remember, kids are involved."

"I know, I know."

We talked a bit more. I felt relieved that my father at least seemed to understand; I knew in his wisdom, he wouldn't offer an opinion until he could really assess the situation.

"If you need anything, you'll let me know?" as he offered to pay the check.

"Of course."

"Your mother and I are here for you."

"Thanks, Dad."

Back in my apartment, I so appreciated that he and Mom would always be there for me, but this journey was one I would have to navigate myself. I took a deep breath and felt ready for the challenge. Something was driving me forward. Looking around my dinky apartment one-tenth the size of my spread, I felt more room here than I had for months, and began to really love it. The crashing waves of the ocean with the vast view of the Pacific right outside helped to give me unlimited psychological space.

Livelihood

At work, my business development was drying up. Other members in my office were mostly independent contractors busy with their own projects. When I stopped to let some colleagues know I needed some time off, it seemed that they couldn't care less.

"Time off? Oh. So how's things?" Jim asked.

"Not so good," I confessed.

"Oh, that's too bad," he said and kept walking.

I felt that nobody cared, that they'd probably be happier if I wasn't around. I overheard one of them whispering, "Be careful when you talk to Adam. He's on a short fuse, nowadays." Quick frankly, I wouldn't have wanted to talk to me, either. My edgy behavior at work had not yet changed. Fortunately, they didn't push for information, because I was quite incapable of talking to them about what was going on.

Solitude

It was not only work colleagues, but also personal friends with whom I began to feel estranged. One long-term friend of sixteen years, Scott, was one of my best companions and golf buddy. Our families often had dinner together. When he invited me out for a barbeque, I wasn't really up for dinner and drinks, but went anyway because he could be a pick-up in the face of my woes.

A bit prematurely gray, Scott had an easy-going demeanor, which I always liked.

"So Scott, how're you doing?" I said, trying to wrap a smile over my problems.

"How are *you* doing is the real question," Scott replied.

"Hanging in there, feeling like shit. My life is in the sewer, and I have no clue which way is up or down any more. Other than that, I'm fine," I smiled grimly.

"I'm truly sorry to hear that," Scott said.

"I heard you and Carol had Gigi and the kids over for dinner. That true?"

"Yeah, Carol really felt bad for Gigi and wanted to be supportive. As for me, I'm Switzerland."

"Switzerland? You're a country?"

"No, no, I mean I'm neutral, not taking any sides."

"Sides? But Scott, it's not about right and wrong, it's about two people who used to love each other, but are now suffering because of a separation."

"Well, Carol doesn't see it that way, and she's the boss," he answered sheepishly.

I took a sip of beer. In spite of all I had drunk, I was getting what he was really saying. He must've believed Gigi's version of events enough to take sides and want to distance himself from me. Was this what I was hearing? I was devastated by my conclusion.

"Look, Scott, the last thing I want to do is cause any problems between you and Carol," I murmured. "You know I care deeply for you both."

We got off the depressing subject of my split-up and made small talk before saying our goodbyes.

Driving home, my sense of abandonment deepened. Like with the guys at the office, here was a "friend" of many years who blithely bails out on our friendship because my problems are a nuisance, too much for them to bother with. I didn't want him to take sides; I just wanted a friend when I was in need. Was I making up all of this? Was this another of Gigi's ruthless maneuvers to exact revenge by poisoning my friendship with Scott? As it turned out, things played out as I feared, because that was the last time Scott and I would get together.

I had a deep respect for what Gigi was capable of doing to get the last word. One day, for example, feeling pangs of loneliness, I impulsively went over to the house to see if I could lay eyes on my beloved kids, only to find that Gigi had actually gotten all the locks changed. No one was home, so I found an open window, climbed in, and drank in the scene of my kids' rooms with their clothes, toys, and books all around. I wrote hundreds of notes—"I love you."—and stuck them everywhere, into their books, under the pillows, and among their CD's before I left.

Gigi called the police, and I was warned about "breaking and entering." Then I found out that she had even gone out of her way to issue an "Unlawful Detainer"! So now, I had received an eviction notice from my own house, for God's sake!

Another time, my daughters told me that "Mom wrote some things on your desk," but that seemed normal, and I forgot about it. But much later when I was moving the desk out of the house, I found that she had scrawled underneath the desk with a felt-tip pen secret messages, "Here sits a dishonest man," "You are a lying cheat," and a dozen other such proclamations. I was shocked at her level of vindictiveness. Had she resorted to some form of Voodoo?

As I struggled with my sorrows, I would occasionally weaken and reopen the question, "Should I go back?" In the midst of a period of doubts, I had a vivid dream.

I'm walking along the beach when something shimmering in the sunlight catches my eye. I pick it up; it's a seashell. Turning it over, I see the word, "Courage." A moment later, the shell crumbles into dust in my hand.

Awakening, the meaning of the dream was clear. The crumbling shell symbolized the disintegration of my life as I knew it. To face the uncertainty that this engendered, to continue my journey, I had to have courage. This dream galvanized my determination to not look back, but go all the way with my seeking.

On the Quest

*Oh, I can't take this anymore. I can barely breathe. Hold on, hold on, don't give up, just another sixty seconds…*Such were my thoughts as I struggled with the pain of my twisted body. I was taking yoga! How it helped me to open up, stretch my muscles, and gain relief from my problems! After years of anxiety, I had finally found a way to release built-up stress. The benefits were so immediate that I began to go three days a week to yoga, and five or six days a week to the gym. It helped me stay grounded in the physical world in spite of all my problems. In addition to yoga, I worked out at the Malibu Gym an hour and a half a day. Physical exercise had become my latest obsession.

With no family life, and less and less work demands, I had much time on my hands. In addition to working out and yoga, I even tried my hand at meditation. Haphazard at first, I borrowed instructions from the end of my yoga classes where we were guided to "breathe, and observe the mind." Trusting my intuition, I simply began on my own and eventually learned a bit about *Vipassana* philosophy, which counseled the observation of the mind's activities. In spite of my good intentions, I felt a complete failure. My thoughts jumped around wildly, a "monkey-mind," as the Buddhists say, but in my case, the monkeys seemed to be on acid: *"You're a cheat... You don't deserve anything... You abandoned your family... You're so guilty... Gigi is right... Whoops, I should be meditating... The bank's squeezing your credit line... What an asshole he was, that vicious cheat... I'm a wimp, sitting here because I can't manage the world out there... What if I lose my kids forever? I'm so scared... I'll end up my life all alone, lonely..."*

Watch my mind? It had gone amuck, racing with anxiety and fear. Is this okay? The instructions were only to watch the mind. What is considered success in regard to meditation? One moment, it would be lamenting over some rage from the past, the next it would be overwhelmed by some anxiety about the future. How, as I had just learned, was I to be in the so-called everlasting present?

Pondering such thoughts one day, as I was going through a shopping center, a word in bold letters jumped out and grabbed my attention, the word NOW. It was part of a title of a book in the window, *The Power of Now* by Eckhart Tolle. Immediately, I went in and picked it up. For the next fifteen minutes I completely lost myself in the book. I was amazed. Here, after fretting about the past and the future, I had stumbled across a book that spoke to this very issue. What sweet synchronicity (although I didn't know the word at the time). The book was so clear, and to me so simple, and yet so profound. It gave hope that I could be freed of my obsession with past betrayals and potential fears, that there was another way to live. It became my daily bible.

By the beach one late afternoon, I thought I'd try to meditate by the water. What a challenge to be in the "now." Even though I had not been able to find absolute stillness, at least I was able to witness my mindless, chattering thoughts. I will not give up; I will be present each and every moment.

As it happened, I could remain "in the moment" a few seconds, and eventually much longer. At the end of my meditation, I felt I had made some progress. My thoughts were truly still for a whole minute! The sun was setting over the Pacific and it was beautiful. I could take in the beauty wholly, simply. For the first time in my life, I noticed my heart beating. My breath, it rolled in and out, in and out; what a miracle. I felt so alive, so peaceful. I will do whatever it takes to make this feeling last, I promised myself. That night as I put my head on the pillow, I fell into a deep, peaceful sleep for the first time in God knows how long.

Lost and Confused

Even after living in Los Angeles most of my 43 years, finding my way through strange neighborhoods was ever challenging. Heading into downtown for a court case, I found myself inching along the 5 freeway. My anxiety level rose by the minute because I absolutely couldn't be late. A former client had reneged on a written agreement and no way was I going to let that asshole get away with it. It reminded me of *another* asshole I had to deal with, a client who had completely disregarded the introduction and meeting we had with a major lender, bypassed me, and did a $100 million loan leaving me out of the loop. "What is going on here?" I asked myself, "Everybody out for only themselves?" It would take years before I could appreciate the irony that I, too, had always thought of only myself.

Filled with bitter indignation, I decided to outwit the traffic and find a short-cut to the courthouse. Though I had never been in this part of downtown, I was running late, so it was worth the gamble. As I drove through, I was disgusted by the scene down there, and knew I'd never come back. Homeless people were everywhere, living in cardboard boxes. Instinctively I averted my gaze when I caught a man defecating on the street. What a wasteland. *People? More like homeless waste*, I thought. A noxious smell wafted across my nose, and I rolled up the window.

To make matters worse, my car was running on fumes, and I had to stop for gas. Thankfully there was a station on the next corner. As I pulled in, one of those homeless waste cases approached the car. Sensing danger, I hit the lock button. He tapped on my window as I stared at him like he was an alien. After a moment, I cracked open the window.

"Hello," he said with a smile. "Would you like for me to pump your gas and clean the windshield?"

"Well…" I stalled, deciding. Suddenly, I granted that he was a human being, and a polite, well-spoken one, at that. "Okay, go ahead."

The cell phone rang, it was my attorney.

"Hello, Adam, it's Ron."

"Hi, Ron, what's up? I'm five minutes away."

"Court starts in three minutes, so hurry up for God's sake. Mr. Gottlieb is here with his lawyers. We're going to have a hell of a fight. I know one of them, Michael Moor, a street brawler of an attorney. It's a good thing I brought *my* fighting team today!"

"Oh great! This is exactly what I want to be doing today, dealing with a bunch of street fighters!"

"Hey, you filed the lawsuit, Adam, what do you expect!"

"Okay, I'm on my way!"

Then I noticed the "service attendant" politely waiting. My tank was full, and the windows sparkling clean. I can't remember the last time I had such good service at a gas station. I rolled down the window all the way.

"Hey, what's your name?"

"Buddy."

"Buddy, thank you for the good service, and here's a little something extra for the effort." I slipped him a five. He accepted it graciously. "One more thing, Buddy, what's the quickest way to the courthouse?"

Pointing for clarity, he tells me, "Head west along Los Angeles Avenue, then hang right at the second light onto Broadway. Go north. When you reach Eighth Street, make a right…"

His directions were so concise, I was impressed. *Here's a man who is in the present*, I thought. Eckhart Tolle would approve. I thanked him again and headed out.

Racing out of the station, I followed his perfect instructions, but found myself caught at a red light. As I looked out, the street was teaming with Latino immigrants. From Mexico? Guatemala? Honduras? Street vendors were everywhere. One man was joking with a buddy, and a mother and her two children were excitedly checking out toys, laughing. It reminded me of good old days as a kid without a care in the world.

From an empty lot, a mariachi band began to play, attracting a growing crowd! More laughter and whoops of joy. Where am I? A parallel universe? They had nothing, but had everything? Whereas with me, I had everything—money, cars, Country Club—and yet, I seemed to be burdened with nothing but alienation, fears, and depression. Thinking like this made me sad, especially when I thought about how often I took for granted Morgan's joyful laugh, Sophia's soft gaze of peace, or Maya's beautiful smile, and instead, I was on the cell phone with some deal or another. HONK! The loud blast of a horn blew off my precious thoughts. The light had turned green, and some asshole couldn't sit still for even a moment.

What street was I supposed to turn left on? I made a left on Sixth, going the wrong way on a one-way street. I made a few more turns, only to find a dead end. I maneuvered a quick U turn and found my way blocked by a huge truck. Leaning on the horn, I tried to blast the truck out of the way, but a big, burly guy holding a bouquet of flowers only shrugged, "It's going to take a few."

The phone rang, my attorney again, "Where are you already!"

"I made a wrong turn, hit a dead end street, and now I'm stuck behind a truck watching two meat heads unload flowers."

"How do they smell?" he asked sarcastically.

"What're you talking about? Just help me get out of here!"

"Well, the judge has delayed the hearing and has suggested we work out a settlement."

"Settlement!" I shouted. "I am *not* going to settle with that jerk. He screwed *me*."

"Let's talk about it later. Perhaps you'll be in a better mood. Don't forget to stop and smell the flowers!"

I threw the phone on the floor of the car, *Assholes upon assholes!* My rage turned into tears of desperation. Everything in my whole goddamn life was crumbling just like that goddamn dream had told me. House, home, wife, children, all crumbling. And now, my business, too, crumbling. My borrowing capabilities were fast diminishing; I was on borrowed time. With that thought, I practically doubled over with burning pain in my stomach.

Trying to escape the mad jungle of downtown L.A., I had a creepy feeling that I was being hunted. No longer was I the hunter; I was the prey just like my mentor had long ago warned me against. But *who* is hunting me? The world? Life? Then a surge of horror shuddered through my body with a new and deeper fear: *I'm mad. I've lost my mind.* Because, didn't I just read somewhere that everything of the visible world is an illusion? But what else is there, what's real? Where's the direction home? *Oh God, please, I need help!*

3

GUIDANCE

Urban Path

Settle with the very asshole who screwed me over? That's why the judge delayed my hearing? It was more than I could take. In spite of the burning in my gut and the madness in my brain, I pushed on to escape the crazed urban jungle I found myself in. Forcing myself to breathe deeply, I impatiently made my way out of downtown in fits and starts, when the phone rang.

"Hi, Adam, your brother Pete. Remember me?"

"Pete, what's going on?" I answered, gamely.

"Well, I just got moved into my new place in West Hollywood. Want to come by and check it out?"

"Sure, it's on the way home, so why not."

Pete! What a welcome distraction. His driving directions were spot on, and so I found his new place with no problem. Off Melrose and Doheny, his house was a beautifully remodeled craftsman type in a super-hip area. With eight years difference in age, we didn't hang out when young, but he was always a very loving sibling with a great smile and gracious charm. I had frequently longed to know him better, but we were both always caught up in our own lives. Knocking on his door, I greeted him warmly.

"Hey, bro, it's great to see you."

"Come in," he said, looking me over. "But what's going on? You, uh, look a bit dazed."

"It's been a rough day," I told him, "and a tough week, brutal month, and shitty year to tell you the truth!"

"Sorry to hear that. Having been divorced twice, I know how it goes. Must be rough not seeing the kids that much, and a wife that's constantly on attack."

"Tell me about it, but let's change the subject. I came to see your new pad."

He took me around on a tour. In the backyard was a lush garden and a swimming pool with a grotto. "Just like Hefner's Playboy mansion," I joked. Inside, there was a light, airy feeling, but my eyes fixated on a bookshelf in the study. I had never thought of Pete as much of a reader, so this was a surprise. "Left over by the guy who lived here before," he explained.

There must have been fifty books, mostly fiction and novels, and all covered in dust. As I glanced over the titles I kept coming back to one in particular that was a tan earth tone with blood-red writing. It was a box set, which included a deck of cards to go along with the book.

"Do you mind if I borrow this?" I asked Pete.

"Sure go ahead. And which is the chosen one?"

"This one here, *The Sacred Path*."

Given how lost I felt, the word, "path" in the title spoke to me immediately. After a few more pleasantries, I gave my brother a big hug, and headed back to my little beach shack in Malibu.

A sacred path.

I could not wait to get home. It had been a roller-coaster of a day that had plunged me from rage and depression from that thwarted court case, to a glimpse of happiness from those poor people in the street, to, finally, a glimmer of hope from my brother with this mysterious book that came with a deck of cards. Once in the door, I changed out of my suit, settled down on the deck overlooking the ocean, and looked over the book.

"What is a medicine walk?"

That question hit me on the first page. *Medicine* walk? Me, ill? I kept reading:

"Medicine is anything that will aid the seeker in feeling more connected and harmonious with nature and all life-forms. Anything that is healing to the body, mind, and/or spirit is Medicine." I liked that definition. The text went on to explain that medicine for personal problems could be found by "walking in nature and observing signs that would assist in healing and wisdom."

Like a thump on the head, I realized that maybe I *was* ill. My sickness was not physical, but mental, psychological. This separation that was tearing me apart, maybe I could find "medicine" by being in nature? What a great concept! I love nature.

Lost in hopeful possibilities, I watched the sun settle over the Malibu skyline. Orange rays of the sun lit the clouds in a blaze and changed the color of the ocean from deep blue to a violet and pink.

Then, feeling ready, I impulsively pulled a card from the deck: *The Medicine Wheel.* That was confusing. I understood the theme of a "path," as in the title, *Sacred Path*, and "walk," as in Medicine Walk. For one who felt so lost, these metaphors seemed totally relevant, but what is a "medicine *wheel?*"

Pouring myself a stiff margarita with a double shot of Tres Generaciones tequila, I took a good look at the card I had just picked. It showed a picture of twelve stones in a circle, the words "cycles and movements," and a diagram involving the "Four Directions" as major points on the circle, south, west, north and east. I didn't understand the meanings, but liked it all immediately, and read on.

Each of the four directions represented one of the four elements—fire, water, earth, and air—that also embodied *significant characteristics of one's journey through life!* Though the margaritas were starting to take their toll, I finally realized that the Four Directions was a map, however, it was a map of *inner* journeys! *I* was on such a journey, and this map could be a godsend. It would give me orientation, tell me where I was at, how I got here, and how to get to where I wanted to go. Every explorer needs a map.

To celebrate my discovery, I poured myself another margarita (by now a euphemism for pure tequila), and became determined to "connect and harmonize with Nature and all life forms." In spite of my drinks and the darkening of the sky, I couldn't stop reading, when the phone rang.

It was my middle daughter, Sophia, a jewel of a twelve-year-old who loved to play soccer, and was always easy going and up for fun. Blinking my eyes, I tried to sober up enough to talk to my little angel.

"Hi, Dad, you okay?"

"Yeah, I'm fine." I could not bear to tell her I was a wreck. Was I slurring my words?

"Where were you today? We had a warm-up game for the season. That was the first game you've ever missed, Dad."

"Oh honey, I'm so sorry, I got caught working," I lied. I had completely forgotten that her game started at four.

"Dad, you don't sound so good."

"I'm not feeling so great. Can I call you tomorrow?"

"Ok, I love you."

"I love you."

Guilt swept over me as I kept hearing Sophia's sweet voice haunting me—"Dad, you don't sound so good…I love you." Impulsively, I threw my entire drink down my gullet, went inside, and continued reading out of *The Sacred Path*.

Regardless of my drunkenness, two things stood out and carved themselves into my brain regarding two pathways:

The Red Road *was the world of living things of physical life, and*

The Blue Road *represented non-physical beings of the spiritual world.*

These two roads showed the cycle of our soul's journey from the spiritual to the physical, and back again….

With my cognitive powers increasingly diminished by drink, I found myself repeating in a slurred voice, "I want to be in *harmony* with nature and all life; I want to be *connected* with nature and all life…" I connected all right, but only with the darkness that comes with a drunken stupor. The last thing I remembered was me yelling silently into the blackness, "Oh God, take me now. Show me the way!"

The Voice

I awoke to complete darkness. My head throbbed, my body ached, and I could barely focus my eyes. *Where am I? I must be dead. God took me and showed me the way…to hell. I'm in hell.* Something was flashing. My clock; it was eleven. I was *not* dead. If I could only throw up, perhaps I would know for sure that I'm not dead, and it could make me feel better. A ray of light pierced through the curtains and stung my eyes. Coiling back from the impact, I bumped my head on something that knocked some sense into me, *Get out of here!* Clambering up to my knees, I rose unsteadily to my feet.

Running blindly out the front door and onto the sand, I felt assaulted by overwhelming brightness. Instinctively, I covered my eyes, and stumbled forward until I fell to my knees at the water's edge. A wave washed over me with a welcome dose of cold water, which made me plop down and surrender completely to the ocean. For a few minutes, I felt like a dead fish with the water pushing me to and fro at will. Then, I felt an urge to run down the beach, anything to alleviate my giant hangover, but after a short jog, my stomach convulsed, and I collapsed back onto the sand.

With the sun bearing down, belly on the warm sand, and face buried in my arms, I succumbed to my old feelings of grief and despair, but my tears were dry. Perhaps they were all shed last night, or maybe I was dehydrated from alcohol, but I felt empty and dry with skin like crackly parchment. Through it all, the sun warmed my back as the sounds of waves rolled in and out, in and out, providing comfort by their mere existence.

Gradually, miraculously, all my misgivings disappeared, and I found myself luxuriating in the joy of the moment with sun and sand, sea and the wind.

"Adam. Adam…."

Someone calling me? I put my head up and looked around. There was nobody for a hundred yards, except for a couple of kids playing way in the distance. *Got to stop drinking so much*, I thought to myself, *I'm starting to hear things.* Dropping back into the pillow of my arms, I began to drift off again.

"Adam, Adam…" It was the same soothing voice, soft and gentle, and from just a few feet away. Jolted back to reality, I sat up and looked around in earnest. The only person around was *me*, no one else. *I'm a businessman, a practical, down-to earth kind of guy*, I thought, *not the kind that goes around hearing voices.*

"I'm here with you now," the voice continued, "here to show you the way."

Completely stymied, I sat on the sand for a long while trying to make sense of what was happening. Like the gentle, warm breeze rippling over the sand blowing over me, the voice permeated through my whole body. It must've had special healing powers because I had the strange feeling that I had been blessed with a moment of grace.

Who was that? Show me the way? To where? As I worked my way back to my apartment, I was torn between hope and doubt. Angels? Spirit guides? Or madness? After all the "separation" I had been going through, this voice gave hope that I was being guided out of my misery and getting me reconnected. But reconnected to what? To "nature and all life forms" like I had prayed for in my drunken stupor last night? Or to madness? To believe an airy voice will "show me the way" sounded like just another lunatic grasping at straws to console his own growing insanity.

As I reached the stairs to my apartment, a surge of life like a dose of pure oxygen came over me so strongly I grabbed the handrail to steady myself. For a moment frozen midstep, I was completely centered on the idea of *connection*, which felt true to my bones. Though it was not clear as to *what* I was connecting to, a conviction that I *was* moving forward had been triggered by that gentle voice. Little did I know, but in time that gentle voice would completely transform my life.

As soon as I walked in the door, I picked up the Medicine Wheel cards to put together all the little pieces that I felt were coming together. I felt I was assembling a big jig-saw puzzle to help me discover a new way to live. Meanwhile, a phrase kept running through my brain: my "medicine" was to *live the mountains, the waters, and the hills*. Once again, I wasn't quite sure what that really meant, but intuitively, I loved it.

Tending to the traumas of my life was a full-time job at the moment, so I was not able to focus on the "medicine" that I hungered for. Where do you even begin? Were those "mountains, waters, and hills" somewhere in the Himalayas? Or maybe right here in Malibu? Was it even physical, or was it metaphoric within myself? Or perhaps both? Caught in this confusion, I got a flash. The clock.

"Oh damn, it's Wednesday!" I muttered to myself. "Kids' night out. For dinner. I was supposed to be there ten minutes ago."

Gigi and the In-laws

Grabbing my cell phone, I ran out the door and hopped into the car. "You're going to be twenty minutes late!" I chided myself. Speeding through the streets, I arrived at the iron gates in no time, pushed my clicker to open it, but nothing happened. *Oh, great! Gigi must've changed the gate code, and now I can't even get into my own house.*

Incensed by her tactics, I blasted with my horn and waited impatiently. I shouldn't have been surprised, because I remembered that Gigi had just filed an eviction notice to keep me out. For the last three years, I had poured blood, sweat, and cash into this mansion, and now I wasn't deemed worthy to enter. How pathetic. Finally, the gate opened, and out came my mother-in-law.

"Hi, Caroline, how're things?"

"What've you been up to? No good, no doubt," she answered coldly.

"The father of my childhood friend just passed away," I lied again. The funeral was the weekend before, but it was the best I could muster up at the moment. "I'm just coming from the funeral."

"Funeral?" she scoffed. "What rubbish. The only funeral I'm interested in hearing about is yours."

What irony, I thought to myself. *She wants to go to my funeral, and in a way, so do I!* Death to my old way of life, my marriage, my career.

Unaffected by my mother-in-law's coldness, I got out of the car and slowly made my way up the pathway as she stood up ahead with arms crossed, defying me to enter. I knew what I was getting into with this whole family, which I confess, I found a bit screwy all around. On one hand, they could be all nice and civil, but if you got on their wrong side, look out.

For example, Gigi's brother, Jack, had happily helped me move furniture one day, but then, without warning, appeared another day uninvited at my house looking mean and dangerous. He was going through a messy divorce at the time and had threatened to kill anyone who got in his way. I told him to leave or I'd call the cops. He glared at me, and slowly backed off, but not before yelling, "I'm going to kill you!" As a black-belt in Karate, it was not an idle threat, especially since he had already been arrested by the cops for "threats of terroristic intent," and had been dis-owned by his own parents.

As I approached my mother-in-law, it was like approaching a toxic cloud. Instinctively holding my breath so I wouldn't choke, I coolly slipped past her and entered the house, only to run squarely into Gigi. Quickly, I assessed that the kids were upstairs and blurted out in a whisper, "Gigi, we have to officially end this marriage." No response. Did the words even register? "Did you hear me?"

"Yes, I heard you," she answered sharply. "So what are you saying? We're not even going to try?"

"We did try. If I thought it'd do any good, I would keep trying."

"You can't do this to the kids." Tears formed in her eyes. I knew she would lay a guilt trip on me, but the truth was I had given a lot of thought to my kids.

"What we have now isn't exactly *nurturing* for them," I said.

"And you're suddenly the expert? Been studying psychology on the side?"

"I never claimed to be an expert."

"Well you're not!" She paused. "But why? Why now?"

"Because we can't keep going on the same path."

"Don't do this," she pleaded. "You wanted some time off, I gave it to you. You needed more time to figure things out, you got it. Now let's get on with our lives, together, as a family. This is a good life."

"But..."

"But what?" Gigi asked. "I thought if you had time away, you would come back and realize you wanted to be with me." Suddenly she gave me a piercing look, "It's not like you're seeing someone else, right?"

I hesitated, looked away, and cleared my throat. Glancing back at her, I was lost for words.

"Adam?" she repeated, while staying surprisingly calm. "Please tell me. You're not seeing anyone...are you?"

I didn't want to lie anymore. Me, a congenital liar, suddenly wanted to end deceptions of any kind. But I didn't know what to say.

"Who is it?" she demanded evenly.

The tension built up until I finally burst out, "It doesn't matter! It's… it's nothing serious, and…"

"How could you?" she cried. Her face turned red, and she spat out her words like a flame thrower, "GET OUT!" and pointed at the door.

With the children still in the house, I retreated as fast as I could. The cat was out of the bag, I had told Gigi the truth, and there was no more lying! At the same time, I had opened Pandora's Box, and to divorce Gigi was tantamount to declaring war. Out of the blue, I knew that my precious affair with April was, among other things, a way of decisively terminating my marriage and moving on.

A few days later, just as I was to go to New York to celebrate my 43rd birthday, I found letters from my kids at my apartment door, which I read on the plane. From fourteen-year-old Maya, "I'm so sorry for what happened. Please come home. We really want you home…" They were so heart-breaking I could barely read on.

Parenting

Feeling emotionally raw, I couldn't help but compare my parenting with that of my folks'. I stopped by one day to update them on the latest and get emotional support. That was hard to come by, but that's how it always was with them. I relished the times that mom encouraged me, like the time I got good grades in fifth grade—"See, Adam, see what happens when you apply yourself? You're doing so great!"—but such encouragements were few and far between. From the viewpoint of an adult, I could now see how her love always seemed to have a catch. Conditional love, that was all I ever knew from her. But then again, she was the one who had to enforce the boundaries, make the rules, and punish transgressions. My father, on the other hand, seemed to lay back and adjust to the ever-changing ebb and flow of life. Good cop, bad cop. Even in those difficult moments I always will remember how she used to scratch my back as she tucked me in for the night.

Around the dinner table, I told them that I had made a final decision to divorce Gigi. A long silence. I drank a gulp of water and waited for a response. Finally, "Would you like to go to church with us tomorrow?" my mom asked. I hesitated; it's not what I had in mind at all.

"No, of course you don't. Why would you want to do that?" my mother answered, matter of factly.

"I think Adam just needs some time to figure things out," my father offered.

"Hasn't he been doing that for weeks?"

"Actually, Mom, it's been months, and it's been hell!" I sprang up from the table, realizing it had been a mistake to visit them. I should have met my father alone, and somewhere else, but he was getting frail with loss of sight, hearing, and memory, so I thought it was best to visit him here at his home.

As I made my way to the door, my father called out, "We're here for you, Adam." I looked back one last time, nodded to my father as my mom continued to sit there with arms tightly crossed, refusing to even look at me. She couldn't wait for me to be gone.

But driving back to my beach apartment, I remembered what my therapist had told me about "taking responsibility." "Try to see things from your mother's viewpoint," she had counseled. My mom did preach to us the values of love, honor, and respect, but then a precious thought jumped into my mind that showed how she did love me in her way. Once, Gigi, in her critical fashion, had told her point blank, "You know, your son, he has emotional problems."

"Yeah? Then I think you need to look into your own mirror," my Mom retorted in my defense.

My mother *had* opened her heart to my new wife after the marriage, but Gigi had never gotten close to either of my parents and kept discouraging me from spending time with them, another contributing factor to my decision to get divorced.

Furthermore, I realized as I headed down the Pacific Coast Highway that in many respects, I, too, was guilty of conditional love by always expecting Mom to satisfy *my* emotional desires. By seeing my parents for who they were (instead of my idealized versions of what they were supposed to be), I felt uplifted. I didn't have to take things personally; she had loved me as best as she could, so I no longer had to be a victim.

That night, in spite of my insights, I couldn't sleep for mourning the death of my marriage, the fate of my children, and my failures as a human being. Sure I had provided financial stability, but lacked in providing emotional support. I was finally beginning to end denial and accept *my* part in creating my sorrowful predicament.

The only positive note of my sorrows, it seemed, was that I was beginning to accept this period of mourning as only natural, and to honor the time it takes to heal. And strangely, the more I took responsibility for my predicaments, the more I felt connected to all living things. *There it was again, the theme of connection*, I said to myself as I sank into a deep sleep.

When I woke, the first thought that jumped out at me was about that mysterious "voice." Insane or not, it gave hope to all the questions plaguing my mind, but even more important, its soothing, feminine quality gave me a sense of peace, of being loved. Over and over again, I replayed the scene at the beach when she first appeared because it made feel so good.

The Garden

As part of my new routine, I made a habit of meditating every morning in my bedroom. *What's going on at work? Do they even care? Oh no, Morgan's sick. Did I take care of that loan payment…* Such were the endless stream of thoughts that pillaged my brain. After fifteen minutes of mindless chatter, I felt as if I were floating from one moment to the next. The intensity of chatter diminished, and I felt an expansion, an uplift…

I was in a lush tropical garden. Sounds of water gently flowing. Flowers, bright red and yellow, emitting perfumes everywhere. It was so peaceful that everything from plants to birds seemed to be floating. I was floating. In this garden of warmth and love, a gentle voice.

"Adam?" It was *her*, my mysterious "voice."

"Adam, I've been trying to reach you. I'm here to help."

On hearing my name from a voice of pure love with an offer to help, it was everything I had prayed for. Everything seemed so simple, so clear. In the clarity, I could also see forty years of my own toxic waste—angers, snide remarks, judgments, self-importance. I shuddered at the complexity of my own faults.

"But I'm here to show you another way," continued the voice. "It calls for surrendering to yourself."

"Surrendering to myself?" My mind went reeling with opposing thoughts. *Wow, I've really gone insane. Not only am I hearing voices, I'm about to follow its advice.*

And yet, everything about her made me feel so good. *What am I to do?*

"Didn't you want to be shown another way?"

"I also put out an intention for God to take me."

"But He has."

"How come I never heard you before?"

"I've always been here, but you just stopped listening."

"I feel so lost," I confessed.

"It's okay to feel lost. Take small steps. You are expanding."

Suddenly I found myself back in my bedroom, feeling exhilarated. I looked around, everything was normal. *But what happened?* In spite of the craziness of "hearing voices," faith and courage coursed through me. "I *can* heal myself!" I told myself, and became even more determined to go all the way on my mysterious quest.

Normal Life

The next couple of weeks I struggled to maintain my enthusiasm. Back and forth, the pendulum swung. I was still drinking, still having doubts, still plagued with worries that I had made the right decision to divorce. The most painful part was the increasing estrangement from my children. Already it had been ten months since I left the house.

One morning as I was coming out of my lover April's house to go to work, I found to my complete surprise Gigi sitting in the car in the driveway with the kids! I was flabbergasted. She had tailed me here? With the kids? Before I could even get my thoughts straight, she stuck her head out of the window, and yelled, "Cheater! Liar! Double-crossing FRAUD!"

I couldn't even look at her or the kids and quickly got in my car and drove away. I must've looked like the guiltiest man in the universe, skulking away in shame. After that, when the children called, they didn't plead for me to return, but instead demanded to know, "Why did you do this to us? You care more for April than us." And when I had my visits with the kids, they would throw tantrums, so my visits became erratic. It broke my heart to be tormented by the very ones I loved the most.

The Showdown

In the ensuing days in the security of my apartment, I tried to follow my therapist's suggestion and put myself in Gigi's shoes. I could truly feel her pain, but I was caught. I couldn't just stop growing and go back to the old order of things. The toothpaste is out of the tube. But with Gigi's stubborn refusal to change, what could I do? I groaned just to think what a battle it would be to legally extricate myself from our marriage. She could do anything, she was so erratic, just like her brother and her mother. When she's up against the wall, anything goes!

The phone rang jolting me out of my thoughts.

"Hi, it's me."

"Hi, Gigi, what's up?"

"I'm sorry about last week, with the kids in the car and all," she said tenderly, "But I feel at such a loss. I feel betrayed by you, Adam."

"I understand, it's a difficult time for all of us, and I'm so…"

"There you go again thinking only about yourself," she cut in.

"But I said *us*, Gigi."

"Difficult for *you!*" she continued, yelling over me in rage. "What about me and the kids?" She was so hot, she had to catch her breath. When she continued, her tone shifted yet again into a voice of cold, focused revenge, "Adam, you have destroyed this family, so I'm going to destroy you. I'm going to *ruin* you. I'm going to take everything you have, your children, your money, and your reputation." Before I could absorb what I was hearing, I heard only the dial tone.

I threw my cell phone across the room, scared. My sphincter tightened, and my stomach ached. She meant business, and I had the foreboding of an ugly, drag-out fight.

Closed Deal, Closed Office

Barely catching my breath from Gigi, I was called back to the office when a deal I initiated had run into some snags. At the office, I felt distant, an outsider peering in through a window of someone else's life as my associate briefed me of our dire predicament. I got on the phone with the buyer of a large apartment project who insisted that the price be reduced $200,000 because of cement repairs and termite infestation.

"This guy's nuts," I thought to myself. It should only be about $50,000. For a moment, I flushed with anger, but then I breathed, made a counteroffer I thought fair, and hung up. I just accepted the fact that the deal wouldn't happen. Deep down, I didn't care. My associate was aghast at me so blithely blowing the whole deal. But a few minutes later, the buyer called back, capitulated, and the deal closed to both our satisfaction.

"That was brilliant! How did you keep your cool the whole time?" asked my associate.

"Easy," I replied, "I didn't care."

"Sure you care."

"No, actually I don't anymore. I just surrendered to whatever. If the deal didn't work out, it doesn't really matter to me."

"But it *did* work out," he exulted. "You're back!"

"Actually no, I'm not," I insisted. "I need some more time off, but you can reach me if you really need to. In any case, I'll be in tomorrow to sign some checks, so see you then."

My associate looked at me, mystified, but I didn't care. The business was starting to show some big negative cash flows. With me not working and huge payouts required every month, I pondered the validity of continuing my business. All my professional life, I had aimed to reach "the pinnacle of success," whatever that was supposed to be. But there was always another peak to conquer, and I, for one, was through with this rat race. That night, I decided to close shop. I was through running a business and was ready to move on with my life.

A few days later, I was back at the office around 10 a.m. Nobody seemed to notice or care. After going through a stack of bills and junk

GUIDANCE

mail, Darren, one the best brokers I had ever hired, came in the office. Sharply dressed in slacks and shirt with his easy-going manner, he was in an especially good mood.

"Hi, Darren, how are things going?"

"Great! I just closed an eight-million-dollar apartment sale." He smiled with a well-deserved sense of pride.

"Congratulations, Darren! That's great news, but I have some bad news. I'm giving you notice. You'll have to find a new place to work because I am closing the office."

"What? You mean…" His face dropped, changing from sheer joy to bewilderment in a few seconds. "You're letting me go? After I just announced that I had closed a huge deal?" he asked, glaring at me.

"I am sorry, Darren, but I'm closing the doors. It's no fun here for me anymore."

"How could you tell me this just after I shared this great news?"

"What can I say, I'm sorry!"

"What an insensitive…" He shook his head in disgust, and stormed out of the office.

A few hours later during the weekly meeting in the conference room with our sales force, I mustered up a speech to let everyone know my big decision.

"Things aren't working out here. With the economic structure of our company, we can't continue, so I'm closing the office." Blank stares. Silence. "Well…I did give you a chance to buy into the company, but none of you wanted to," I continued, trying to justify my decision. Still no response. "I guess that's about all. Thank you for your time."

Nobody reacted much. Word must've got around through Darren. Barely glancing at me, everyone ambled out of the room until I was left all alone in the aftermath of their revulsion for me. It could've been a momentous event, a rite of passage, but I was filled with self-pity and feelings of "poor me." It took me a couple of years to realize what a complete inconsiderate asshole I had been. There was no compassion, no kindness, just the utterances of a cold-hearted, self-absorbed schmuck obsessed with his own problems. (Over the next few years, thank God, most of the guys were kind enough to forgive me. On occasion, we still get together to have a beer and a few laughs.)

Beach Meditation

The next morning while meditating on the beach, I tried to stifle apprehensions from losing my family, my office, and self-identity to stare out into the vast black void of my life. Utilizing breathing exercises learned from my yoga instructor, I closed my mouth, slowly breathed in, slowly breathed out, and repeated this seven times. It was designed to bring *prana* (life force) into the body, and stillness to the mind. Deeper and deeper I went until, once again, I dropped into a trance-like state that gave me an experience of being in my favorite spot in nature (real or imagined), that tropical garden that I had visited before. Again, the peace, the perfumes, the beauty of blossoms.

And then, a welcome surprise, that gentle, loving "voice."

"Hello, Adam. Remember when you were a child, when you thought anything was possible? That daring adventure you did, remember?"

With her question, a stream of memories flooded over me. But I didn't know exactly what she was referring to.

"You had courage. A fearless spirit. Remember…" For ten or fifteen seconds, my mind continued to reel through countless memories, and suddenly I saw myself as a boy, exhilarated as I flew inches above the pavement. I knew what she referring to.

The Storm Drain

I was eight, riding around with a couple of buddies, they on their bikes, me on my *Flexi-Flyer*, a wooden platform with four wheels and a handlebar to steer. A giant skateboard. Lying belly-down, I would find sloping streets and parking lots, and scream along inches above the pavement, pretending I was flying. With a primitive braking system—a couple of paddles that pressed against the tires—it was truly dangerous, but at eight, I didn't care; I wanted adventure, thrills.

With my two buddies, we raced around a parking lot until we found an open storm drain at one far end. We all slowed, stopped, and gaped at it.

"Here's where all the water goes. Wonder where it goes from here?" I asked. "Let's go into it and find out!"

"Nah, too spooky in there," one of them replied.

"C'mon, don't be a chicken. I have a flashlight," I said, gesturing at the one taped on to my *Flexi Flyer*. "Don't you want to know where the water goes? It'll be fun."

"You're crazy," the other boy said. "Way too dangerous. Who knows, maybe you'll drop down into a big hole and disappear."

"Okay, you guys can stay here. But I'm going. I'm gonna find out where the water goes."

Before I knew it, I was all by myself, gliding smoothly down the gentle slope of the storm drain. With no water, I fancied myself going into the belly of a giant snake, I was so excited. The storm drain took a turn, and the light diminished dramatically. After a few more twists, it was totally dark except for intermittent flashes of light from overhead drains and gutters.

Gradually I picked up speed until soon, the overhead flashes of light hit me like a staccato strobe. Blinded by the on-off lighting, I could barely avoid clumps of debris that whizzed past me. Terrified, I sailed deeper and deeper into the twisting blackness until I reached what I felt was the point of no return. With heart pumping, it was all I could do to hang on to dear life as I got swallowed by the yawning blackness.

I wanted to go back, but *couldn't*; the speed had whipped me along well past my ability to brake. Anyway, part of me *didn't want* to go back. I was exhilarated by the thrill of adventure, driven by invisible forces sparked by the need to know, *Where does the water go?*

Zipping along faster and faster, I descended deeper and deeper into the bowels of the earth towards an unknown void. Poised between terror and exhilaration, I was totally focused in the moment when everything suddenly appeared to move in *slow-motion*. I was in an altered state beyond my control, tearing along at breakneck speed, yet feeling weightless, timeless…until everything suddenly turned into blinding white light.

After a few moments, I realized that I had burst out of the storm drain into bright sun. My *Flexi Flyer* slowed as the pavement leveled out, and I ran over a small river in the middle of a culvert. Before my eyes could fully adjust to the brightness, I looked up and saw a magnificent rose. What a beautiful conclusion to a scary thrill ride through the dark.

Looking around, I practically laughed in recognition. I was in the Arroyo Seco culvert that runs by the Rose Bowl in Pasadena, and that rose was the logo on the stadium. What's more, now I knew where the water goes.

"You see, Adam, you've always been brave," said the voice. "Use this same courage to go into the dark unknown you face now, and you'll find the answers you seek."

Suddenly, reality shifted again, and I found myself back at the beach where I had been meditating. For a while, I sat there silently to absorb what had just happened. I let the warmth of the sun wash over me as I half waited for the voice to say more, but she didn't appear, nor, for the moment, did she have to. I felt a new level of conviction that no matter how bleak and uncertain my journey may appear, I *do* have the courage to keep going like I had done as a kid. Just plunge into the darkness, go through my own fears, and on the other side, I *will* find my answers. And, perhaps, light and roses besides! As I gazed out at the vast Pacific, I reveled in my new sense of hope. *And no matter what*, I chuckled to myself, *I know where the water goes.*

The Roads of the Sacred Path

With my new conviction, I dove into my studies to expand my understanding of the "roads" as described in the *Sacred Path* cards:

- The Red Road is about the physical body and material life.
- The Blue Road concerns the spiritual world.

Although it would take me years to comprehend the full meaning of these roads, I felt satisfied at the moment because, for the first time, I had a *structure* to give clarity to all my uncertainties and endeavors, a map to show me on which paths to proceed.

It sparked in me an interest to create a map of *my own life*. I didn't even know what that meant, but the idea seemed meaningful, exhilarating, and scary all at the same time. *If successful,* I mused, *could I then completely recreate for myself an authentic life of connectedness with all living forms in love, peace, and joy?*

Now here was a dream I could stake my life on.

4

THE RED ROAD

A Map of My Life

On a large piece of paper, I drew a big circle with two lines running through it, one orientated North–South, and the other East–West. Guided by the Medicine Wheel from the *Sacred Path* book, I was inspired to construct a map—a "Map of My Life"— to help me, hopefully, find a way out of my trials and show me the way forward.

Not knowing how to start, I had no choice but to begin, and just trusted that the answers would come when they came. Isn't that what the "voice" kept counseling me to do? So, plunging in, I drew that circle to represent "wholeness," and those lines cutting through it to mark out the "four directions."

As I worked with my colored pencils, the act of drawing allowed thoughts related to my new endeavor to flow by in a constant stream of consciousness:

"Thank you, 'voice,' for reminding me of that brave *Flexi Flyer* adventure into that drainpipe. It gives me courage to plunge into this Map of My Life…

"Remain loyal to your instincts, and you'll find the answers you seek. Again, like that *Flexi Flyer* adventure, by following your instincts, you found out where the water goes?

"If the Red Road is about life in the physical world, why not begin at the beginning when I was born?" That stopped me. I stopped drawing and considered the audacity of that thought. It tickled my sense of adventure.

An hour later, I was meditating deeply in my living room, and soon…

I feel so still and calm I can feel my skin tingle. How nice and warm, safe, and connected I am. I am in my mother's womb, and all's right with the world. My mother is at a party, relaxed, having a good time.

I was born, and my life in the physical—my journey on the "Red Road"—had begun.

I snapped out of that meditation, and wondered, *Did I really experience what I had just experienced? The nerve of it all, to see yourself in the womb!* Whatever it was, it hit me deeply. Vision, fantasy, or daydream, it didn't matter to me, because I felt I had found a way to begin at the beginning. Where it would lead, I had no idea, but I've begun! I'm on the path. As I had read somewhere, one must "break down to break through." That was exactly what I had been doing, and I laughed at the wonderful craziness of it all.

Between Heaven and Hell

As the weeks rolled by, I became impatient to hear from the "voice." Where is she? *Who* is she? In spite of my daily meditations, I wanted so much to sound her out about my birth vision. I knew I was supposed to be patient and accepting, so once again, sitting on the couch in my living room, I forced myself to continue with my usual meditation with no agenda. Easily, I drifted back into what I now called the "Sacred Garden," and saw flowers blooming, radiant and alive. Then, in a plume of intoxicating fragrance, her voice simply reappeared.

"Adam, you are finally willing to see the full richness of physical life, the Red Road, half heaven and half hell."

"What? I'm on a path to hell? My life may be difficult, but it's not hell?"

"Do you remember, once, when you were on fire?" she answered softly.

Body on Fire

Involuntarily, I winced as I immediately recalled that horrible day in Pasadena when I was twelve, playing with Brad and his older brother, Tigger, in the schoolyard with another buddy, GR. We were experimenting with a homemade bazooka gun. A series of Folger's coffee cans, minus tops and bottoms, were taped together to create a long cannon. Propped on a bicycle, we angled the bazooka for maximum effect and stuffed a grapefruit into the end as a missile.

When we were all ready, one of us shook a can of compressed kerosene (so dangerous, they took it off the market), then another took the can and squirted the fuel into the lower end of the bazooka. The third person lit it with a cigarette lighter. KA–BOOM! The grapefruit shot way into the distance. Straining our eyes, we watched as it sailed over the entire length of the football field to…hit the basketball backboard! Whoops of glee! Though we hadn't aimed at anything in particular, we considered it a bull's eye, a direct hit! How we cheered and congratulated each other!

Inspired, we quickly reloaded with another grapefruit. This time, it was my turn to squirt the fuel. We all got in position—timing is of the essence—but somehow in the excitement the can got dropped. Fuel splashed over my entire leg and chest, and WHOOSH, *I was on fire!*

In panic, I ran twenty yards to where there was dirt and rolled on the earth as my friends frantically threw soil on me to put out the flames. After interminable seconds, I was extinguished, and I felt so relieved. But then, I almost fainted from excruciating pain. The burn peeled back my skin, leaving me in the worst agony. Somehow, however, in a hazy nightmare, I was rushed by one of the parents to the Huntington Memorial Hospital where I was treated for second- and third-degree burns. Every day for thirty days, I returned to the doctor's office, where my bandages were painfully replaced.

"All right, I got the point," I said to the voice, "The Red Road can be hell, but what's the point with all these terrible memories? What're you trying to do to me?"

Ignoring my complaints, she continued smoothly, "Can you remember that traffic accident in Malibu?"

Once again, my memory raced back to the very day our whole family moved from Pasadena to Malibu. At twelve, I had felt a mix of anxiety and excitement as I began a completely new life in a part of town where I knew no one.

An Omen?

As traffic slowed along the Pacific Coast Highway, I fixated on the sight of the ocean, so vast and calm. *I could like this place*, I thought to myself. I had always responded so well to nature. When traffic really slowed down, I tore my gaze from the ocean to see what was going on up ahead. Blinking lights. Cop cars. Ambulances. An accident?

Before I actually saw anything, a feeling of dread washed over me. Slowly, as our car pulled by the scene of the accident, I saw smashed cars, twisted steel, and on the ground a big lump with a yellow sheet pulled over it. Glistening dark blood stained the asphalt all around it. Somebody had been thrown from their vehicle in a most horrible way.

"Uh, Dad, is that man…dead?"

A long silence. My father wouldn't answer, which only added to my growing anxiety. But I knew. I had laid eyes on a real dead body. This was not TV, but the real thing. Fearful, yet curious, I couldn't tear my eyes away from that image of death as it seared its way into my brain. I wondered if it were a terrible omen on my first day in this new town of Malibu. Just then, a terrible memory from when I was eight came before me: Heading home from my grandmother's house, we saw an entire family strewn on the freeway. They had been thrown from their car, and they were all dead.

Before I could digest this image, the "voice" spoke again.

"Good, Adam. Now, can you remember the evening you tried to visit your brother?"

Flirtation with Death?

"Hey, Adam," my Dad suggested one evening in high spirits, "let's head over to the beach and see what your brother's up to." He and a friend were camping right on the beach.

"Sure, let's go!" I said. In spite of the corpse on the road, I was really beginning to have fun exploring my new home, complete with mountains and what I considered the world's largest sandbox—miles of beach with fine white sand. Seventh grade would soon begin, and that added to the excitement.

It was a moonless night in summer, so warm I thought for a moment that I was in Hawaii. Tooling along in my mom's Pinto station wagon, I rolled down the window to feel the hot Santa Ana breeze blow across my face. Well-tanned with long, blond hair, I must've looked like the prototypical Malibu beach boy as we made our way up the hill towards Paradise Cove. From the front seat, I loved seeing the beautiful coastal ride unfolding before me with the ocean at night decorated by twinkling lights of houses where the land meets the sea.

"Dad, I'm sure beginning to like Malibu."

"Yeah? Me too."

Two bright lights came racing down the hill. A thrill of fear coursed through my body as everything went into slow motion. Those lights were coming straight at us, in our lane! A wrong way driver heading straight at us. *A head-on collision*! In shear terror, I SCREAMED, my father, too. SCREEECH of brakes, but closer and closer the car came. I could even see details of colored tags on his bumper. *We're going to die!*

Just in the nick of time, my Dad swerved the wheel, fishtailed until he could regain control, slow down, and pull over to the side. My heart was pumping wildly. I was so scared, I had peed in my pants and began to cry. My dad hugged me, which gave some comfort, but my terror remained.

Foregoing our visit with my brother, we turned around and went home. Once there, my Dad tried to console me.

"Want some ice cream? It'll make you feel better."

"No, I just want to get in bed." The image of the dead body on the highway from a few weeks ago, that I was just beginning to forget, reared its ugly head again. *That dead body could've been me!* Together with this near accident, a fear was embedded in me far, far deeper than any ice cream could relieve.

I crawled into my covers, put the blanket over my head, and trembled in the private terror of a young boy. Over and over again, I couldn't stop replaying the scene, those lights coming at us, "Look out! Look out! You're going to die!"

How strange that my "voice" would continue to steer me towards all these dreadful memories. A wave of paranoia swept over me, *She's messing with my head. By overwhelming me with memories of death, fear, and pain, she's trying to do me in!* But that thought evaporated, because every other time she came, her presence left me inspired, hopeful, and peaceful. But the question remained, "Why all this attention on tragedy?"

Visits with Children

Having closed my office due to minimal projects and lack of interest, I could finally spend more time with my kids. But what irony, because nowadays, they didn't want to see me. With each passing day, they receded farther and farther away, which tore my heart apart. Though we still had our meetings—a few hours for dinner, a walk on the beach—our visits became more erratic as my own kids became increasingly alien to me.

I knew Gigi was ruthlessly trying, as promised, to "destroy me," and thought nothing of using our children to her own ends. I was now the enemy, and it was utterly painful to watch my kids reflect Gigi's rage and judgments. For the most part, I remained disciplined about not getting the kids involved in our fight, but still, now and then, my guard would slip. In the beginning, things were peaceful.

"You don't care about us. You're always on the phone," Maya would say.

"That's not true. I care about you a lot. Anyway, that sounds like your mom talking."

"No, Dad, that's what *I* think. I know what's going on. You don't care about us."

Through the weeks, the accusations would escalate. For example, once I drifted through a stop sign, and before I knew it, Gigi would rail against me for being a "reckless driver." From here, it was a short step to hearing from the kids that I had turned into "an abusive, negligent father." I had to take deep breaths to remain calm.

In the face of these difficulties, I focused on my kids' inherent beauty and innocence, which could shine through everything and bring a smile back to my face. But over and over again, Gigi would succeed in sabotaging my best intentions. For instance, sometimes she would appear before our visits were over and simply take the kids away. Or intrude in the middle of our time together with phone calls.

"Hi, Gigi," I answered, as I breathed deeply, ready for anything.

"Adam," she said sternly, "the girls are having a really hard time visiting you now. Your irresponsibility and inattentiveness makes the kids detest their visits with you. Did you hear me? *Detest* their visits with you."

"How do you know?! Part of the problem is that you keep calling every twenty minutes when we're together. So please leave us alone! And don't come early."

"No, the problem is that you don't feed them on time. And you get drunk watching golf on TV instead of playing with them."

"Oh sure, Gigi," I said hotly, "that's exactly what I do with my precious time with them. Anyway, this conversation is going nowhere. See you later." I slammed down the phone in frustration. "She is nuts!" I yelled out to no one in particular, as my kids looked at each other knowingly, "Dad is losing it."

Once again, I had failed in my struggle to remain cool and show my kids that we *can* have a loving, peaceful time together. Pretty soon, I had to admit that Gigi was winning the battle, because after a few short months, the kids simply did not want to see me anymore. I could not blame them; who would want to subject themselves to all this drama?

Beyond Fear

Through such heartaches, I soldiered on through my days. Sometimes I'd go to the Club to play a round of golf or eat alone at a restaurant, but always in the background I'd muse on the meaning of my torments. Not only did I have to withstand the agony of my receding kids, but also my "voice" had forced me to dig out my series of painful memories. *What was that all about?* Because of her, I found myself constantly revisiting the pain from setting myself on fire, the horror of seeing dead bodies on the road, red blood on the red road, and the terror from almost dying in a head-on collision.

Why?

I did realize, though, that it was *then* when my youthful innocence was forever destroyed, only to be replaced by a deep-seated fear that *I am nothing but my body—fragile, vulnerable, and perishable. Any moment, I could die.* Of course, now I know most certainly that this isn't true, but this knowing wouldn't come until many years later.

Gradually, on the other hand, I began to see what my "voice" was driving at about life being half heaven and half hell. By making me revisit the hellish part—*by ending denial*—I could see with unblinking candor from where came the seeds of some of my deepest fears. They weren't because *life* is inherently so frightful; they were only because I happened to have undergone terrifying experiences when I was so young and impressionable. Something deep inside had begun to stir and shift the perspective of my entire life.

Meanwhile, I wondered, if the world of the physical—the Red Road, as I was beginning to call it—was half heaven and half hell, what about the heavenly part? Why dwell on so much negativity? Immediately, I recalled the beautiful times when I fell head-over-heels in love with Gigi.

Courting Gigi

I was thirteen, feeling my way around the new junior high school in Malibu when something caught my eye in the playground. My heart began to pound when I first laid eye on Gigi Darling. She was tall, a brownish blonde, and tan, and carried herself in a fun, easy-going manner. In the cool manner of budding teenagers, we checked each other out, but not a word was said. Later, in the hallway, I introduced myself and asked, "Would you like to go on a walk with me after school?"

After class, Gigi and I found ourselves strolling through the fields, chatting away about our eighth-grade teachers, cool music, and everything under the sun. From then on, I couldn't wait to go to school and be with her. After my previous year of death traumas, I could finally relax and open my heart to the joys of life.

That summer with her was the best I ever had. On the beach at night, Gigi and I would kiss and talk about the moon, smooch and point out constellations, and kiss some more as we made plans for other things to do. Everything seemed possible. We became best friends, broke up, got back together, and spent hours at the beach kissing and talking about our vision of a future together. We both loved to hike, and oftentimes swam naked in the watering holes in the Malibu Mountains in joyous innocence. On the sand, she spelled out "I L Y T M M F V," but wouldn't tell me what it meant unless I caressed and kissed her to her satisfaction. A tough bargainer she was, but five minutes of intense smooching later, I finally got the letters decoded, "I love you the most, my forever Valentine."

After some fits and starts—we both went out and lost our virginity with others—we became like two magnets that fell into each other's force fields. On the beach, when we were fifteen, we made love for the first time. It was not in the spirit of "sex, drugs, and Rock and Roll," as I had experienced with others, but rather it carried a feeling of purity, innocence, and caring.

For a year, I had saved money—as a street vendor selling dried flowers that I had picked in the hills above our home, and delivering papers for the Pasadena Star News—so that when I turned sixteen, I could buy my first car, a '68 VW Bug. Proudly, I surprised Gigi by picking her up on a date with it. How she loved the blue color and the feeling of freedom it gave us. Finally, we could go out in style, like real adults.

Spending less and less time at home with my parents, I was living the way they taught me—freethinking and independent. Though my mother sometimes said that I was "self-centered," when I was with Gigi, I felt inspired for the first time to put someone else's feelings before my own.

Summer of love

That summer, we were so deeply in love, it didn't matter where we were so long as we were together. Feeling foot loose and fancy free, I was hit with a moment of inspiration.

"A summer hiking trip in the Sierra Nevada Mountains, that's what we should do this summer!" I blurted out to Gigi. When I was a kid, I had had many great experiences hiking in the pristine wilderness with my dad. Gigi, who had never been hiking, thought it sounded fun.

But there was a big problem. With my VW on the blink, we needed to borrow Gigi's parents' ancient 1970 Opel sitting in the driveway. As I looked it over, I wondered, *Will it even make it out of the driveway, much less the Sierras?* With Gigi's folks out of town, we had to approach her auntie, a tough-minded woman just like her sister. Working up our courage, we went inside to ask permission. There she was on the sofa, reading a magazine.

"Hi, Auntie," Gigi said in a most friendly tone. "Sorry to interrupt, but Adam and I want to ask you if it would be alright to…"

"Don't even think about it!" her aunt cut in without even looking up.

"But I haven't even told you what we're asking for," Gigi fired back.

"Doesn't matter. I know what you're thinking. Your mom and dad gave explicit instructions that you and your brother are to stay close to home."

"Well, in that case, I don't really care what they said!" Gigi retorted. "Nor what *you* say. Adam and I are going on a hiking trip for a few days."

"Like hell you are," her auntie exclaimed, as she began to rise to her feet.

"Adam, get in the car," Gigi whispered defiantly. We ran outside and jumped into the Opel. With Gigi at the wheel, we sputtered out of the driveway, and once on the street, burned rubber like two bank robbers who had just broken free from jail.

Whooping in glee, I was thrilled to see such chutzpa in Gigi. She was certainly not one to take no for an answer.

"Awesome, Gigi, simply awesome!" as I gave her a high five. Looking so hot, sexy and wild, she flashed me a beautiful smile. We were like Bonnie and Clyde, and never felt so alive.

But then there were *my* parents to deal with. When I stopped by to broach the subject with them, they simply said, "Wonderful. Have a great time." Oh, they were so cool about allowing me the freedom to explore life. *How awesome!*

Heading north up highway 14 for the next four hours, the Opel managed to move along just fine, though when we climbed uphill, even big rig trucks could pass us. We headed towards Bishop, a little town nestled in the foothills of the Sierras, a place I knew well from trips with my family.

Arriving at South Lake late in the afternoon, we set up camp, and that night we snuggled under the stars lakeside. What a dream to curl up with Gigi; the warmth of her body made my heart sing. Early the next morning with backpacks full of supplies, we climbed higher up the mountain, and ended up at a perfect campsite at 9000 feet, Chocolate Lake.

The next morning, we woke up to a beautiful summer day with clouds, big and puffy. Flowers gave off perfumes, bees buzzed for honey, and all around, snow-capped mountains watched over us as we puttered around in communion with nature. In the midst of this pristine wilderness, the focal point for me was Gigi, who wore a T-shirt with the words "Loving Stuff" written over her heart.

At sunset, the sky was ablaze with slashes of scarlet among blue-violet storm clouds. Cozy in our tent, our passion exploded in sex, rising ever higher as sleet pounded our tent. Afterwards, spent, we lay together relishing our afterglow as we fell asleep in each other's arms.

As an adult, the recollection of these happy experiences helped lighten all the horrifying pain, death, and conflict that seemed to materialize all around me. After all, concerning life in the Red Road, didn't my "voice" say *heaven* and hell? It's not all tragedy. *Must keep things in balance*, I told myself.

The Swing of the Pendulum

Everything sailed along famously with Gigi and me, teenagers in a state of grace. As we matured, our connection only deepened. Many times, we'd be on the phone so long that we'd fall asleep talking. With hormones raging, we'd think about birth control, but passion would sweep all caution aside. Then one day after school, she told me she was pregnant. Shocked by the cold reality, we could only remain silent and stare at the ground. With barely a word uttered, we both knew we were far too young to raise a child.

On the way to the Venice Clinic for Planned Parenthood, neither of us spoke a single word. All during the ride, I felt cold and wrapped with an eerie feeling. At the clinic, I paid the nominal fees for the service of an abortion. Thoughts of "taking a life" and its implications barely flitted across my mind; they were considerations well over our heads. Though I didn't know if it was "right," I felt it wasn't *wrong* what we did. Neither of our parents knew about this; we were two youngsters out on our own.

Afterwards, our relation seemed more frail, but still, we went out, had great times together, and simply moved on. Of course we tried to exercise more caution regarding birth control, but it was scatter shot. About a year later, she got pregnant again! More shame, guilt, and shock, and again, we went through another abortion.

Afterwards, something changed. She wouldn't return phone calls, and at school, I felt shunned. When I was able to corner her, she was polite enough, but cold, and refused to talk about what's really going on with her. How it drove me nuts to be left in the dark about our relationship. This agony of being in limbo was more than I could bear. Refusing to believe rumors that she was interested in someone else, I was left angry, abandoned, and victimized.

A couple of months later as I was hitch-hiking on the Pacific Coast Highway, a red Subaru came into view, and my spirits lifted. It was Gigi, who pulled over and stopped. How fine she looked, all dressed up for some party, as my old desires for her got inflamed.

"Where you going?" she asked evenly.

"Beverly Hills," I said, even though I was only going to Santa Monica. I just wanted to be with her longer. By the way she was dressed, I was struck by a terrible foreboding.

"You're going out on a date. You're dating somebody else! That bartender from the Charthouse."

"I don't want to talk about it," she said.

Before I knew it, a big argument flared up. The pain of rejection! Our shouting became so intense, she pulled over and yelled.

"Get out! Just get out!"

My temper erupted, and in blind rage, I hit her! In the stomach. She screamed and ordered me out. Before I was fully out of the car, she gunned the motor, leaving me spinning and off balance. Stunned, I watched her disappear into the distance as I stood all alone with my own rage and guilt.

As an adult, I had never hit anyone, and here, I struck the very person I felt closer to than anybody in the world. Utterly distraught, I broke down and wept. Blindly, I walked up Chautauqua Avenue, and up the hundred stairs going up Santa Monica Canyon, sobbing uncontrollably all the way. Joggers who used the stairway for their training passed me up and down, oblivious to my torments as I continued to weep. At the top, I staggered over and collapsed on to a curb, and sobbed. Two teenaged girls came by and tried to console me, "Are you alright?" but nothing could stop my agony. *I had hit the very person I love the most.*

For the next few days, I called Gigi, desperately trying to apologize, but I could never get through to her. For months, I was left with nothing but the agony of overwhelming guilt. The shame of it all, hitting her, a woman, and in the stomach of all places! Was this a subconscious reaction to the pregnancy that was our undoing?

Hope Rekindled

For the next year as a senior in high school, I struggled to mend my heartache, forget Gigi, and get on with my life. Then she dropped out of school, and lucky for me, "out of sight, out of mind." Now I would really try to move on, and a short time later, I saw in the quad of Santa Monica High a girl that seemed to have a light around her, a glow of innocence and friendliness. With frizzy blond hair and a relaxed, artistic temperament, she seemed much more grounded than Gigi, who was all fire.

New to the school, her name was Julie, the first girl that I dared open my heart to since Gigi. Raw and vulnerable, I would not be able to bear another heartbreak, but still, when I saw Julie, my attraction for her grew way stronger than any reservations I harbored. Before I knew it, I was totally smitten by her. *I'll ask her out for the prom.*

For prom night, my friend Doug and I went all out and rented a limo, dressed up in tuxedos, and had champagne to the ready. As I presented Julie—Jewels, as I loved calling her—a fragrant corsage, I felt honored to have such a loving beauty as my date. It was a lovely evening that was unfolding like a dream. Hope rekindled in me as I luxuriated in our perfect evening and the good times awaiting us. Once again, I felt like the world was my oyster.

The next evening after the prom, a group of friends and I went clubbing in West Hollywood. Though Julie was not with me, she was with me in my mind as I danced and drank, and unabashedly sang her glories to my friends. Around midnight with three stiff gin and tonics under my belt, I felt exhausted and was ready to go home. Though drunk, somehow, I was able to get into my car, and maneuver all the controls, and find my way on to the 10 Freeway heading home towards the Pacific Coast Highway.

Fighting off fatigue, I blinked and found to my horror that the landscape had totally changed. *Where am I?* Screaming along at sixty miles an hour, I struggled to get my bearings because I was now on a completely different freeway heading in a completely different direction from where I was going! What happened?

Traumatized, I pulled the car over in a state of shock, fearing for my own sanity. In spite of my drunkenness, I reasoned that I had fallen asleep at the wheel, swooned over four lanes of freeway, and instead of smashing into the side barrier as would be expected, it had opened up to accommodate the connecting ramp to the 405 Freeway, and that was where I had found myself when I had woken up. All this without hitting anything! What a miracle I was still alive. Thank God for waking me up in the nick of time, for saving my life and limb, and for keeping intact my dad's spiffy 240Z Datsun.

After pulling myself together, I cautiously continued on my way to Malibu, got on and off the freeway safely, drove respectfully on the surface streets, when CRASH! I had dozed off again, and hit a sign at a bus stop! Damn, that took out the front side of the 240Z. Limping home, I made it to our driveway with no further incidents, thank God, but I didn't have the presence of mind to turn off the headlights, which woke up my parents, who saw the damage.

"Someone backed into me," I lied once again. My parents shook their heads in utter disgust and went back to sleep. The damage to the car and my obvious lack of honesty only distanced them from me. They demanded that I pay the insurance deductible.

Back in school the next Monday, my spirits lifted when I thought about Julie. I couldn't wait to see my beloved and see what she thought of our big night at the prom. For me, it was an evening with no equal. I asked everyone everywhere for Julie, and found her nowhere. When she did not show up the next day, I called her as soon as I got home. *Was she ill*, I wondered? A man in a soft tone answered.

"Hi, I'm Adam, Julie's friend. Is Julie there?"

"Adam, Julie was killed yesterday on her way to school," the man replied, almost in tears. Stunned, my mouth went dry, and I couldn't speak. Apparently, on her way down Topanga Canyon, there was a freak accident with a tractor-trailer that killed her instantly. I uttered a thank you for the news, got off the phone, and wept in agony. Once again, my hopes had been dashed to smithereens. Since then, June 6th, 1979, has been etched in my heart forever.

Nightmares

I am in deep sleep, so deep all I'm aware of is nothing, an endless blackness. Suddenly, without warning, something utterly terrifying makes me fly out of bed, screaming, in a prodigious leap.

Waking up completely disoriented, I find myself a few feet from the end of the bed, face down on the floor. What happened? How did I get here? Bathed in sweat, I notice my heart beating so fast, I'm struck with a new layer of terror, *I'm having a heart attack!*

During my last year of high school, these nightmares occurred every three or four months, and went on for years. One time, it happened while I was with a girlfriend, flying out of bed screaming. She became so petrified at what she saw she looked at me as if I were possessed by demons. "It's not humanly possible. Nobody who's sound asleep leaps through the air screaming to land way past the foot of the bed!" she exclaimed. Unfortunately, I couldn't alleviate her fears because I, too, was completely mystified at what happened.

But where did these nightmares come from? What did they mean? Of course, I tried to figure them out, but there were *no visuals* to give me the faintest clue. Whatever terrified me came from pure, unfathomable black, which made these nightmares even more frightening. They instilled a profound fear in the deepest part of my being. Is *horror* at the source of who I am? It would be many years later before I would be able, or willing, to confront these traumas.

Light at the End of the Tunnel

But those years were happening…*now*. All those old traumas were running around in my brain *now*, especially since my "voice" had been goading me to face them. I must've been ready, because here they were, all this blackness.

One morning during the usual meditation in my beach cottage, a warm sensation flowed through my body. Once again, with lightness in my heart, I slipped into my "magic garden" that signaled the appearance of my mysterious guide, the "voice." It had been over a month since I had last heard from her. With no ceremony, as is her fashion, she spoke to me.

"No matter how dark things appear to you, have faith. I am always here. You are being protected, guided, and watched over, so be still. Listen, and you'll know."

I waited for more, but that was all I heard. In spite of the brevity of her comments, peace and stillness lingered on a long while until suddenly, I got an insight about my nightmares. They were triggered by that night I had fallen asleep at the wheel. From that momentary blackout, I had woken up to come face to face with fear and death. Now that I knew, it seemed so obvious.

Those nightmares had crystallized all those profound terrors and guilt I had been carrying. Finally, I was at ground zero of all my fears, and knew what to do next: deal with these fears. What that entailed, I had no idea, but at least I knew where to put my attention. Once again, my "voice" had steered me right.

Quite unexpectedly, revisiting my nightmares filled me with a deep sense of gratitude for being alive. In spite of all my trials and tragedies, in spite of all the errors of my ways, I'm still here. I *am* being protected and guided.

Initiation into the Red Road

As I digested these memories, I began to see my tribulations not in terms of being a victim, but rather as a willing participant in the richness of the Red Road. It's called *being alive*. From joyous courtships to agonizing burn pains, all that happened…happened, as befits the full spectrum of life from heaven to hell. Is this what my "voice" was trying to make me see? Through the weeks, a new strength welled up in me. My new awareness gave me the feeling that I had been *initiated into the Red Road*.

With this perspective, I wondered about Gigi and me, why my life had been so intertwined with hers, she who has caused me as much anguish as anyone on this earth. But I knew the answer. In spite of our present conflict, it was through *her* that I had first opened my heart, fell in love, had beautiful children, and experienced the *joyous* part of the Red Road.

What Is Love?

A couple of years after the explosion of my relationship with Gigi, we bumped into each other during a Christmas holiday. All my anxieties from years of rejection and guilt welled up immediately, but within minutes they all evaporated. How so much can be transformed by a glance and a smile. Filled with new hope, I casually invited her to visit me in Berkeley where I was going to school. "Let's just have some fun," I told her easily, and thought nothing more of it.

A few months later in Berkeley, feeling forlorn in the driving rain, I recalled how I saw an impassioned TV evangelist shout out the question, "WHAT is love? What is LOVE? …Love is JESUS!" Though I had passed it off as crazy entertainment, I did ask myself, "Yeah, what *is* love?" With Valentine's Day right around the corner, I felt lonely and unwanted, so it was a legitimate question.

Shaking off the umbrella, I entered the bakery shop, and immediately got hit with the words, "What is love?" Written in bright red letters, it adorned a big, heart-shaped cake. I burst out laughing at the coincidence, and before I knew it, words flew out of my mouth, "WHAT IS LOVE?" Heads turned, and sparked the counter girl to echo me, "Yeah, what is love?" All the repetition of this question got my mind spinning, not that any conclusions came my way, but finally, I realized, I was ready to seriously consider this fundamental question.

A couple of months after that, Gigi *did* visit me in Berkeley. What a pleasant surprise. After a marriage and divorce for her, and a launching of a career for me, ten years had passed, and now we were seeing each other again! Within a year, we were married and joyfully expecting our first child, Maya.

And so the pendulum swung again, from joy to misery back to joy. Such is the nature of the Red Road, always changing, never staying the same. Isn't this why all the spiritual wisdom traditions keep reminding us to remain detached because, in time, everything changes to its opposite? Is *this* what my "voice" was guiding me towards seeing, that the nature of the Red Road swings back and forth between heaven and hell?

Gigi and April

And sure enough, the swings of the pendulum never stopped. In a blink of an eye (that included fourteen years of marriage and the birth of three children), my relationships had drastically shifted once again, this time from joy back to misery. One evening in my beach apartment while totally engrossed working on my "Life Map," my serenity was rudely interrupted by the phone. It was Gigi.

"Your girlfriend just attacked me!" Gigi declared hotly.

"What? April?" I breathed deeply to center myself. Newly impregnated with the idea of life being "half heaven and half hell," I was determined to handle this situation with a touch of equanimity. "Gigi, what on earth are you talking about?"

"The sheriff is on the way, and I'm going to file charges against her!"

"Wait a moment. Start at the beginning. What happened?"

"I was driving on Point Dume, when who is right in front of me, but your *girlfriend*"—how she spit that word out. "We stopped at a stop sign, but when the light changed, she wouldn't move. The guy right behind me pulled up closer so that between the two of them, they boxed me in. This was planned! Then, that guy from behind bounds out of the car, sticks his ugly head in my window to yell at me."

"Yeah? So? What did he say?"

"He threatened me!"

"What did he say?"

"If I don't stop following April there'll be hell to pay!"

"You've been following April? Why in the world would you do that?"

"I was not following her."

I groaned to myself. I did not want to get caught in this squabble.

"Gigi, this has gone way too far! You really need to chill out."

"Me? Chill out…?" She was so irate; she couldn't muster up a retort.

"Yeah! And quite frankly, I'm sick and tired of your anger and crazy behavior." I slammed the phone down before I had to hear another word.

Catching my breath, I felt sick of everything, sick of Gigi, of April, and most significantly, myself. Here I had wanted to be a peacemaker, but I ended up getting sucked in by the craziness. After a few minutes, I called April.

"Hi, what the hell is going on?" I demanded hotly, just like Gigi.

"Your fucking wife has been following me, and I am sick and tired of her."

"Why would you have someone attack her?"

"He did not attack her. He only told her to stop following me!"

"April, I told you to stay clear of Gigi, she's…she's crazy. Not doing well."

"Whose side are you on, anyway?"

"Nobody's side. I just want peace and…"

"You know what?" she cut in, "to hell with you! And to hell with your wife!" she slammed the phone down.

Damned if you do, damned if you don't! I couldn't help but feel sorry for that goddamn phone, for *all* phones. With so many of them slammed down on my account, I was beginning to have compassion for those poor plastic messengers who were just trying to do their job.

Recoiling from Gigi and April, I tried to get back to the creative flow with my "Map of Life," but I was too off center by what had just happened. I realized that just because I'm starting to change and grow doesn't mean the world and its problems are any different. Be that as it may, I promised myself that I would act like a warrior, and be even more vigilant in monitoring my own angers, fears, and judgments. This time, I had failed and blew my cool with both Gigi and April—guilty as charged— but it only made me more determined than ever to remain vigilant in the war against my own inner saboteurs.

End of April

As it turned out, I never spoke with April again. Though, nowadays, I have no idea what she thinks of me, I'm forever grateful for the support, friendship, and love she had given me during a critical point on my journey. The book that she had given me for my birthday, *The Man Who Tapped the Secrets of the Universe,* was a godsend. Many times I had pored over it, and gained a moral compass to navigate through all the storms I had to endure: "To attain peace and creativity, stay balanced, be present." A noble thought that I am still determined to live up to.

In the morning, I had had enough contemplation and headed out to the beach. On the way, I noticed a magnificent Monarch butterfly resting peacefully on the sand, gently flapping its wings. *How strange to be on the beach, and how beautiful,* I thought to myself, and moved on. An hour later after a long walk on the shore, I happened on the butterfly again, only now it was no longer moving. It had passed on. Hypnotized, I had the thought that I, too, am like this butterfly. "Let it be, Adam," it seemed to say to me, "let the old world die, and find your new freedom." With this thought, I gently picked up the fragile creature and put it alongside the other treasures on my living room altar.

The Name of the "Voice"

With the closing of my business, April out of the picture, Gigi at war, and my kids rejecting me, I tried to forge a new path with new values, but it was psychologically exhausting. All my memories of death didn't help, and to continually stare at the great unknown of my future was daunting, but I kept reminding myself that I do have the requisite courage. "It's inherent in your bones," I'd remind myself, thinking of my *Flexi Flyer* adventure into the storm drain. I moved to a new smaller office in Santa Monica, and twice a month (a far cry from my old schedule of twice a week), I went to the golf course for a little relief. My game suffered accordingly, but who cared? Golf in those days was pretty far down my priority list.

Instead, I relished my time alone reading, meditating, and working on my "Map of Life." Through explorations into spiritual matters, I was learning to "surrender" to it all. "Seven steps forward, two steps back; four steps forward, one step back," this was how I progressed towards redesigning a new life and myself.

One day, half asleep on the beach, I lamented on how everything I touched had turned so bad. *Maybe I just don't know how to love.* As hard as I've tried, my life was still a mess. *What's wrong with me?* But my sorrows would be tempered when I reminded myself what the "voice" had said, "Take little steps. It's alright to feel lost; it's all part of the process." Just the thought of her helped make me feel better. But who is she, anyway? Isn't it odd that I've pinned my hopes on a nameless, invisible voice? I chuckled to myself on how my sense of reality had so changed.

All of a sudden, I heard a voice near me say the name, "Lila," (pronounced Lye-La).

I sat up. It was *not* the mysterious "voice" that had been guiding me so much lately; it was someone else. Then all around me within five or six feet, I heard the name, "Lila...Lila...Lila," repeated from different locations, but then I knew: I had been given the name of my mysterious "voice," who then spoke to me for the first time in a month.

"Hello, Adam."

"It *is* you!" I answered. "I know your name. Lila."

"Yes you do. You've learned so much about the Red Road, the world of the physical. Now, what do you think is beyond the Red Road?"

For a while, I waited for more, but my "voice" had no more to say. As usual, her cryptic statements set things in motion that would change my life. *Beyond* the Red Road? I wondered. Soon enough, her question would open me up to a whole new dimension, the rich world of thoughts and feelings, and the beginning of the "Yellow Road."

5

THE YELLOW ROAD

Mind Gone Amuck

Stumbling half-asleep through the kitchen, I met the challenge of a new day with the aid of a cup of tea. Heightened by the soft refrigerator hum and the barking of some faraway dog, the silence all around was palpable. And, as always by the beach, the sound of waves.

How peaceful, it would seem, but how incorrect. It only brought to relief my crazy mind filled with thoughts like a head full of prancing monkeys, leaping about, questioning this, judging that, driving myself crazy:

Simple soups, simple salads. That's all you know how to cook. Aren't you a little sick of the same old tuna salad?...Ouch, my poor stomach. The pains are sharp, different than before. Popping Tums doesn't help anymore, so what's going on? At least I've cut down on my drinking...

But so what? Drinking or not, who cares? It's all illusion, anyway. Isn't that what all these good books have been cramming down your throat?

I feel restricted, can't get a full breath of air. Just yesterday on the beach, I had to keep sucking in deep breaths to get enough air. Maybe it's cabin fever. I need air... Maybe I should get out of town. Or at least mix with people, because...I'm lonely.

What I'd give for the sweet embrace of a warm woman, some sensual gratification. So what's the purpose of my self-imposed isolation?

Purpose? Haven't you learned anything? There is no purpose; it's all illusion. Everything *is what it is*. Just stay in the "now."

But I hear the seagulls cawing. Do I really hear them? Am I supposed to pretend I'm not hearing them? I love the taste of this tea going down my throat. Do I really taste it? If I can't trust my senses and can't trust what I see right in front of me, what can I trust?

You know what's your problem? You think too much. You keep sucker-punching yourself, believing in physical sensations and appearances. *Beyond* the Red Road, remember?

So I can't trust my senses, and now I can't trust my thoughts, so how am I supposed to survive? My tethers have all been cut. I'm adrift in deep space.

You're starting to scare me. You are quietly, deliberately losing your mind, I'm sorry to say. You're going insane. Coo-coo. Nuts. Am I clear? Why, you've even been hearing voices! And following its instructions…

Beyond the Red Road

I stopped sipping my tea, disturbed by the thoughts of my own insanity. I gasped for some fresh air. Working my way down to the water's edge, I forced myself to stop all negative thoughts. I had been warned; *doubt* is a most debilitating demon. By sheer will, I focused on wistful thoughts of happier times—my kids' faces of excitement opening Christmas presents. Our family trips into the High Sierras. Attending my kids' soccer games…

But what has it all lead to? The complete upheaval of your family, career, and identity.

Oh, how demon doubt creeps back in given the least opportunity. But I had to be vigilant. No self-pity, and no judgment, I had promised myself. Those days are over. I must keep the faith and use this time of upheaval to see *beyond* the visible world of appearances, *beyond* the Red Road.

I watched blindly as a flock of pelicans floated by when suddenly one of them contracted its wings, turned into a dive-bomber, and plummeted thirty feet down, down into the water, SPLASH, and disappeared.

A moment later, it was back with a fish wriggling in its beak. *It's a sign,* I smiled to myself. *I'm that pelican, and I, too, will dive below the surface of things to catch my prize.*

With Lila encouraging me to look *beyond* the Red Road, I studied my Sacred Path Cards for clues of what that could be, but only found discussions about the Red Road of the physical world and the Blue Road of the spiritual. *Yes, beyond the physical lies the spiritual, but there seemed to be a huge gap between these two extremes. What's missing,* I wondered.

A Vision of Yellow Light

Meditating one morning in my beach cottage, something took over my mind and...

I find myself walking in nature that is so dark I can't see my hands in front of me. The air is dank and smells awful. Suddenly, something utterly terrifying overwhelms me. With heart pounding, I run blindly in the dark only to smash headlong into a tree. A wave of excruciating pain. Crumpled on the ground, I hold my head, and whimper in agony, "How do I get out of here?"

In spite of my closed eyes, I "see" a sunny yellow light a few feet in front and above me. I can feel it in my heart—warm, comforting, peaceful. I open my eyes and find myself in the same darkness. Shutting my eyes, the warm golden light returns.

Upon waking, I wondered about its meaning. It was so vivid, it must've had some special significance. Was it a sign of hope, a beacon in the storm? Was it yet another reminder that in spite of darkness all around, light and warmth can be found within?

A few days later while working on my map, a light bulb went off: What's beyond the Red Road is *the world of the mind—the place of thoughts and feelings.* Fears, joys, judgments, and sorrows, beliefs, hopes and anything psychological—these are the contents of the mind.

This is the missing gap between the physical and the spiritual that I had sensed with the Sacred Path Cards. After all, in terms of a journey, do we not need to travel through our thoughts and feelings before we can truly connect *consciously* with spirit? And so another "road" found its way into my map. Inspired by that vision smashing into the tree and feeling peace from that warm yellow light, I knew to call it the "Yellow Road."

As I began to draw the road into my map with colored pencils, thoughts came up supporting this insight. "If you're into love, joy, and peace," I said to myself, "*this* is where the action is, because love, joy, and peace are all feelings. What's more, so much of our predicaments in life are dependent on our attitudes, and our thoughts and judgments. Here, we can work on the *cause* of things, rather than merely on the surface outcomes of life." Coming together like this, I became so excited I couldn't wait to re-examine all my recent ordeals in terms of the Yellow Road.

Investigating the Yellow Road

After this epiphany, I had a brief moment of doubt, "Who am I to go defining such major aspects of the human condition?" But by now, I could recognize the voice of my impetuous inner critic, so, trusting my intuition, I had no further qualms and plunged ahead into this newly opened road of my journey.

There is no other way to explore the Yellow Road but to look *within*. It's an inside job. So any incident that came up, whether of the past or present, I strove to look *behind* the event to see if I could perceive the emotional/psychological conditions that gave it significance.

For example, death. All my experiences with mortality—the dead bodies on the road, being on fire, the death of Julie—used to terrify me because I saw death only in terms of the visible, physical aspects, the Red Road. From this viewpoint, death is *the end*.

But from the viewpoint of the Yellow Road, I could see that what's more important are my *attitudes* about death. Was it a tragedy, or just a natural part of nature? Does consciousness go on with or without the body (like we experience in dreams) so that even if the body is inert, our thoughts and feelings continue? If so, then…*does death even exist?* As I opened my mind to these other possibilities, my feelings changed dramatically. No longer was there the automatic terror that I used to experience about mortality.

For instance, I used to be tormented by why beautiful Julie had to die so young, but then, thanks to the Yellow Road, I read somewhere that nobody dies "a second before his time, or a second later." *That* shifted my belief system! If I accepted this viewpoint, I could not only find a measure of peace that she had died at the exact right time, but also that somewhere, somehow, there must be a Great Spirit watching over us all, Julie included. *All things are exactly as they should be.*

Then, I thought about a "positive" experience. At seven, for example, I got "married" to my next-door neighbor, Kimmy, also seven, with freckles, bangs, and a little red dress. Looking like Darla from the Little Rascals, she was cute as a button, complete with a piece of chiffon to serve as a veil. Seven-year-old Ted performed the ceremony witnessed by half a dozen of our friends. With no experience or authority but our desire to do it, we created a beautiful ceremony. Some had even gone home for rice to throw at us at the right moment.

From the viewpoint of the Red Road, this "wedding" would have been nothing more than a cute, child-like event of the past. But from the Yellow Road of thoughts and feelings, it was as pure an experience I have ever had of *innocence and joy,* which is why I've cherished this event all these years. Every time I remember this ceremony, I know that innocence and joy are still within me.

With my parents, the viewpoint of the Red Road showed how we spoke little, led somewhat estranged lives, and exchanged love with conditions. If I had stopped here, I might have harbored secret resentment (like I did through my twenties), and might have felt angry and victimized by "imperfect" parents the rest of my life.

But, thanks to the Yellow Road, I could see below the surface and realize how their detachment had also instilled in me (perhaps inadvertently) an *independent mind.* Also, I learned by their example that life is a great joy of exploration and adventure, which remains fundamental to my life. Thanks to the Yellow Road, this shift in perspective brought forth deep gratitude and appreciation for my parents just the way they are.

Then there was my work. I shudder when I think about a financing deal where I was offered $15,000 from a broker as compensation for helping on the deal, which I angrily refused. This is as far as the Red Road would take my ordeal. But the Yellow Road showed how I had been so filled with false pride I wouldn't accept it because I thought it should've been much more. What hubris! If I were to do it again, I would have graciously accepted it, and not let my self-importance get in the way. A lot of nice things can be done with $15,000.

As I can see now, my old business was totally obsessed with the Red Road: How much money can I make, amen? What a joke. I had completely ignored the qualities of the Yellow Road, how I *really* felt about my work. On the surface, I was proud, confident, and competent. But deep down, my stomach churned with anger, mistrust, and anxieties: "Eat or be eaten. Every day is a death struggle if you want to be victorious." The so-called victory that this attitude produced was filled with fear, stress, and rage within.

Now, with my office in the final phase of unwinding, I sighed with relief that I could get out of my long-term lease obligations because I couldn't wait to get out of there. My precious business that I had poured so many years of my life meant nothing to me now. Except for a little 8-by-8-inch plastic memorabilia involving a "big win" with the Windsor Hotel Portfolio, my big-time business was nothing but a giant reminder of *failure*.

Breathing in deeply to face this failure from the perspective of the Yellow Road, I forced myself to see with unblinking candor that psychologically, I felt humiliated and defeated, and that, yes, I had made a lot of mistakes, big ones, even, but…so what? I may *feel* a failure, but that doesn't mean *I'm* a failure. Didn't all the books I've been reading remind us that we are much bigger than the normal ups and downs of life, that we are part of the Great Mystery, infinite, imperishable, and free? Hmmm.

So, what should I do about my feelings? Beat myself up? Be in denial? Make excuses? Forgive myself? *Forgive myself?* But it would take more traveling down the Yellow Road before I could understand this and put it in practice.

On my deck facing the ocean, I mused on my predicament as the Rolling Stones' song "Emotional Rescue" floated through the air. How perfect! *I* was the one in desperate need of an emotional rescue. *Maybe a girlfriend?* It would be nice, but at this point, not nice enough to do anything about it. My plate was already full with more urgent concerns, so I decided to remain celibate for at least half a year. Anyway, the emotional rescue I needed could only be performed by myself. *I created the mess, I intended to undo it.*

Angel of Death

One evening in my beach cottage, instead of reaching for a beer, I decided to take a few deep breaths to relax after all my self-reflection. Relaxing— what a new concept for me after years of running the rat race—but before I could slip into the zone, the phone rang.

"Hi, Sophia," I said excitedly. "How're things?"

"I'm okay," she said in a tiny ten-year-old voice.

"What's going on, sweetheart?"

"I'm so sad since Pepper was killed, and you and Mom broke up."

"I'm sorry, honey." I sighed with empathy for what she must've been feeling. During a moment of silence, I could feel my poor baby so far away. "Why don't we get together tomorrow, and do something fun?"

"That sounds great, Dad!"

"I'll call you in the morning, okay?"

As soon as I put the phone down I was deeply moved. My newfound awareness of the emotional/psychological dimension of life made me see clearly that *Sophia* was the one who really needed emotional rescue. Enough about me. Her dog, Pepper, had gotten out of the fence and had been missing all day. After a couple of hours, we gave up the search, fearing that she had been killed on the highway near our home.

By nightfall, she was still nowhere to be found. That evening, our neighbor called saying she had seen a dead dog out in front of their house. Knowing Sophia's delicate state, I grabbed a shovel and a cardboard box, secretly snuck out of the house, and found, near the neighbors, cute little Pepper lifeless on the road. I was glad Sophia didn't see her in this state.

After retrieving the dog, I returned home without being seen. The other kids were busy elsewhere, so I focused on helping Sophia find closure with her beloved Pepper. Through my experiences with death, I felt centered, and intuitively knew what to do. With candles and flowers, I created a simple, but elegant altar on the porch outside the kitchen.

With no denial or fear, my feelings flowed freely. The death experiences of *my* past surfaced—the dead body I saw on the road, the death of my girlfriend Julie, and all the rest—as I went upstairs to get Sophia to join me in a final farewell.

She looked at my face and knew that Pepper was gone, and cried as I held her tightly. After a while, we went downstairs to the candlelit altar, and held a silent vigil except for her sobs. After twenty minutes, I spoke a few words on her behalf.

"Pepper, you were a great, loving dog. So much fun. We'll miss you, and will always love you."

Sophia sat through it all, so moved she couldn't talk, but I knew she had benefitted from the ceremony. Leaving her alone at the altar, I returned only to wrap a blanket around her, and whispered, "I love you." She nodded and sank back into her private sorrows.

She didn't want to watch the burial, so the next day, I dug a hole and buried Pepper in our garden. For a while, all the emotional pain, death, and loss suffered not only by me, but now, my children, distressed me, *Where, dear God, is the joy? Haven't we seen enough death and suffering?* But still, the remnants of wisdom I had been gaining allowed me to see beyond appearances even by the Angel of Death. I could keep centered even as I felt the loss.

Freedom in Europe

During these days when I was trying to figure myself out, wandering around in Malibu, I woke each morning with no plans, no appointments, and no obligations. I hadn't lived this way for over twenty years, since I was twenty-one in Europe. During that trip, as now, I could change my schedule on a whim, harbor no idea of where I'd land at nightfall, and move through my days with the exhilarating feeling of freedom.

During that trip in Europe, I had leapt into the great unknown. On each cobblestone street, in every face I passed and flower I smelled, I felt a great affection for…life. With no expectations, everywhere I turned revealed something new to explore or a fresh concept to grasp. I lived my days connected to all, moving to my own rhythm in total freedom. Love was everywhere…except for one time over a *jambon* sandwich.

At a train station cafe, I had ordered a delicious-looking *jambon* (ham) sandwich. But where was the *jambon*? I opened the bread and showed it to the waiter, "I'm sorry, sir, but there is no meat! No *jambon*!" He dismissed my complaint, rattled off something in French that accused me of having already eaten it. Indignant, I refused to pay. As I got up to catch my train, he tackled me to the floor! Two grown men writhing on the ground fighting over a piece of missing *jambon*. What has the world gotten to?

Eventually, I had to pay him if I wanted to catch my train. Heavily shaken and irate, I watched the landscape shoot past my train window, and before I knew it, I was at my next destination, Champagne Province. A tour group of white-haired wine connoisseurs, all old enough to be my parents, sauntered by, and on a whim, I slipped in, unofficially, and joined them. Nobody questioned me, all thought I was somebody's son, I surmised.

Soon, I found myself in an opulent chateau, engaged in small talk, receiving sympathy for being tackled over my missing *jambon*.

"Oh, don't worry about it. Those Parisians, they're so snobby," said one English gentleman as he sipped from his glass of Dom Perignon. "Instead, taste this. Only thing I drink anymore, so…tense, rhythmic, and vibrant. What do you think?"

As I received my sample, I thought, *Wow, with an attitude of no judgment and no expectations, I was now even "enjoying" having been tackled over that damn jambon.* Slowly, I took a sip of that exquisite Dom Perignon. Relishing my crazy adventure, exhilarated by the fine champagne coursing through my taste buds and nasal tract, I believed that *anything* was possible, even…God. *Did I really say that? The "G" word coming out of my own mouth?* I looked at that glass of Dom Perignon with new respect.

All during college years at Berkeley, I had often boasted to friends that I was a "devout atheist," although little thought was given to that quip. But now, in Europe, with no schedules and obligations, I could really examine such deeper questions of life.

One sip in, and *God* came out. Relishing my Dom Perignon, I gazed in concentration as I finally found words to describe my drink, "Full of surprise, and profound."

Vision of Bill

One magical event during this European trip, I was sitting by the magnificent Lake Windermere in the Lake District of England. Feeling completely at peace on a clear, cool spring day, I saw how dark and murky the lake was beneath the glass-like surface. I thought about my girlfriend, Amy, and her recently deceased brother, Bill. Less than a month ago, he had been riding on a motor scooter in Hawaii when he was hit by a truck and died instantly. He was only twenty-four.

And then he was "here," right beside me. Not physically, but I could feel his presence as if he were sitting beside me to my right staring over Lake Windermere. I took a few deep breaths and carried on as if it were a normal day.

Silently, I flashed on the last time I was with Bill at his funeral in bright, sunny Southern California, but all the sunshine in the world couldn't cheer up the many sad faces. Then his body was lowered into the earth. The sobs of Amy were punctuated by the sounds of dirt as I threw shovelfuls onto the casket, which slowly disappeared from view.

As I recalled his funeral, I saw in my mind's eye Bill's face as calm and accepting as I had ever seen in anyone. Though I was alone by the lake, the *life* of him was alive and well in spite of his recent death. What a strange paradox, and yet the whole experience made me feel that death was not the end. It was a beginning of something new. It was the first time I had gained options on how to face the Angel of Death other than with fear.

Traveling had given me new attitudes that I now sought to apply towards my divorce and the demise of my business. Open-minded, with no expectations or judgments, I was trying to accept everything with equanimity, even death. Even when someone during this European trip had gone off on a tirade against America and ugly Americans—"You are materialists! Imperialists! You talk peace and freedom as you bully the world!"—I could listen with detachment, interested in his viewpoint whether I agreed or not. *Now*, I challenged myself, *can I hold this attitude with Gigi?*

Death Ritual

Several years after my trip to Europe, in a house in Malibu, I was playing with the notion of giving up smoking pot. Get clean, get pure. I told my girlfriend, who suggested giving up the habit in style by taking all my last bits of dope and baking it into brownies as one last blow-out indulgence. And so we did, and came up with delicious brownies, which we began to devour. Thinking that they were not taking effect I had an extra one or two.

Before I knew it, we were so high that if we had bumped our heads on the ceiling, I wouldn't have been surprised. For the first hour, we were filled with nonstop laughter. My stomach ached. Everything was funny. How nice to laugh! I had read how it could even heal disease. *Dis-ease?* The idea launched me on another laughing fit.

After an hour, my well-being went downhill fast. Filling up with gas, my stomach welled up like a balloon, and I was utterly in pain. Staggering to the bathroom, I tried everything to get the brownies out of my system. Which end it came out made no difference as long as there was some relief, but no such luck. Desperately, I whimpered for help.

"Honey, help me. I feel awful. I think I'm going to die." She couldn't hear me, so I put out another plaintive cry, "Help me! Please, help."

But to no avail. My girlfriend had turned into an inert lump on the couch, completely passed out. Having trouble breathing, I gulped air as I felt my stomach was about to burst. I barely made my way to the bedroom and collapsed on the bed. Within moments, I began to hallucinate wildly:

Lightning bolts! Flashes of bright colors! A freshly dug grave with moisture still oozing from the sides. A few people standing overhead. I am lying on the raw earth at the bottom of the grave. A clump of dirt hits my stomach, then my legs. And my face! I scream in terror, but can't move, as dirt continues to fall from above. With earth covering my face, I can't see. I'm being buried alive. *I can't stand this nightmare, I'd rather die.*

Suddenly, my vantage point changes. I'm now standing beside the grave along with the others. With shovel in hand, I plunge it into the pile of earth, and throw it onto my own face, onto my chest, everywhere until I am completely buried...

I woke up in the morning feeling like I had been hit by a truck. The pot must've eased its effects. Though I didn't know it at the time, I've come to see this experience as a shamanic Death Ritual, a death of the ego, the death of the old me, the death of thinking the body is the real me. It was a rite of passage for my early twenties.

Between this vision and the presence of Bill's spirit by that lake in England, my old fears about mortality and death became greatly reduced.

But what about the time when Lila made me face all the death experiences of my life and my old fears of death and mortality reared their ugly heads again? Yes, five steps forward, and two steps back. My old fears *did* come up, but only for a while. When I reminded myself of my graveside vision and Bill's spirit by the lake, I knew that there's much more going on than the physical. I was beginning to see *behind* the Red Road, and one by-product of my new perception was the growing awareness that *death does not exist.*

Compassion for Gigi

In August 2004, shortly after I had broken up with April, I invited the entire family on a boat ride from Santa Barbara to the Channel Islands. It was a beautiful summer day, everyone was in good behavior, and the hours on the open sea served us all well. Afterwards, Gigi sent me a letter.

"A nice trip. Wouldn't it be nice if we could be together as a family again?"

For me to go back to our old ways? Impossible, but something in the letter made me see our break-up from *her* perspective. With newfound awareness of the Yellow Road, I saw just how sad and frightened she had been, and what *she* had been going through. Our family was torn apart for reasons she couldn't really understand. For this, I felt responsible, and a bit of guilt.

She had believed in the marriage vows we had taken years ago, and wondered why I had abandoned them. To her, marriage was "for better or for worse, in sickness and in health," and my departure was a breaking of this vow. To me, however, I was still carrying them out, still caring for the kids, not only financially, but also, as much as possible, emotionally. But most importantly, I was caring for them spiritually. I didn't want us to be trapped by a materialistic life filled with smug judgments, which was where we were all headed.

My arrogant, narcissistic ways had finally given way to the simple truth that life was much bigger than me, and much bigger than I had thought. As a start, I had to be truly happy and whole if I was to be a true head of the family, so I had willingly trashed a life run by ego in order to rediscover a true identity, one rooted in spirit.

All these psychological insights were beginning to settle into my daily life, and as a consequence, compassion and understanding began to enter into all my actions. Ultimately, we all want the same thing, love, peace, joy, and happiness—all feelings. No wonder Lila urged me to look behind the physical into the Yellow Road. *No matter how things may appear in the outside physical world*, I kept reminding myself, *their true value lies in the invisible realm of thoughts and feelings, the Yellow Road.*

Mind over Matter

One afternoon, Angie, my first yoga instructor, asked me to stay behind after class. I was flattered and couldn't help but notice her slim, muscular body draped casually in sexy yoga pants and a tank top. But, by then, I had matured a little, and categorically dismissed any thoughts of having another involvement. With newfound dedication to my spiritual quest, I didn't need any distractions.

"I sensed you're going through challenging times," she told me, "so I've got something for you. I thought you might be up for a challenge." With that, she handed me a large paperback book.

I stared at the cover, *The Disappearance of the Universe* by Gary Renard. I chuckled, because immediately, I could relate to the title. *That* was how I saw my universe, fast disappearing. Home, family, business, all gone.

"It'll blow your mind."

"Is that the goal?" I quipped.

"It's one of the most profound ones I've ever read, and trust me, I've read plenty."

"So tell me," as I unconsciously weighed the book in my hands, "after reading so many, many books, do you feel any more…any more…."

"Happier? Closer to God?" Enlightened?" she cut in.

"Yeah, exactly. Any of the above?"

"Well, what can I say? I live a day at a time, grateful to be myself, express myself, and, you know, keep on searching."

"Excuse me, but that doesn't sound like a concrete answer."

"Hey, there are plenty of answers, but first, what's your question? That's a process in and of itself. And, like they say, gather up all your questions, and when you don't feel the need to ask them anymore, that's when the answers come."

I looked away, not completely satisfied with her reply, which, to me, bordered on a platitude.

"I don't know, but I keep coming up with the need to surrender," I murmured.

"Yes, surrender to all challenges!" she answered gleefully.

"You're one of *those*, are you?" I asked.

"One of what?"

"The type to dot their I's with little hearts."

"Meaning, I'm light-hearted?" She studied my face after my hint of sarcasm, but then continued with conviction, "Yeah… I guess I *am* light-hearted. I'm happy because I'm grateful, and gratitude begets more happiness, and all together, I feel light-hearted. Yes, I'm light-hearted."

"Now that sounds like a concrete answer," I said with a smile. Kissing her on the cheek, I thanked her for the book and started to leave.

"Just promise me something. When you get your answers, share them with me, okay?"

"And vice versa," I replied, "although I have a feeling you're going to find them sooner than me."

"Hey, come on, it's not a race you know. Enjoy the read!"

I left class infected by her high spirits, and looked over the volume on the way to my car. Is this another one of Lila's tricks to make her point, I wondered, guiding me to this book because when the Universe disappears, what's behind it? The Yellow Road?

Looking through *The Disappearance of the Universe*, I came across statements like, "Nothing real can be threatened. Nothing unreal exists." Along with the *Sacred Path*, such books opened me up to an invaluable alternate perspective on reality, love, and forgiveness.

The Course in Miracles

That night I stared at the increasing number of books lying on my kitchen table. When you're lost, everyone has a book to recommend. Remembering how enthusiastic Angie was with *The Disappearance of the Universe*, I scooped it up and dove in. After only a few pages, I was mesmerized. It forced me to re-evaluate all preconceived notions beginning with the declaration that all life is an illusion, a dream. *There it is, again!* And it kept referring to another book, *A Course in Miracles*, which *also* declared that life is an illusion. *All right, I get the point. I'll look into it.*

After a morning yoga class, I approached Angie and stared at her for a few moments.

"What's wrong?" she finally asked.

"Sounds weird, but since this is all illusion, I'm trying to figure out if you're real or not."

"Wonderful! You've started reading it," she laughed.

"I feel like it's some sort of endorsement for *A Course in Miracles*."

"And that's a bad thing?"

"Well, depends on what's in it? Although, I like the miracle part."

"Still looking for easy answers," she said shaking her head.

"Sorry. Didn't mean to be so flip."

"The *Course* is very challenging. Not for everyone."

"But is it right for me?"

"Get the book, read the book, and then we'll talk."

I plunged into the *Course*, and found it dense and profound. "Channeled" by a woman, the content is supposed to be the thoughts and words of Jesus. I had no way of knowing the truth of that, but ultimately, it didn't matter. The quality of material was so profound, that it has since become a pillar of my spiritual quest, and for years, now, I've read it every day for spiritual nourishment. No wonder it has proven so influential in a wide range of spiritual circles of our times.

Using Biblical language, the *Course* made a strong impression on me with simple, but powerful declarations that walloped me like a hammer:

"There are only two emotions, fear and love."

"Only when you live in love can you return to Source, or God."

"Universal love can be gotten only through forgiveness."

I chuckled at how things had worked out. My father had asked me to "give Jesus a chance," and here I was in a roundabout way fulfilling my promise.

Back in my beachside apartment, a thought from the *Course* kept running around in my brain: *The road to enlightenment requires forgiveness*. But forgiveness requires love, and I was filled with fear. What a big part it has played in my life with the fear of losing my children, the fear of "being eaten" in business, and the fear of the great unknown that I was facing this moment in my life.

Working Through Pain

"Breathe…breathe…be in the moment," Solvei urged me as a way of encouragement. A full-figured, blonde yoga teacher from Norway, I had hired her to give private instructions in yoga after Angie had moved out of town. Upside down, sweating profusely, body trembling, I tried to follow her instructions as I was approaching the fourth minute in a handstand against the wall. Seeing my arms shake, she urged me once again.

"Remember, strength from inside. Use your strength from inside."

"I can't do it." I gasped.

"Hold still, work through the pain. Go deep into your own core."

It was all I could do to practice mind over matter, and I found myself breathing deeply and deliberately. A tough task-master, Solvei taught an intense form of yoga, *Astanga yoga,* and was not one to indulge in weaknesses of any kind. So I focused on my breathing to enter into my "core," my heart center. No wonder they say yoga builds core strength.

I remember April had also encouraged me to do headstands.

"You ought to practice this regularly. It's not only good for health by promoting youthfulness, but it also turns your life upside down. You get a new perspective on everything. You'll be surprised by what you see."

Sweating freely, using my will to continue the stance, I saw a stream of thoughts pass by my mind—my usual fears, doubts, and old beliefs—but who's able to linger on them with the physical duress going on? After a while, being so focused on my breathing and working through my pain, I felt a profound peace descend over me and experienced a few moments of *just being,* no doing required, *just be.*

Faith of the Father

On my weekly visits with my father, he'd sometimes check up on me, "Bills still being paid?" I'd assure him, yes, and move on to other topics, like how much I'd been studying recently.

"Haven't read this much since college," I told him. "The difference is that, now, I *want* to. Then, I was forced to."

"Anything interesting?" he asked.

"Just a lot of spiritual books."

"Maybe it was my fault," he replied, frowning.

"What?" How fast guilt and judgment came into the picture, but that's to be expected since he's such a devout Presbyterian.

"I keep reminding myself that if we had just brought you kids up with a little more religious structure, maybe..."

"Dad, you can't force religion down somebody's throat. You know how many kids I grew up with whose parents made them go to church? Not only did they resent it, but I guarantee you, most of them will probably stay away forever. At least with me, I'm studying the subject."

"Gigi didn't help," my father sighed.

"C'mon, Dad, now you're looking for someone to blame. It's not you or Gigi or Mom. There's nobody to blame. What you gave us kids was even better, the freedom to choose. And, believe me, you did expose us to your faith, you did."

"Well, how about adding the Bible to your reading list. At least the New Testament. I want…it would make me so happy if you'd only give Christ a chance," he insisted, firmly.

"I'll think about it, Dad. I will, I promise." I was struck how my Dad, by his own standards, was uncharacteristically insistent. But, deep down, I could see that the faith in my own heart was not the faith of my father's. Every generation must rediscover the truths for their own time.

Forgiveness

Taking my cue from the *Course*, I threw myself deeply into the power and practice of forgiveness. Forgiveness had always implied to me that someone did something wrong, which implied judgment and guilt, which in turn created separation. *Who are we to judge, anyway?* an inner voice kept shouting. The judge and the guilty will, for the most part, remain at odds with each other, so it seemed to accomplish nothing in terms of true healing. But now, thanks to my books, a breath of fresh air was blowing through my preconceptions.

First, I had to take responsibility for my actions and own up to wrongdoing on my part. For example, with Gigi and my children, I had to admit how my departure had caused them to suffer, and ask for their forgiveness.

However, on a deeper level, I had to forgive *myself* for all my errors, real or imagined. For breaking up the family, I had to come to terms with my own guilt and remorse, and forgive myself. My "inner Judge" had been raking me over the coals endlessly condemning me for my imperfections. Once I could forgive myself (and I'm still working on it), I could readily forgive others (Gigi, for example) since I had already gone through the most ruthless of all saboteurs, my own demons.

Finally, thanks to the *Course*, I could see forgiveness in a third way, the most powerful and transcendent way: *Give love, kindness and*

understanding to everyone with no expectations and no conditions, period.
Seen this way, forgiveness means, "for giving." Give love. Give kindness.
Give understanding. With this attitude, my heart opened wide, and my
mind went spinning. How liberating! I could even hear myself declare to
the world at large, "I'm a blade of grass. Walk on me. Let me give cool-
ness for your feet."

Equanimity with Kids

"Dad, you don't take care of us," twelve-year-old Morgan shouted at me
one afternoon during a visit at the old house. "You're a cheater! You're
a liar, and you don't take care of Mom. You think about everybody and
everything except us!"

I was ready to pounce on her and prove her wrong, but this time,
equipped with my new attitudes about no judgment and forgiveness, I
checked myself and silently breathed to calm myself. I was determined to
practice new ways to respond. (As fast as I learn something, life, it seems,
plops me into some predicament to test me.)

"You love your girlfriends more than us. You don't even work anymore, but waste all your time watching golf on TV…" she continued,
and went on bitterly attacking me for another five minutes.

How I cringed with righteous indignation—*How dare she say that!*—
but I forced myself to listen, and hear her well. Sweat went down my
armpits, but I remained cool. When she was spent, we sat there for a
moment in silence. Finally, when all was calm, I spoke.

"Morgan, I want you to know that I heard what you said. Thanks for
sharing your feelings. They're not things easy to talk about. I know I've
caused you suffering, and I'm really sorry."

Taken aback by this new response from me, she studied me for a
while.

"I feel love for our whole family," I continued. "We've *all* suffered—
you, me, Mom, your sisters, all of us. We've all gone through a lot. I really
care about you, and about Mom, and would love nothing better than to
have us all work together through this difficult time."

Tears filled her eyes, but she remained silent.

"I hear what you're saying, too," she finally said with a pout, "but I still think you've gotta' do more for us."

"You're right. I'll try, I really will try."

She remained silent, so we just sat there a bit awkwardly. Then we went to dinner at my mom's house. We ended up playing together on the piano as she proudly taught me a new rhythmic duet. By the time we returned to my house, her energy was completely different. As we sat on the couch, she leaned against me, "Thanks, Dad, for taking me out."

Once again, I found myself up against the wall upside down in a handstand sweating and shaking while Solvei egged me on. It was a particularly intense yoga session with me upside down for nearly five minutes as I battled disparaging thoughts, epiphanies, and distractions when, once again, I found myself sliding into another world. It was all peace and bliss.

Sitting on my deck after class, I could still feel that sublime peace. I only needed to exist because I was enthralled by euphoria. Suddenly, I panicked. I had almost forgotten to go to Malibu Junior High. My eldest daughter, Maya, was going to graduate.

On the drive over there, I reminisced about all the wonderful times I had had with her. Being the first child, she held a special place in my heart. Just last year, we had both participated in an outdoor adventure outfit in Canada called "Back Roads." With hiking, biking, rock-climbing, and mountain air all around, it was a perfect place for father-daughter bonding, especially since we both love the great outdoors so much. It has remained one of the highlights of my life, but how elusive these magical moments are.

Now, with the family split, and she maturing through another rite of passage with this graduation, a feeling of loss swept over me. I just had to remind myself to be in the moment, take things one day at a time, and keep faith that when one door closes, another one opens.

Rites of Passage: Maya's Graduation

I could have burst with pride to see Maya, my firstborn, looking so radiant and beautiful in her special graduation outfit. Gigi was on good behavior, the kids were in great spirits, and all in all, it was a great event.

After the ceremony, I scanned the sea of a thousand faces in the outdoor amphitheater, imagining what each parent might be feeling. Each student there represented thousands of hours of love, caring, misunderstandings, and magic. As I looked over the crowd, my gaze was magnetized by a woman with a beautiful, radiant smile and an aura of lightness. It was Lizanne! She and I had gone out briefly years ago.

With Gigi and the kids busy with friends, I saw Lizanne laughing at the buffet table. I worked my way over to her and gave her a warm embrace. Her hair was lighter, and she seemed genuinely happy.

"It's so good to see you," she said. "I saw Gigi inside, and... Are you..." She stopped herself. She sensed that we were separated.

"We're done, just not officially," I stated evenly.

"Mine is official," she replied sadly.

"Really?" My curiosity was piqued. "The last time I saw you, everything seemed so fine." She shrugged lightly with a smile. "But, then again," I continued, "all the real action is behind closed doors. Who knows what really takes place between two people? Sometimes not even those involved."

She laughed. "So true. Sometimes you get so caught up in the day-to-day you don't see that it's all going to pieces right before your eyes."

"I wish it were that easy," I groaned. "Gigi has taken our kids hostage."

"I'm so sorry to hear that."

"We had just reached the point..."

"Of no return," she cut in. "Been there," she sighed. "By the way, we don't have to talk about this if you don't want to."

"That's probably best. But would you like to get together sometime?"

"Just to talk?" she asked, caught off guard. "Okay, that would be nice."

"Absolutely, I'm not ready for more than that..."

"You don't have to explain. I feel the same way."

"It's just that...I feel broken right now," I blurted out. "Before you stands a broken man, with a lot of baggage in my trunk, stuff nobody's going to want to deal with." I felt a bit awkward by my own candor, but it was part of my new modus operandi, *truth*. One of life's little tenets I had finally decided to embrace.

"So I will give you a call to talk," I continued, "it would be great. If not, no worries I won't be offended, I promise. So take care of yourself."

"You too," she replied. We embraced, and she headed off.

I had always been attracted to her, but the timing was never right. Either I was involved, or she was seeing someone. We had dated briefly nearly twenty years ago, but she had left me for a wealthy older man. Though we had each moved on, I had always kept a special corner of my heart for her.

As she walked off, I couldn't take my eyes off of her. There was something in the way she tilted her head, a certain sparkle in her steel-blue eyes, and an easygoing manner in her stride. For reasons beyond explaining, our meeting gave me a sense of hope and a breath of fresh air for my heavy burdens. As it would turn out, this ceremony was not only a rite of passage for my daughter, but for me as well.

Did that afternoon visit in the quad set the stage for my own graduation?

A Shamanic Session

A few months later in a short get-away from my normal routine, I was meditating in a garden in Carmel when a gust of wind blew over me so suddenly that my eyes popped open. Just then, I saw coming towards me a tanned, normal-looking man with no pretensions, who I sensed right away as being super bright. It was Jon, who I had met through April, the masseuse. With Jon, I was to have my first "shamanic session," not that I knew exactly what that meant, so I just kept an open mind and saw it as a way to go deeper in reclaiming my connection with Spirit.

In the Tower Room of the Cypress Inn, I found myself laid down on a blanket on the carpet surrounded with crystals, feathers, and rattles. As Jon slowly passed hands and feathers over me, working on my invisible "energy body," he told me he had picked up something about one of my "past lives." This was an idea new to me, but I was open. Intrigued by his shamanic perspective, I thought it could be useful in helping me expand my conceptions of life. He was careful to say little about those past lives, but alluded to something about "anger and violence." Immediately, a shudder went through me. He had hit upon one of my sore points, for I well knew I was capable of sudden explosions of rage.

He also mentioned "soul retrievals," another idea new to me. Could this mean *"spirit retrieval?"* If so, could I relate to it with my recent focus on reconnecting with spirit? Lying on the floor, I felt that my mind was indeed expanding, because until now, all I knew was that there was only one life, the one I was living. *The one which felt like I was dying. Something was dying in me and I desperately needed to know.* The idea of reincarnation I had always dismissed as irrelevant. What made this session powerful for me was that there was relatively little talking, little intellectual discourse. Instead, Jon's ideas burned deep into my psyche through ritual, body, and emotions.

KNOCK! KNOCK! KNOCK! Rudely shaken out of my reverie, I realized that it was past my 10 o'clock checkout time. Jon opened the door a crack, and the manager peeked in and saw a man lying on the floor surrounded with exotic paraphernalia. Had he smelled the sage and thought it was some wild marijuana spree? Did he think we were in the midst of some satanic rite?

"What's going on in there?" he demanded, as he tried to peek inside the crack in the door.

"Everything's all right," Jon answered quietly.

The manager became even more suspicious, until I sat up like a corpse coming back to life and shouted, "Everything's alright! Now shut the door!"

Quietly, Jon shut the door in the manager's face, and we continued with our "shamanic full-body energy cleanse."

Accelerating the Journey

One morning in my beach cottage, I took in the daily affirmation from *A Course in Miracles,* "I will be still even for an instant, and I'll be home." That inspired me to meditate in earnest, but I was anything but still. Instead, an inner voice kept shouting out, *I feel in prison. Enough of my beach cottage. Enough book knowledge, I need action, adventure, direct experience. I need to break free! But where? How? When?*

Whoops, I had gone well off my meditation again, but slowly, with the power of the practice, I began to calm down, and ever so gently slip into a familiar calm that usually announced the appearance of my mysterious "voice," Lila. It had been months since I had last heard from her about the Yellow Road, but sure enough, she was here. Peace permeated the air all around.

"Lila, thank you so much for coming. I could use your guidance right now. I feel so…restrained. What can I do?"

"Accelerate your journey," she replied in her sweet and soothing voice.

"What is that supposed to mean?"

"Go on a Vision Quest."

"A what?"

I waited and waited, but she didn't say more. Typical. She says a few words and leaves me squirming and scrambling trying to find out what she meant. But her few words always packed a punch for the better, so I was left with the words *Vision Quest* running around in my brain.

Busy working on my Map one evening, I had labeled the southeast quadrant "The Red Road," and the southwest quadrant "The Yellow Road." As usual, when I worked on the Map, my mind became so calm that inspirations often burst into my head like fireworks. Recently, the Map seemed to come alive, become vibrant and responsive. I'd sense it talking to me, silently, of course, saying, "Look here, draw there," and I'd be moved to develop something on a certain quadrant.

It was a perfect activity to muse upon the concept of a Vision Quest. Though I had heard the phrase before, I had no clue as to what it really meant. Am I supposed to go out in the world and find a vision of… myself? My direction in life? What does that really mean? Or is it a rite of passage, an initiation? If so, initiation into what? And who's conducting it? *The Sacred Path* book counseled that Vision Quests should not be undertaken without guidance from a "trained Medicine Person." So, who would guide me? My invisible voice?

Or, alas, I'm going crazy? I hear unseen voices, I follow its instructions, and step-by-step, I'm going mad. *But no, it's that damn Demon of Doubt, again, trying to wreak havoc with the greatest transformation in my life*. By sheer willpower, I forced myself to keep faith and trust my inner knowing. But it wasn't easy.

I had always assumed that I came from the world, that *the world created me*. But now, inspired by the *Course*, I was introduced to the idea that *I create the world*. My thoughts and feelings create my reality. Is this what a Vision Quest means for me to do, to go out into the world to receive a vision as to what kind of world I'm to create? What are the criteria to know you're doing it right?

Recently, I had been tired of book knowledge, bored with my long walks of contemplation on the beach, and ready to get away from Malibu. For the past six months, I'd been holed up like a monk, tossing and turning in the stew of my own guilt, fears, and hopes. And insights. Like that butterfly on my altar, I was ready to burst out of the cocoon to fly free. Lila was right, her timing perfect. It was time for me to "accelerate my journey" and go on a Vision Quest. But, still, what did that really mean?

Choice

In 2004, following the family tradition, I, along with my brother Peter, attended church on Christmas Eve with my parents. The service was pleasant enough, and it was nice to be with my family, but after just a few minutes into the sermon, I started to squirm. When they spoke of Christ as the *only way out of eternal damnation*, or how we can be saved from our *original sin*, I literally started to cringe. "*What happened to love and kindness?*" I screamed silently to myself. The morality, the guilt, the judgment, they were everything I was desperately trying to liberate myself from, thanks to *A Course in Miracles*.

After the service, in the spirit of Christ, I managed to be polite and gracious to family friends, but I couldn't wait to get out of there. With my new attitudes of no judgment, I reminded myself that ultimately, there's no right or wrong, but only personal choice. They've made their choice, I've made mine, and we just have to be ready to take full responsibility for the consequences. But still, *Let me out of here!*

After the service, my parents invited me back for tea, but I said I was too tired, kissed them goodbye, and headed home. I was riled by the pastor's insistence that only through the church would I find salvation. *No, no, no*, I declared to myself, *I, for one, will look inward, and trail-blaze my own path to enlightenment.* I felt so imprisoned by those old ideas of Christianity that I wanted to explode again, *Please, get me out of here! I need relief!*

And just on time, my brother Peter invited me to go with him on his annual trip to Brazil. It sounded absolutely terrific if you appreciate fine foods, sensual women, and endless booze. Hedonism at its exotic best, enhanced by a samba backbeat. But, alas, I wasn't the old Adam anymore. The excessive carnality was exactly the opposite of my new hungers, so I had to make my regrets.

But then, I was offered another choice. Gary, a friend from the gym, was kind enough to ask me to join him on his annual pilgrimage to Mumbai (Bombay). He was going to see his childhood friend from Chicago who had transformed himself to become a Swami. Now that was a theme dear to my heart, someone who was able to transform himself completely towards spiritual values. In any case, I had always wanted to go to India and, thanks to all my recent research, had become doubly fascinated by Buddhism and Hinduism. My altar was filled with Buddhist artwork of lotuses, *thangkas,* and Hindu sculptures. What I could learn from cultures with such long traditions in spirituality!

But, thinking it through, I realized that this was Gary's journey, and not mine. I couldn't see myself giving over my life to follow a guru, no matter how loving and wise. For better or worse, I still needed to forge my own path. So, if Brazil was too sensual, and India did not belong to me, where should I go?

Vision Quest

That evening when I got home to make tea, I stopped in my tracks, gazing at my Sacred Path Cards on the kitchen table. *They* could give me a clue as to my next move.

I washed my hands, got into "sacred space" by reciting an invocation, and decisively surrendered to whatever the cards wanted to tell me. Then I picked up the cards. With the question of my next move firmly in mind, I shuffled and spread them out like a fan, face down. With eyes closed, I moved my right hand slowly, slowly over the cards. At one point, I felt a subtle pull from one of the cards and turned it over: *#3, Vision Quest.*

I got goose bumps! It seemed too perfect! But then, I *did* promise myself to surrender to whatever came up. The card included the image of a young warrior and the words, "Seeking/Finding." *That's me, exactly,* I thought.

Before diving into its full meaning, I decided to pick one more card, and repeating the movement, pulled *#16, Power Place* with a picture of Monument Valley and the words, "Earth-Connection/Empowerment." The words "Indian Nation" flashed in my head, and in that moment, everything came together.

I knew how I often felt a profound stillness and connectedness whenever I was in the wide open spaces of Mother Nature. She's filled with dolphins, birds, trees, and mountains, each a friend, a healer, and a perfect example of unconditional love.

What if I headed east towards the Indian Nations, towards Monument Valley of the rising sun, towards the place of my…salvation?

Having just seen my kids and folks, I told no one what was brewing in my head. The only person I *did* tell was my "newfound" friend, Lizanne, because I needed someone to water my plants, and more importantly, because she was the only one around that I felt emotionally safe to reveal this deeper stirring from my heart. Still, she was a bit perplexed, and told me later that she was as curious as she was impressed.

"What kind of man would go off blindly to find himself?" she had wondered.

Before dawn the next morning, I was roaring down the empty 10 Freeway watching the sun beckoning me on as it rose over the City of the Angels. How auspicious; it was Christmas Day, the universal Holy Day for resurrection. Feeling as exhilarated as that first time I had gone off to Europe at twenty-one, courage and faith welled up from my gut. In a few minutes, I left it all behind. L.A. was but a distant silhouette in the rearview mirror, and the sun was lighting up the world for a whole new day.

Though I didn't know exactly *where* I was going, I was going! I was on my first Vision Quest!

6

VISION QUEST

Sedona

Cactus and sagebrush whizzed by as my car raced through the desert towards Sedona. Thanks to my yoga practice I felt calm in my excitement, and saw myself as a hummingbird—being still while in motion. Up ahead, it looked like the road was submerged underwater, but it was just a mirage. *How perfect*, I thought to myself. *Truth and illusion, that seems to be one of the themes of this trip. Whatever unfolds, I must be open and just receive.*

As I rounded a bend, I gasped in surprise. I forgot how majestic this landscape could be. A cluster of massive red sandstone soared hundreds of feet high, piercing the bright blue sky. In the distance, more outcroppings of colossal stones created, all together, a unique and wonderful announcement of the nearing of Sedona.

I pulled off the road to take it all in. On the flat desert, those giant rocks standing so tall and proud turned golden red from the setting sun. What character, what power. If one of them came to life and spoke to me the wisdom of the ages, I would not have been surprised. For a few moments, I stood there and absorbed their mighty presence.

Known for its natural beauty and powerful "energy vortexes," Sedona had long attracted mystics, healers, and seers, and served as a Mecca for those seeking inner truth, healing, and rejuvenation. In the past, whenever I had asked people why they had come here, I would often be impatient with their "supernatural" answers of a "lucky accident" or an "inner calling." But now, I had to chuckle at myself because I was here having been "invited here by the Medicine Cards."

I was on a "vision quest." With absolutely no regard for pleasure or luxury, I saw my "vision quest" as *not* about going to a definite place to visit a specific attraction, but rather a journey of faith that *I'd be at the right place at the right time for finding my true identity. I had officially become a pilgrim, aspirant, initiate, one who gets on the path to remembering their higher Self.*

Arriving in town at the magical hour when the sun has just set, I noticed how every living object could show off their own luminosity. It inspired in me a sense of purpose. The end of this day signaled the end of my old life forever, and I, too, can radiate my own luminosity. How I burned with determination to find the new path awaiting me, whatever that could be. I wondered what secrets the red earth of Sedona could reveal to me.

I hadn't felt this excitement since I had gone to Europe when I was twenty-one. How freely I had roamed! With no time constraints, no reservations, and no schedules, I had traveled with no expectations but that of joy and discovery. That, too, I could see now was a vision quest, a transformative journey that had impacted my life forever. So, trusting my instincts, I could think of no better way to launch my vision quest than to immerse in the ineffable energy of Sedona.

Inn on the Creek

After cruising around awhile, I found a room on a creek at The Briar Patch Inn. That evening, I sat before an outdoor fireplace and "burned away my past." A friend, involved in shamanic traditions, Jon, had introduced me to the practice of releasing unwanted habits, beliefs, and thought-patterns by "blowing them into a stick" and then throwing the stick into a fire to release those old habits through "ritual burning."

With the warmth of the flames on my face, I thought of my "failures" in business and marriage and occasions of reprehensible personal conduct. With each thought in mind, I would literally blow it out into a stick, throw it into the fire, and watch it burn. Hour after hour, I threw sticks into the fire; I had so much to burn. For the next four evenings, I would carry out this practice, and gradually, magically, I felt lighter and freer.

One night, something whizzed by among the canopy of trees. A huge owl had flown by in the dark to settle in his own turf. I found it inspiring: I will be like that owl and peer into my dark past, and find my rightful home. I noticed that recently, intuitively, every incident of nature seemed to be a sign, an omen, an inspiration for me. Nature was constantly talking to me, and I was ready to listen.

Bell Rock

The first morning in Sedona, I awoke up at the crack of dawn ready for anything that would give me an overview of my trip. But even before I went to sleep, I knew it would be Bell Rock, a famous Sedona landmark of sandstone that shoots up into the sky for over 500 feet. This prominent outcropping is shaped roughly like a bell, hence the name, and is revered in this area for holding special vortexes of energy. What this really meant I had no idea, but there was only one way to find out, and that was to see for myself.

Not even the chilly weather could dampen my spirits as I walked around its base. Craning my neck to look up to its apex, I was inspired by the notion of meditating at the very top, which meant somehow scaling up its vertical sides. Hmmm. During my last trip here years ago, I had watched with a touch of envy as rock climbers scaled the massive rock to the top, but today it was my turn. If they could do it, I could too, I reassured myself.

With determination trumping my fear, I began my hike up a steep slope to where the vertical sides began. Exploring for a way up, I found a two-foot crevasse that could allow me to work myself up eight feet high until I found another ledge. Exerting pressure with my legs to increase friction on my back, I jimmied myself up, foot by foot until I had ascended a good ten feet and reached the top.

After walking some distance, I found another route that gave me the possibility to climb to the next level. This time it required scrambling thirty feet straight up with the narrowest of footholds. The moment of truth.

Though I had never practiced rock-climbing, I began my ascent, but suddenly my body froze with a wave of anxiety. I remembered when I was a kid of eight falling from an avocado tree. I had plummeted fifteen feet or so, and in trying to break my fall, I had broken both my arms. Thank God I didn't break my neck, but still, ever since then I had a fear of heights. *Perhaps I am now supposed to overcome this fear because now I am hanging on the edge of a cliff. Should I take the easy way out and just jump?*

Taking a deep breath to shake off the fear, I began once again, inch by inch, to climb up the rock. Knowing the importance of keeping focused, I categorically refused to look down. Taking things one step at a time, I found footholds and ledges that allowed me to continue, but only barely. Once, when I couldn't find anything, I had a moment of panic. I was stuck, and couldn't go up, and couldn't go down. Again, I forced myself to breathe and remain centered. After a few moments, a foothold appeared that I had somehow missed, and I moved up another foot.

And so it went. One foot after another, one ledge after another I worked myself higher and higher. After 45 minutes of intense concentration, I found myself at the top! Standing tall, I felt a tremendous sense of accomplishment with the utter conviction that clear intentions made great things possible. Now, finally, I allowed myself to look down and scanned the 360-degree panoramic view 500 feet above the desert floor.

How magnificent! Just the overview to start the trip that I had looked for, just like the view the eagle sees as it flies. Here and there dotting this whole area were those gargantuan outcroppings growing out of the desert floor. Each a sculpture, each a living being with character and dignity, each magnificent against the perfect ultramarine sky.

The Overview

After taking in the view, I made myself comfortable to meditate. No one was around, which was only natural considering it was the dead of winter, so I had the whole place to myself. As I settled down cross-legged to meditate, I began to hear music. *I must be advancing in my meditation,*

I thought, but after a while, it didn't seem to be coming from within. It sounded so clear in a normal kind of way, and vaguely familiar. But from where is it coming?

Finally, I realized that it came from deep within my backpack. My iPod had been accidentally turned on, and to my surprise, it was a song called "Transcendence" written by a musician named Robin Miller whom I had met in Sedona years ago. What sweet coincidence. Out of 7121 songs in my iPod, "Transcendence" was playing, so what could I do but take it as a good omen of things to come. For a while, I listened to it as a perfect transition into meditation.

As I meditated, I began feeling energy swirling around and through me. It seemed to flow from deep within Mother Earth, up through Bell Rock, though my body, and on up to the heavens. For twenty minutes, I let this powerful, rhythmic force go through me, hoping this energy could help end my aching sense of separation. *Is this the vortex of power that they talk about?*

When I opened my eyes, I felt a little dizzy, and so light that it seemed my spirit could leave my body and soar free. But doubts crept in, and the moment was gone. I was still imprisoned by reason and logic, and knew I would work on liberating their hold on me. For a couple of hours, I sat there taking in the panoramic view as thoughts of self-pity and self-doubts dissolved away into feelings of euphoria and invincibility. I felt Lila's presence giving me courage.

The Crystal Shop

After lunch that day, I ended up browsing through the local stores. In one crystal shop, my eyes were quickly drawn to a piece of rose quartz shaped like a heart. I felt it belonged to Lizanne, who I had just "re-met" at Maya's graduation. "Do I know her well enough to buy her this gift?" I asked myself. I hesitated a few moments, until I trusted my instincts and bought it for her.

Just then, a woman bumped into me who acted like she knew me.

"Have we met before?" she asked.

Meeting her dark, probing eyes, I replied, "No, I think I would have remembered."

"Maybe it wasn't in this lifetime," she replied easily. "My name is Antarah. Antarah Rose." Later I would find out that she was a well-known psychic in town. "What brings you to Sedona?"

"I'm...seeking my truth," I said, although I was thinking about the solution to my constant theme of "separation."

"Continue your journey, and what you seek will *find you*. All you need to do is to keep open, and show up," she stated with calm authority.

I thanked her and started to leave. As I reached the door, she called out with one last remark, "And don't worry, your children will be fine."

I was stunned by her words, "just show up and what you seek will find you," another sign that I was on track.

A Visitation

The next day I sat in the middle of a creek next to the Inn on a big rock with precious sunlight hitting it. *Perfect*, I thought to myself, and hopped stepping-stones until I found myself sitting cross-legged on the big stone to meditate. Blue jays flew above, and the creek flowed past on both sides into a tunnel of willow trees fifty feet away. I smiled to myself with the idea that Mother Nature had set up this perfect setting just for me. Shutting my eyes, I could hear in stereo the soothing babble of the creek on both sides as I gradually drifted into a deep meditation.

After twenty minutes or so, I began to feel tingly. I thought I could feel a presence of something—a spirit? A brush of wind chilled me so much that my eyes popped opened. There, right before me in the tunnel of trees, I saw an old Indian man staring at me. Standing erect and proud, he seemed suspended with no visible sign of support. The edges of his outline gently shimmered. *Wait a second here, what's going on here? Am I seeing what I'm seeing?*

A moment of doubt came over me, and I didn't trust my eyes. Though I was still in a meditative state, I felt uncommonly perceptive and alert. I didn't dare move, barely breathed, and glanced elsewhere for a reality check. It was as if I were seeing everything for the first time; the textures of the willow trees, the shades of blue in the water, the silver and feathers the man wore, all seemed perfectly clear and more vibrant than usual. Strange as this experience was, I did not feel alarmed, and simply accepted whatever was happening. His regal beauty was not threatening, although his stern gaze demanded utter respect.

He quietly continued to gaze at me. He had such a regal bearing, and remained so still, it put me in awe. When our eyes met, I felt a profound communion with him. *I must be in some altered state between dreaming and waking,* I thought to myself.

"Who are you," I finally stammered.

"Your ancient father," he said, flatly, betraying no emotions whatso-ever. A chill went through my whole body. I knew what he said was true even though I didn't know what it really meant.

As he continued to gaze at me, it dawned on me that something was amiss, I had betrayed him, and something dear had been lost. Tears welled up in my eyes. Yes, I had done something terribly dishonorable even though I didn't know what it had been. Filled with remorse, tears rolled down my face as I wept openly.

"Please," I asked him, "please forgive me."

By degrees he became more and more faint until he was gone, leaving me all alone again, aching with guilt at what I had done. *But what had I done?*

That evening, I reviewed in my mind every instant of what had happened. Staring into the fireplace, I felt diminished at what I had done, and utterly humble at how little I knew in the face of the mystery, of past lives, shamans, and loss. The only thing I knew to my bones was that this beautiful, noble Indian was my ancestral father, and that I had somehow done him a grievous wrong.

A couple of days later, I wandered through Boynton Canyon. No one was around, so I found a nice spot and sat cross-legged, as usual, to meditate. It was about noon so the day seemed warmer than usual. In the middle of this flat, empty desert, I was surrounded by sage bushes and big rocks. The power and the silence of the desert, I hoped, would help me assimilate all that I had already experienced.

In spite of the wintry air, a gentle heat came up from the earth. Countless tiny wildflowers proudly declared their presence, a lizard scampered about here and there. This empty desert was actually teeming with life! I felt so present, so safe, and so connected that I felt I was beginning to have a deep communion with my true mother, Mother Earth.

As I closed my eyes to meditate, I thought, *In my strange trip, what will be revealed today?* As my meditation deepened, I again felt a presence so powerful that I opened my eyes for a reality check only to see about 150 feet away an Indian man on a brown horse. They looked larger than life, maybe 30 feet high. Again, my perception was clearer than normal. It was my ancestral father looking as dignified and powerful as ever.

Again, he gazed sternly at me, betraying no emotions, but I felt he was more relaxed. In my altered state, I knew his appearance was a gift, that Spirit was reaching out to me, and that whatever this gift meant, I would honor and accept it with gratitude. Surreal as his appearance may have seemed, it all felt perfectly natural. Much more work and study on my part would be required to fully understand my connection to him, but I was more than willing to do whatever was required.

As if reading my thoughts, the man and the horse began to get fainter by degrees. I stared after him until he completely disappeared, leaving me feeling lighter. A burden had lifted, a burden I didn't even know I had as tears welled up into my eyes, this time of gratitude and awe.

That night as I digested this powerful visitation, I knew my attunement with Spirit had taken an irrevocable turn. Though my burdens were still with me, I distinctly felt lighter. Before the fireplace, I held a stick with both hands as part of the ritual in seeking forgiveness. Even though I didn't know the particulars of what I had done, it didn't matter; forgiveness is of the heart, and I blew fervently into the stick to release my remorse.

A few days later, at New Frontiers, the local health food store, I ran into Antarah Rose again.

"Adam, it's good to see you," she said, as psychically, she gave me a once over.

"Had a great experience out in the desert. It's so alive. I felt so connected."

"Looks like Sedona is doing you good, awakening your energy centers," she smiled. "Your healing has begun."

"Really?" I didn't know what energy centers were, but I took it in stride.

"I see people come in and out of this town, but most are their own worst enemies. Don't let this happen to you. Let this place do its healing, tune in to the positive, and when you're ready, move on. You'll know when it's time."

After a couple more days, thanks to Antarah's gentle guidance, I felt it was time to "move on." After the powerful meeting with my "ancestral father," I was ready to leave Sedona.

Seven Sacred Pools

On the way out, I saw a sign for the "Seven Sacred Pools," which immediately brought up fond memories of family trips to the "Seven Sacred Pools" in Hawaii. So, spontaneously, I pulled over to have a look. As I sat on a rock formation overlooking the pools, I reflected on my past, and in spite of all the difficulties I had gone through (and would still have before me), I was filled with gratitude and a deep sense of well-being.

As I climbed down the rock formation and got closer to the pools, something bright and shiny caught my eye. A golden, reddish yellow stone glistened in the creek. Dipping my hand into the freezing cold, I retrieved it.

It was about three inches long with layers of reddish brown and yellow. Intuitively, I saw the yellow as the golden glow of my youth of innocence, and the reddish brown layer as the ordeals of my youth such as when my legs caught on fire. As I pondered it, it helped me see how I had always been caught in judgments of one layer over another instead of seeing it all as parts of a whole. No wonder I was plagued with sufferings and feelings of separation. Considering the stone a real find, I asked its permission to come home with me. It was destined to be the first sacred stone in my Medicine Bag.

Medicine Bag

As a technique of using physical objects to help cultivate one's inner being, I learned that shamans and Medicine Men and Women often utilize what is called a "Medicine Bag" or a "Mesa." These bags, often made of cloth or leather, contain objects of super-ordinary powers for healing, visions, and self-transformation. Through fasting and prayers, vision quests and other techniques, common objects become charged with power and are then placed inside the bag.

My shaman friend Jon, who suggested that I collect stones for my own medicine bag introduced me to this practice. I was to collect three stones for each of the four directions, twelve in all, to represent my journey through life. Now, finally, I knew I had the first stone for my Medicine bag, and I was off and running. These stones are found or gifted when one becomes initiated on the path.

Also, from my research with *The Sacred Path Cards*, I knew that stones were the "keepers of memories," and could serve as "allies" that would support my newfound journey beyond selfish ego into the world of Spirit. With my first stone, I became very excited because I was now a participant in all these practices, and not just a bystander.

During a rainy afternoon, I thought I'd get one more massage before I moved on to…who knows where. The masseuse was about sixty with grayish sandy hair, and called herself Rainmaker.

"You moving on? Because there's a lot of rain coming."

"Did you do a rain dance?" I asked half jokingly.

"Not this time."

An hour later, I was on the move in a light rain. I wasn't sure where I would go, but decided to drive north towards the Navajo Nation. This destination was inspired by *The Sacred Path Cards*, and also from having met my ancestral father, whose image kept appearing in my mind, prompting me to dig deeper to find our connection. Soon the rain picked up and began to pound the roof of my car as if announcing what's coming next on my journey.

After a few hours on the road, I pulled over for gas and food. As I waited in line for a sandwich, I spotted some postcards that depicted

Monument Valley. I plucked one from the metal stand and immediately felt a tinge of energy at the base of my spine. I knew it would be my next destination, and asked for directions.

"Excuse me, sir," I said to the store clerk, a Native American in his fifties with red skin, black hair, jeans, and a cowboy shirt. "How do I get to this place?" as I pointed to the post card.

"Why do you want to go there?"

"No particular reason. Just a place to check out on my journey."

"This is a place of power for our people. If you have no reason to go, then I cannot help you." He turned and walked away, shaking his head.

"Did he say *place of power*?" I asked myself. He *did*, and those were the exact words on The Sacred Path card I had drawn.

I walked back out to the car and figured that I would just ask another person for directions, but not a soul was in sight. Standing by my car, I stared at the postcard and asked myself, "Yeah, why *do* I want to go to this place?" A lone bird flew overhead heading north. Another omen? As he flew off into the distance, I knew my answer and went back into the store, all excited. Impatiently, I waited for the Indian clerk to return, but after a few minutes by myself, I yelled out, "Hello? Anybody here?"

A few seconds later, he reappeared, "What do you want now?"

"I know why I want to go to the power place."

"Why?"

"Spirit has called me to return to this land to make peace," I blurted out.

"Make peace? With whom?"

All his damn questions would've made me explode in rage in my old days, but now I paused and considered his question. Tears welled up inside.

With ancestral fathers. With myself, I wanted to say, but I felt so vulnerable, I couldn't answer, especially in front of this total stranger who was not accommodating in the least. I turned my face to avert my tears from his gaze. Feeling so exposed, my whole identity as a man seemed to be at stake.

The old man took stock, sucked in a deep breath, and from behind the counter took out a greasy map. With a wizened finger, he pointed at the map.

"Follow this road. After 90 miles, you'll come to Four Corners. Only street light around. It's Kayenta. Small town of 500 Indians."

I nodded, gratefully.

"Looks like weather moving in. Good luck. I hope you find the peace you look for."

"Thank you, good night," I replied, and left.

For a couple of hours or so, I plunged through the rain that was pounding the flat, barren terrain of the Navajo Nation, until, finally, I saw a lone streetlight. I checked into the first motel I could find, the Holiday Inn in Kayenta.

After a shower, I had a light meal at the hotel café. Being the dead of winter, there were only a few people staying there, and the place felt forlorn. For a moment, I started to wonder why I had chosen this time to come, but then I thought that I was here now, and nothing was going to stop me from continuing my Vision Quest.

I drifted off to sleep thinking of the old Indian who had seen right through me to my inner turmoil, but who had still relented and given me instructions. As sleep took over, I found myself whispering over and over again to myself, *Peace, peace…*

At first light, I awoke to flurries of snow. I had brought a ski jacket, but when I stepped outside, I was chilled to my bones. After a steaming cup of tea, I asked the clerk for directions to Monument Valley. Short, stocky, and in her forties, she carried a stern demeanor made more apparent by a beautiful turquoise necklace.

"No point in going out there today," she said.

"Why not?"

"It'll be closed down."

"What are you talking about?"

"Look!" she gestured. "Blizzard."

"It's…only snowing. I can deal with snow."

"We all can, but many of us choose not to if we don't have to. You're welcome to drive out there. But if you get stuck, nobody will rescue you."

"I'll take my chances."

Monument Valley

As snowflakes drifted down gently from a white-grey sky, I followed the directions I had been given as best as I could. I could barely see through the windshield, much less see any landmarks.

Located in northwest Arizona, Monument Valley is familiar to many because of its frequent usage in movies and commercials. In truth, it really isn't a valley. It's a series of giant rock formations that rise steeply over a wide, flat, desolate landscape. Native Americans have deemed it sacred land, and it was now my next destination, but it looked nothing like my cheery postcard image.

At one point I had to pull over because visibility was non-existent. I could barely see the edge of the road. Whiteout all around. Way too dangerous. Frustrated, I pulled over and closed my eyes, fighting off negative thoughts, *What if my car breaks down and I get stranded? If you freeze to death, what would happen to your children? Your remorse, your Vision Quest. How can you be so selfish? What humiliation. All those Indians shaking their heads, 'Another dumb white man, so sure of himself.'*

Rainbows

With eyes remaining shut to focus my intent, I reminded myself that now in the face of obstacles and uncertainty was the time for patience and faith. Silently, I tried to lift my spirits. After ten minutes or so, I opened my eyes and gasped in awe.

The sun had peeked through the clouds of the whiteout and had turned the newly fallen snow into a carpet of tiny glittering jewels. In the sky, every direction was practically white on white except the east where, in the distance, a vague silhouette of a huge outcropping loomed over the desert floor with a brilliant rainbow floating directly over it like some heavenly crown. The vibrant colors of the rainbow were made more magnificent by the monochrome white all around.

Behind it, there was another rainbow, and yet another—one after another going back as far as I could see. The swaths of color arched perfectly across the sky so beautifully that it was more than I could bear. I watched, mesmerized, as they appeared and disappeared, appeared and disappeared like evanescent beings of a celestial dance. I pulled out my iPod and clicked on the four renditions of the song, "Somewhere Over the Rainbow," listening to every note. Over whelmed by joy, tears rolled down my face.

As I witnessed this miraculous play of nature, all my fears, guilts, and doubts disappeared. I took it as a sign that, blizzard or not, I was on the right path. After another fifteen minutes, I started the car and continued driving. Street markers became visible and told me I was only minutes away.

When I got near the official entrance to Monument Valley, another sign! Perfectly arched over the road, another rainbow appeared. What could I do but act as if I were in some Hollywood movie and drive right under the glorious arch and enter Monument Valley.

In the Visitor Center parking lot, I stepped out of the car to a ferocious wind, fierce and cold. With my hiking boots crunching in the snow, my feet quickly became wet, but I didn't care. Doubled over against the wind, I felt exhilarated as I made my way to the Center. No one was in sight as I trudged on through driving white flakes.

A Moving Shadow

Coming closer to the Center, I approached a half-dead tree, but as I got closer, I was momentarily startled by what I thought was a shadow coming alive. It was a Native American man. *Who in his right mind would casually hang out in this freezing wind?* I wondered to myself. He was tall, powerful-looking, and looked in his forties. In spite of his jeans, cowboy hat, and a heavy overcoat, he looked like a warrior. Emotionless, the man merely nodded as I walked towards him.

"Hi," I said cordially.

"You seem not at peace," he replied in a matter-of-fact monotone.

Where am I, anyway? I said to myself. *Like that storekeeper, another total stranger piercing into my psyche telling me I'm not at peace.* A bit shaken, I stared back at the man, who watched me impassively. In the past, if someone had been so painfully direct, I would've found cause to attack with sarcasm, but I must've really changed. Encouraged by

Antarah's counsel that all I had to do was "show up" and let whatever is supposed to happen, happen, I answered with utter candor.

"I'm here to find my truth… Can you help me?"

He looked me over, and murmured, "Our people see the Cloud People as our heart. Snow and rain washes away the gloom of the past."

"What?"

"You've been here before?" he asked, curiously.

"No…" I replied, but before I could really finish my sentence, I thought of my "ancestral father" and a past life here that it implied, and I stopped talking.

"We must all return to places that haunt us," he continued. "And seek out places that call us."

Had this place been calling me? I wondered to myself. There has been enough signs and synchronicity to make that a possibility.

"You need to hire that guide over there, the one with the Jeep. It's treacherous out in the valley today."

Immediately on guard against being prey to somebody's hustle, I told him, "I'm a young man and need to get my feet on the ground, so I would like to walk, if that's all right with you."

"Fine with me. You may not find what you're looking for, but then you'll just have to continue your search."

I shook my head. A bit miffed by his condescension, I definitely wasn't going to hire his Jeep guy. Anyway, I had my ski parka and boots, and wanted to connect directly with the earth and remain vulnerable to whatever might come. Besides there is no bad weather, just bad clothing, I said to myself. After getting my bearings, I passed the Visitor Center and began wandering into the area of "Mitten," which featured a huge rock outcropping shaped roughly like an upright mitten complete with a thumb. With this weather, though, I could barely see anything, but still, I thought I could tune in to its energy.

As I walked off, the man yelled out with a big grin, "Hey, watch out. Wild Indians out there!"

I laughed and waved, warmed by this last comment.

Mud Man

Into the snowstorm I went. The light dusting had turned into a blizzard. I tightened my parka to ward off the gale at my back, and leaned way back, practically carried by the wind.

After an hour or so, I figured that I must've trudged a couple of miles, but there was no way of knowing because part of the time I was walking blindly in the whiteout. Thank God I could always feel, if not see, the monstrous silhouette of the outcropping that is Mitten, which helped orientate me. As I soldiered on, thoughts of my ancestral father came and went. With no one around, with visibility near zero, and the biting cold and unrelenting wind, I began to feel myself sliding into an altered state. It seemed as if I were in a waking dream.

After another half hour, the wind diminished greatly. Though I still felt everything was a dream, I still had enough wits to figure that I must be at the leeward side of Mitten, which was blocking me from the wind. If so, I must be at the exact other side of the outcropping from where I started. *Well here I am. Now what?* I said to myself.

Within minutes, things became a lighter grey, and suddenly, low on the horizon, sunlight peeked through the clouds, creating right before me a magnificent rainbow. Then other rainbows joined it, appearing and disappearing like I had seen before. Once again, I felt reverence for this celestial display. My spirits lifted. Far from my normal way of being, I was *beside myself* as another force took over me. In awe before the spectacular dance of the rainbows, I fell to my knees. My hands, by their own accord, plunged into the freezing snow and mud, and kneaded it like a child playing with precious Play-Doh.

The cold was a shock, but the earth felt so alive that before I knew what I was doing, I had scooped up palmfuls of the slush and smeared it all over my forehead, cheeks, and nose. The freezing soil stung my flesh and made me groan involuntarily, but it also gave me an overwhelming connection to the power and glory of the earth. I shivered as some of the mud slithered down my neck, but primal thoughts of the deepest conviction welled up from within, "I love you, Mother Earth. I never want to be separate from you ever again. I promise to honor you. You are my life. I love you, beloved Mother Earth..."

After ten minutes or so, the sun disappeared behind a cloud, and everything became much darker. The snow had turned back to freezing rain that shook me out of my reverie, terribly alarmed. *What are you doing. You're going to die out here! Get a grip!*

But then the sun came out again, and another rainbow appeared. Its arch spanned from one end of the earth across the sky to descend beyond the horizon. A double rainbow appeared with its vibrant colors bringing life to the otherwise grey canvas of earth and sky. In face of this magnificence, I felt overwhelming humility, and reconfirmed my devotion to the earth. I thought to myself, *I'm an Indian now, war paint and all.*

It began to drizzle, and looking upward, I allowed the rain to wash over my skin. The mud dripped all over my cheeks, chin, and down my neck, but I was beyond caring.

The sun disappeared, and everything turned dark grey and, again, shook me back to reality, *What are you doing? The sun's going down. You're lost. Find your goddamn car!* I was so far out of my norm, it took a while to fully come to my senses. I rose to my feet trying to assess my situation. In spite of my "right clothing," my pants had gotten wet, and I was chilled to my bones.

Another rainbow appeared, but this time I remained focused on survival. The driving rain turned back to snow. A true blizzard. A moment of panic. *Keep centered. Breathe. Use your wits.* I decided *not* to go the way I came, because it was much longer. I figured that as I worked my way back, I would always keep it to my left to keep me orientated. I could see that the sun had sunk behind Mitten, which was west, and where my car was.

Losing Myself

Though concerned with my own safety, I was not afraid. Tightening up my parka, I huddled down to begin my trek back. A moment of humiliation as I thought about the old Indian whose wisdom I had not heeded.

"Watch out, it's treacherous out there." But I refused to dwell on negative thoughts.

Suddenly, a rustling sound! I looked up and saw a coyote staring at me. He looked hungry, I thought, but too frail to attack. If I fell over or died, however, I could be his next meal. I calmed myself as the coyote stood his ground, staring at me. A gust of wind literally rocked me to my heels. Somehow it made me take stock and assess my predicament.

Remembering that I had an energy bar in my pocket, I quickly took it out, opened the package, and threw it towards him. It fell through the wind into the snow with a light plop. The coyote didn't move, but after a few moments it cautiously moved towards it, snatched it up, and devoured it in seconds. Without so much as a passing glance, it scurried off.

"You're welcome," I called after him, and began my trek towards my car.

After just a few minutes, I was suddenly bowled over by a powerful wall of freezing wind—sixty miles an hour, I later found out. It hit me so hard I was knocked off balance. The chill cut through my garments like daggers as I staggered back to where Mitten had protected me from the wind. I must regroup; things were getting serious.

Tightening up my parka, my hands and feet were so icy that I could barely maneuver my zippers and ties. I didn't think I'd get frostbite, at least not yet, but I knew I had to keep moving. Sizing up my situation, I got my bearings in relation to the silhouette of Mitten. If it got too dark and the blizzard reduced visibility, the wind coming directly from the west right into my face would keep me orientated. A growl from the coyote reappeared. I took it as a great incentive to not fall over, and keep moving.

A thought fleeted by, *Is this one of those Vision Quests where you must lose yourself to find yourself?* But I refused to believe I was lost. After finding all the favorable omens, rainbows, and my profound connection with Mother Earth, I didn't feel Spirit would let me get lost. With this faith lighting up the encroaching darkness, I braced myself and took the first steps back into that fierce wind.

7

AWAKENING

Lost and Found

In the shadow side of Mitten protected by the ferocious wind, I braced myself for re-entering that terrific blast of Artic air. With the first steps back into the gale, I was momentarily dealt a body blow that threw me back upright, but this time I could instantly lean way forward to maintain balance. Icy snow stung my face and ears, but I was partially protected by the mud I had glopped on my face. *See? There's method to my madness*, I told myself. Pressured to get moving by the encroaching darkness, I could see the vague silhouette of Mitten to my left, which reassured me that I was heading in the right direction. Putting one foot in front of the other in the slush, I began my trek back to my car.

In my hyper-sensitive connection to Mother Nature since kneeling before the rainbows, I felt unseen eyes watching me in spite of the blizzard. *Am I imagining things?* Glancing back, I saw it was my old friend the coyote. Perhaps it thought I was worth watching because I could be its next meal. Trailing behind, he disappeared only to reappear a few minutes later fifteen feet in front of me. Was he stalking me? Playing with me? Keeping me company in the storm?

With eyes narrowed to slits against the driving snow, I was nevertheless acutely sensitive for any signs of a trail. Here and there, I saw sagebrush and markers, clues of a path. But the next moment, everything would disappear in a whiteout as I forced myself to keep moving. The wind, even with its stinging cold, was a lifesaver. Its constant direction directly into my face kept me orientated. And time and again, my little coyote friend would appear and disappear, sometimes ahead, sometimes behind, to keep me company. I began to fancy him as a totem animal guide.

After a good part of an hour, the sun peeked out wanly one last time and then retired for the night behind clouds. Sensing the end of day, the wind seemed to pick up its fury, but I just leaned more into the wind and trudged along at a steady pace. As the sun got lower, the desert floor, rock outcropping, sage-brush, and sky all blended into a greyish-blue version of a whiteout, which progressively got darker and darker. Even the faintest visual clues to guide me receded into that grey-blue oblivion. But what the eyes couldn't provide, the gale did, as long as I kept heading towards it head-on. I didn't dare think of what could've happened if the wind had shifted.

Slogging on and on through the slushy snow, time passed as I followed the coyote, the coyote followed me. Thanks to him, I was kept alert and grounded in what otherwise could have been an abstract jaunt that would drive me batty. About an hour and a quarter after I had started, I was drawn to a vague lump in the distance. As I got closer, I could barely make out one lone vehicle looking forlorn. Faithfully waiting for me in the empty parking lot, it was my car! *I had made it!*

I picked up my pace, and just as I reached it, I caught a glimpse of something fleeting in the distance and spun around catch a better look. It was my little coyote. "Thanks," I shouted, but it had already dashed off and disappeared. I guess it wasn't one for much sentimentality. Hopping inside my car, with icicles for fingers barely able to move, I turned on the ignition, and it cranked up immediately. Was I relieved! Then I turned on the heat. How nice to be out of the wind. I felt pain in my ears, but thank God I still had feeling in them.

As I sat in my car letting the engine warm up, I clicked on the radio to hear a deep voice declare, "You may see a thousand bright lights, but none as bright as the one within..." *How appropriate. I can go with that*, I said to myself. For a while, I just sat there with a deep feeling of accomplishment as I silently repeated the words. *A thousand bright lights, but none as bright as the one within.* I had made it! *No one in their right mind would have chosen to explore Mitten today, so why did I?* But I knew the answer: Obsessed with connecting to Mother Nature, I was beyond caring about creature comforts or anything external if I could make my connection. Although I probably didn't have to put my life on the line. Or did I? To show Spirit my level of commitment?

Anyway, I had made it. Though I didn't know all the implications intellectually, I knew in my gut that I had just undergone a life-changing experience, that I had put my life on the line, that it would never be the same, and that I was alive to tell the tale. *I had died to live again!*

Being Navajo

As I headed out the entry to the parking lot, the old Navajo man was still lolling around outside, seemingly oblivious to the fury of the weather. Slowing down to greet him, I rolled down the window.

"Mud on your face," he said immediately in a monotone. "You some kind of Indian, now? A warrior, maybe?"

I felt so self-conscious; I couldn't say a word, and half turned away.

"Where you were today, it's called Mitten," he continued. "Our people, we leave all our darkness there. Did you?"

"Yes. At least, some... What's your name?"

"Sonny."

"So where are you from?"

"New York City," he said, smiling for the first time.

"Yeah, right. You lived here all your life?"

"Not yet. Where you from?"

"I grew up in California," I said, but I wasn't so sure anymore. "Are you 100% Navajo?"

"100%," he said with great pride. "And you?"

"Me too," I replied, joking along with a straight face. "101%."

He gazed at me awhile, and shook his head, "Once a Navajo, always a Navajo."

As I slowly headed back to my hotel, I thought about my jaunt around Mitten. Among many other things, it seemed to be about *moving forward*—leave the past behind, honor each step of the journey, and trust that what will come, will come. How often in the past I had wasted so much time analyzing, questioning, judging, and defending each and every one of my actions. Those days are over, because today, I had truly honored each step of the journey, lived in the moment! With no false modesty and no false pride, I recognized that I had faced fear with courage, witnessed miracles, and experienced, if only briefly on my knees in the snow, a profound sense of connection and peace that transcended time and will never go away.

Holiday Inn

Back in my room, I couldn't wait to take a hot shower, but one look at myself in the mirror made me giggle. I couldn't recognize myself with that mud and slush all over me. I looked much better. How primal. What character. Yes indeed, I will never be the same.

After a steaming shower, I ordered some tea and began to feel comfortable again. Casually, I leafed through a tourist book on the table about Northern Arizona filled with spectacular photographs. My eyes were wide open. One of them showed a flat desert with a deep canyon incisively carved into it with almost perfectly vertical walls. Never saw anything like it; it was called Canyon de Chelly. Into the vertical cliff were carved Indian villages, now in ruins. Sipping some tea, I smiled to myself. Like bread crumbs left by Spirit as clues for my next destination, I knew where I was to go next.

At the front desk, I asked the clerk, a rotund Native American lady, for directions. She laughed.

"Canyon de Chelly? Now?" She shook her head. "A crazy idea. Wait till Spring." But I felt determined. After what I went through, I felt invincible. *Anyway, I'm here now, and will simply move forward*, I thought to myself.

"I'll be fine," I told her.

After a long pause, she let out an audible sigh, "Fine... have it your way."

Looking disgruntled, she scribbled some directions on a piece of paper that I could barely make out, and handed it to me, "Hope you find what you're looking for."

"So do I," I answered, and thanked her.

Old Doubts

As I went to bed that night, the "confidence pendulum" swung to the other extreme. From the exhilaration I had felt in the midst of rainbows and blizzards, I found myself feeling depressed by my smelly old motel room with pillows and bedding like lumps of detritus. It proved to be a perfect setting for a stream of old doubts plaguing my mind—

Stop running away. Go home, and face life…

Who do you think you are to indulge yourself with these big questions..?

Don't you read the papers? Life is not supposed to be happy. Just have a girlfriend on the side and soldier on...

For all you say about your kids, your kids, why are you so willing to abandon them?

I know, I know, I know! These doubts come from my old self after years of conditioning, I chided myself, but still they kept going on and on. How depressing. I decided to take a few deep breaths and meditate to see if that would help.

After just a few minutes, good old meditation came through, and I felt calm to be in the presence of a crystal clear pool in the garden that I now called "Lila's home." It was like Eden to me, and was beginning to feel like *my* home, too. Suddenly, she was there.

"Adam, your doubts. Are you sabotaging yourself again?" she asked.

"Lila! But, what… How did you...?"

"I know your thoughts."

"Well, can you blame me? When I'm all alone, it makes me question everything."

"Adam, you may be lonely, but you are not alone. Remember today in Mitten when you felt so at peace? That feeling is in you every moment."

Like a wise grandmother, Lila's mere voice calmed me, not to mention her words of wisdom. I took a deep breath and thought about being in the shadow side of Mitten where that Navajo man had told me that that's where his people dumped out "their darkness." What had I dumped? Guilt? Doubt? Apparently, I had not dumped the beating up of myself.

Patiently, I waited for more counsel from Lila, but she didn't return. However, she had already set me straight. Gone were my doubts, *in* was a new quest with the resolve to look deeper into my "darkness," my shadow side.

Canyon de Chelly

The next morning I headed out for Canyon de Chelly. As I drove out, I remembered a book I had been reading, *Sacred Contracts* by Caroline Myss. It was about contracts we make with ourselves. In it, she asks, "If you had to choose just one archetype figure, and one astrological sign, which would you choose?"

Without hesitation, I had chosen "Shaman" as the archetype figure representing my aspirations, and "Capricorn" as the astrological sign. The shaman was one who intermediates between the world of the visible and the invisible.

And Capricorn, in my interpretation, had to do with Gigi, a Capricorn, who mirrored back to me my own shadow side. I had to free myself from this shadow side if I were to travel between the world of the earth plane and that of the spiritual. So my next assignment for myself had to do with deep examination of my shadow side. And, as Carolyn Myss had said, this requires forgiveness. Hmm, this theme of forgiveness was coming up a lot for me lately.

It wasn't a very long distance to Canyon de Chelly, maybe sixty miles, and upon arrival, I hit the tail end of a powerful rainstorm. The entire area had sank underwater when the rivers had swollen to flood stage levels. The sun was beginning to set in the west, so I pulled over to take in the view as the bright yellow sun turned the stark cliffs a warm reddish color. This beauty of nature inspired an insight that I felt down to my bones: I saw a shift in my journey. Thanks to this sacred Indian land, I had faced and purged some of my "darkness," but I had also begun to open myself to embrace the light. I felt the dawning of a new life for me.

The Mustang

At Canyon de Chelly, I drove past another Holiday Inn (enough of those places) and found a small motel called the Thunderbird Lodge. After checking in, I jumped right into the shower and rolled right into bed. My mind was eager to explore, but first, a good night's rest for the body.

Bright and early, I went exploring and found that flooding had made many parts of the road difficult to cross. How did I miss all these treacherous stretches last night? At one spot, the road looked so precarious I was forced to turn around, but at the last moment, I spotted horses off in the distance. Curious, I drove toward them, slushing through a mud-strewn road that lead to a ranch.

A couple of young Indian men in their late twenties and thirties came out to greet me. Resembling overweight cowboys, they looked uneducated, drunk, and stoned. I rolled down my window.

"Good thing the water spirits did not wash you away," the older of the two said.

"You lost?" the other one asked.

"Well actually, yes and no," I replied as I sized up the situation. They stared at me, shaking their heads, wondering what this white man was doing there. Getting out of my car, I approached a fenced-in area containing horses. The younger one went back inside a trailer while the other one kept an eye on me as I checked out their horses.

"Haven't been on a horse in a long while."

"How long is a while?"

"Well…" *A while? Be real!* I scoffed to myself. *Last time you were on a "horse" you were a four-year-old tot sitting on a Shetland pony!* "What I mean is, uh…never," I finally replied to the cowboy.

"You think now is a good time to start? See those clouds over there," he gestured, "we're going to get a real downpour in about ten minutes, give or take, and you've never ridden."

"I don't care," I told him as I took out my wallet. "I'm not sure why, but I really need to do this now."

"Yeah, but there's a big problem. Park Service, they've closed the canyon. The river's too high, and nobody rides today." He gestured at huge puddles of water all around.

"All this land, and no place to ride?" I scoffed, as I slipped a twenty into his palm. After a moment, I slipped him another twenty. He looked around, deciding, as I discreetly slipped a third bill into his palm. Suddenly, he had an idea.

"Tell you what, crazy man, this area is washed out, but there's some land on higher ground. I'll take you out there personally."

"Great. We don't need no approval from some stinkin' park service guy."

"I'm Patrick, by the way."

Looking into his deep, dark eyes set in a poker face, I introduced myself and shook his hand. He gestured for me to follow.

"You ever been on a mustang?"

"No, but I'm game. Where do you get them, anyway?"

"Oh, out in the high desert. They run wild, but we lasso them and break them," he replied. "Mustangs are wild, but to us they mean freedom. When you ride a mustang, you feel...*the pure power of the horse.* They're independent, so you gotta' let 'em run, and just go for it."

A wave of fear passed through me, *What am I getting myself into?* "Maybe you... can you give me a few pointers?"

"Nah, the horse'll teach you. Today, you'll ride Angel. She's proud and strong."

"Great, let's do it," I said blustering through my fear.

Following Patrick to a rough-hewn barn, we each grabbed a saddle and swung them on our horses. Black as the moonless night, Angel looked gentle and intelligent as I looked into her eye. With the first stroke, she snorted, and I could immediately sense her power.

"A pleasure to make your acquaintance, Angel," I said.

Within minutes, I was up on Angel, slowly heading down the path away from the ranch.

A cold wind blew strong. Heavy rain clouds were approaching fast.

"We'll just take it easy, okay, Patrick?"

"Just go for it," he repeated, nonchalantly.

After fifteen minutes, the path ended and we were on our own in the open expanse of the desert. It felt like I was thrust into another world. With my last equestrian experience as a tot squatting on a pony, I felt totally unprepared, so I kept repeating Patrick's words, *Just go for it, just go for it.* I was jolted out of my reverie when Patrick suddenly spoke.

"Thought you might want to know, this is the land of the Anasazi."

"Yeah?"

"We'll pass by some of the ruins. I grew up here. I'll take you where I used to ride as a kid."

"I'm right behind you."

"Yeah, for now, but remember, you're on Angel. She's a strong one. We'll ride out to an ancient ruin called Little White House."

Just then it started to sprinkle, and Angel, on her own, picked up the pace to a trot and easily bypassed Patrick. Hanging on tightly to the horn, I was completely at her mercy. As if she could read my mind, she again picked up the speed. Alarmed, I glanced back for guidance from Patrick, but having just been joined by his girlfriend, he was busy talking and smooching with her.

Angel suddenly jolted into a canter, momentarily throwing me off balance. I was white knuckles around the horn, but after a few minutes, I could relax into the rhythm, and my fear subsided tremendously. I could appreciate the thrust and power of my mustang, and instinctively just "went for it" as Patrick had told me to do.

Cutting through the rain, I took in the majestic scenery all around as Angel again quickened her gait, and we cruised through the wide panorama of this sacred ground. Though I was still holding on tightly, my fear had been replaced with a feeling of invincibility and exhilaration. I didn't want this ride to ever end.

After an hour, we were well within the canyon with its sheer 1000-foot cliffs, and Angel slowed down and pulled up to a stop beside some Anasazi ruins at the foot of the canyon wall. About fifty feet above, there were more ruins that looked stunning, having been carved deep into the sheer walls of the cliff. I got off, stretched my legs, and tied the reins onto some brush as I patted Angel and thanked her for the great ride.

Patrick, I assumed, was far behind, but I knew this was the White House he had spoken about. With rain gently falling, I absorbed the profound tranquility of the canyon. As if to protest this moment of peace, fast approaching storm clouds flashed lightning that set off powerful rolls of thunder that rumbled through the heavens, echoing between the walls of the canyon. Angel snorted, but remained calm.

In ten minutes or so, Patrick came trotting up with his girlfriend and nodded towards the ruins.

"Little White House. Used to ride out here bareback and check out the petroglyphs."

After another ten minutes of idle chatter, he looked up at the approaching storm and gestured that we should head back. With this signal, I got back on Angel, who sprang to life as she headed back to the ranch in a spirited trot. Easily she bypassed Patrick and his girlfriend as I hung on for the ride.

The rain began coming down in buckets. Suddenly BAM! BOOM! Lightning struck right above us, causing Angel to bolt into a full gallop. Thunder rolled through the sky. Terrified, I gripped the horn tightly as Angel raced wildly through the canyon. The scenery shot by, but I hardly noticed as I hung on for dear life. But then, something shifted; my body relaxed. I was in an altered state. With my spirit in charge, I began moving naturally to the rhythm of the gallop. No more thinking. Within a few minutes, I was totally absorbed in the ride, I was *at one* with the horse, we were one being. I was the ride, I was…rhythm.

FLASH! BOOM! More lightning exploded right on top of us. Caught between terror and exhilaration, we flew through the canyon. With adrenaline pumping, Angel galloped with no restraint, a raw force of nature propelling me into…death, life? I didn't know and I didn't care! I fully surrendered to the moment, I was the mustang, I was that kid on my *Flexi Flyer* shooting through the storm drain, I was an Indian warrior riding off into battle, crying, "It's a great day to die!"

BOOM! BA-BA BOOM! Again, lightning flashed above us! Thunder boomed! Angel hurtled us forward, wildly and free, with me merged with her, a rider in the storm. More lightning, like arrows from Great Spirit, flew all around trying to hit us. But we were outrunning them! We were invincible! A memory flashed—I *was* that warrior, confident of victory, but this time, I was not riding out to do battle, but racing forward into my new life. Beyond time, beyond caring, we charged through the storm into a timeless realm. FLASH! FLASH! BOOM! Lightning bolts all around. But we can outrun lightning, outrun time! The audacity of it all! The magnificence of it all! We can ride forever! *It's a great day to die!*

As our charge continued through the driving rain, I gradually realized that the lightning storm had blown over. In time, Angel's gallop came down to cruising speed as we came out of the canyon back into the open plain. Soon, Angel slowed to a relaxed canter, allowing me to catch my breath and take in the beauty of the landscape. The rich colors the rain had brought out! Nature, this natural earth, *this* is where I belong, where I have always belonged, where I'll always belong. With every breath, I took in deeply the fresh, rain-washed landscape of Mother Earth.

Eventually, we found our way back to the corral where my heart could finally beat more normally. I dismounted, but with feet on the ground, it seemed as if the earth was gently spinning. Still in an altered state, I walked around to help ground me. I patted Angel and thanked her for the magnificent ride. She snorted, seeming to agree. To Little White House and back had been a two-hour ride.

After a few minutes, Patrick and his girlfriend rode up and dismounted.

"Had quite a ride out there," Patrick said. Though his voice was flat as usual, I could tell he was impressed. "Come back tomorrow. You're ready to go bareback."

"I don't think so," I groaned. I could barely walk. My whole pelvic area was aching and sore. I had never been on a saddle, much less a ride like this.

"So did you get what you came here for?" Patrick asked.

"Guess you could say that," I smiled. "It was incredible. Thanks."

"Anytime. Anything else we can do for you?"

Though I had had my fill of adventure, I found words popping out of my mouth asking if anyone around here did ceremonies.

"Ceremonies?" he chuckled. "Well, we sure don't need no rain-dance." After sizing me up a moment, he finally spoke, "You're serious, aren't you? Tell you what, crazy man, my grandfather has a sweat lodge. Maybe you can join us. Come by tomorrow morning around nine. I'll introduce you."

"That'll be great."

Still feeling the effects from the ride, I ambled back to my hotel with body trembling and aching. It was hard to relax after my exhilarating ride, so I clicked on the TV and spent an hour watching mindless drivel. My butt had gotten so swollen, I felt like I had two painfully bloated tomatoes where my butt used to be. Not being able to sit on it, I had to lay on my side if I wanted to catch up on that drivel.

Between my butt pain, and my freezing, decrepit room (worse than the Holiday Inn), I felt my old friend, Mr. Anguish come visiting again—*What am I doing? Why am I here?*— but I reminded myself that my job was not to reason why; it was merely to "show up" for whatever Spirit had in store for me. In short order, this thought put Mr. Anguish back in place, and he disappeared, leaving me at peace with my swollen tomatoes.

Sweat Lodge

The next morning I met Patrick at the local Ranger Station. He motioned for me to follow him into the nearby mountainous terrain behind a large ranch. Driving for ten minutes, I followed him in agony because it was so painful to sit on my butt, but finally, we reached a Hogan, a small dwelling built right into the side of the mesa. As we approached, I saw an elderly Native American man sitting outside. He wore jeans and a faded wind jacket, had little hair and no teeth. His light brown eyes looked quizzically at me as I came up. He was 88, and when he got up, he stood tall.

"This is my grandfather, Gus," Patrick said. "We all call him Chief G. Over fifty years ago, he was given that nickname by the head of the Navajo Nation because he can clean poisons and evil spirits out of the body. He just makes them rush out. He belongs to the coyote clan." *Coyote clan? That was my totem animal friend that accompanied me behind Mitten.*

For a few moments, I could feel Chief G.'s steady gaze on me. Finally, he spoke in Navajo to Patrick, who translated.

"Why are you here?"

"I'm…here to heal my life and find my way forward."

After a few exchanges with each other, Patrick said, "My grandfather wants to know if you'd like to join him for a sweat."

I lit up, "Absolutely." Though I had never done one, I had a hunch that this would be right up my alley.

"Looks like you got your ceremony, after all," Patrick said, deadpan as usual. I nodded and smiled.

Following Patrick and Chief G., I came to a structure dug into the side of a hill with a façade of wood and mud.

"Entrance to the sweat lodge," Patrick explained. "Faces east, the direction of the rising sun. It's the gateway into the womb of the Mother. Inside, you can release all your poisons into the earth and get back nourishment."

I peeked inside. The heat struck me immediately as I glanced around a space about ten feet in diameter topped with a half-dome ceiling, all carved directly into the hillside. There was a pit for hot rocks, and room for six people or eight or so skinny ones.

"You will go into the lodge four times," Patrick continued. "One sweat for each of the four directions and four elements. In the South, it's the path of the red earth. It's the divine ground of being. Here you can release physical pain. In the West, you let go of the material world… release your past… any darkness you're carrying…" He went on, but he mumbled a bit, and I couldn't follow him. I was impressed with how much he was steeped into his tradition.

"In between each sweat you will drink sage to purify your body. The last two directions, north and east, they will be for your nourishment… You will honor those that came before you, and those that are yet to come. You will regain the vision of the eagle," he concluded. With that, he excused himself and traipsed away, leaving me wondering what it all meant.

Uncertain what to do, I could only watch Chief G. and follow suit. He removed all his clothing, so I quickly took off my slacks and pullover, and put them aside in a fairly neat pile. Chief G. looked directly at me, assessing me as I grew uncomfortable to be so buck-naked and vulnerable in front of a total stranger that I felt could see right through me.

He then handed me a short piece of rope and demonstrated that I was to tie up my penis, and began showing me how to do it. *Tie up my penis? Normal day.* I watched and tried to do the same, but it was so cold, I could barely find the damn thing.

Later, I would learn that it was a symbolic gesture of respect because we were entering into the womb of the Divine Mother. With penis well tied, I followed Chief G. as we crawled through a three-foot opening to enter into an overwhelming embrace of fiery air. It was like crawling into an oven. Within a minute, I was sweating profusely as I sat directly across from Chief G., who seemed relaxed and unaffected by the heat.

Patrick reappeared through the opening with a pitchfork on which a red-hot stone about half the size of a big watermelon was precariously balanced. I shuddered at the thought of what would happen if it rolled off onto my naked body, but he expertly deposited it into the pit. One after another they came, each one increasing the level of heat until there were eighteen in all. Then, he crawled in himself, and closed the opening with a flap of hide. The heat was fiery; I was starting to bake.

Chief G. began to chant, as Patrick, here and there, translated for me.

"He's calling in the four directions. You should say a prayer of gratitude for each direction and for Chief G. for being here with you." I did as I was told, but my concentration began to diffuse. I was feeling suffocated and gasped for air, but the heat going direct into my lungs was more than I could bear. Patrick told me that if I couldn't stay in here long, it's because "you're full of evil spirits." I was determined to stick it out, although it was becoming unbearable.

After an eternity, which was probably only ten minutes in clock time, the Chief began to gulp air and suck in very deep breaths. His body began to shake violently. Before I knew what was happening, he was crawling outside, leaving me alone with Patrick in the lodge. Outside, I heard agonizing sounds of Chief G. retching. They sounded painful. It gave me pause, because if someone as experienced as Chief G. had to undergo such a torturous experience from the heat, what's in store for me?

A few minutes later, he returned. Though I was starting to feel dreamy, I peered through the sweat in my eyes and could see that he didn't look so well. He nodded at me, closed his eyes, and resumed chanting. Suddenly, intuitively, I knew what was happening: He had taken on my poison and was releasing it for my own purification! A wave of gratitude washed over me. Here was someone, a complete stranger, taking on my pain for my well-being.

After another ten agonizing minutes or so, the prolonged heat had so cooked my brain I was swooning. My insides seemed to be filled with toxins as my body continued to bake. It was all too unbearable, and just as I was on the verge of bolting out of there, I felt a nudge from Patrick, who gestured for me to exit the lodge. Dreamily, I crawled out, with him following.

Outside, a chill swept over my body as I crawled out into a light drizzle with air close to freezing. After all that heat, it was utterly refreshing. I could breathe again, and sucked in deep breaths as we all drank some sage tea. But after a scant five minutes outside, I was freezing, and I couldn't wait to crawl back in. All together, we went in and out of the sweat lodge four times. Although Chief G. did not get sick the next couple of times in the lodge, he kept grunting and clearing his throat, as if he were still clearing out my toxins.

Coming out the fourth and last time, I followed Chief G. out, and emerged from the Womb of the Mother feeling utterly drained and spent. Luckily, the rain had stopped, and a bright sun had come out from behind a scattering of clouds. Once our bodies had air-dried and we had put on our clothes, I felt purified and transformed as I followed Chief G. back to his dwelling.

His hogan was simplicity itself with a dirt floor, a skinny cot, a dirty sink, and a bare light bulb to illuminate a space about fifteen by twenty feet. He heated up a pot-belly stove for some heat and some tea. With Patrick translating, he said to me, "You released some of your past. I felt your pain."

So my hunch was right. He had taken on my poison. "I'm sorry you had to suffer on my account," I told him.

"Purification doesn't come without pain. I'm glad I could help," he replied in translation.

Then Chief G. handed me a pouch full of "Indian tobacco" and explained that it was high desert brush and sage.

"Put this in your peace pipe, and smoke it beside a body of water. A lake or a river."

"Sure, I can do that. Thanks."

"My spirit will guide you as you heal and find your destiny."

I nodded and embraced him. Addressing Patrick, I said, "Your grandfather is a good man."

"Did he help you?"

"Yes. It was a wonderful experience. What can I give him?"

"A C-spot?"

I reached into my wallet, took out $100, and handed it to Chief G. Patrick nodded and looked me over, "Your face, it looks good."

"Thanks for everything," I replied.

"I'm glad we could help. Anything else?"

"No, I'll be leaving tomorrow."

"Well, be safe wherever you go."

Santa Fe

When the sun rose the next morning, I thought about going home. After all my intense experiences, I had had enough. But once on the road, instead of heading west back to Malibu, I found myself going further east to New Mexico.

I ended up spending a week in Santa Fe. There were no mustang rides, no blizzards, mostly quiet time, which allowed me time to relax and digest all that had happened on my momentous Vision Quest. I went to a spa, got a massage, and indulged myself in some much-needed pampering.

At one point, I looked up an acquaintance of Jon's, my shamanic friend. Jeannie was in her 50s, a trauma therapist and medicine woman with a practice set up in Santa Fe. I saw her as an elder, both wise and friendly, one who had seen it all.

We met at a local cafe for breakfast, and over fruit plates and muffins, I recounted highlights of my trip. Feeling that I had died to my old self, and now reborn, I asked, "So don't you think everyone should die at least once in their life?"

"Once in their life? How about dying every day," she laughed. "But dying is easy. The trick, at least for me, is in the rebirth when you have no guarantees whatsoever as to what, when, and if you're going to get reborn at all. Now that's faith. To be at peace with all the uncertainty paradoxically makes things certain. At least that's what I think about when I think about getting reborn."

"To me, to be reborn is to transform," I replied.

"Well, yeah, of course, transform to our true being, and all that. But that's the end game. The real challenge, at least for me, is what do you do with all those crazy steps along the way? Like you, for example, after all these fabulous experiences you've had—a wild ride through lightning on a mustang, kneeling before rainbows in a blizzard—what're you going to do with them all when you get back home and have to deal with your wife and kids?"

"Yeah, a good question." I sipped some tea, musing about my past life that seemed of another era. "And to think, it wasn't too long ago that I thought money and possessions and my golf club membership would bring me the love and peace that I wanted. What a joke," I laughed.

"Well, you're a different person now. Sooner or later, we all have to walk the talk, no exceptions, but it sounds like you're doing it. So whatever comes next, act on your highest beliefs, and let the chips fall where they may. But you don't need me to tell you all this. You're your own man, now, with Great Spirit as your ally…"

8

INTEGRATION

Back to Reality

Coming home to Malibu after all the transcendent experiences from my Vision *Quest*, I practically floated back into my beach cottage, but, as life would have it, I was quickly brought back to reality with a half dozen letters crammed into my mailbox from Gigi:

"You're such an asshole; I have to take care of everything…"

"Why are you so narcissistic, always thinking only of yourself?"

"You're a thief. You stole thousands of dollars from our account."

"Why do you favor Sophia over the others…?"

"Do you remember in the car how you were touching yourself inappropriately in front of the kids?" At first, I was utterly caught off guard, but this last one was so outrageous, I had to laugh.

A few days later when Gigi got wind that I was back, I felt the blow from her assault by phone, in person, or through lawyers: "You are guilty of child abuse!" This was because I had given one of my kids some cranberry juice for her irritation when she went to the bathroom, when, according to her, I should have taken her directly to the emergency room. Or, "You are negligent, continuously watching TV when you're supposed to be with the kids." And so it went…

To me, her focus on life back in those days was to estrange me from my children, and to flood me with guilt for breaking up the family. The truth was that I *did* feel estranged from my children, and I *did* have guilt. My stomach would knot up in tension, my chest would feel as if a ton of stones were stacked upon it. So she did achieve a level of success in her goals.

Fortunately, I was now seeing my predicament with more clarity. Even as Gigi was spending so much of her waking moments blaming me for her own unhappiness, I knew that everyone must take responsibility for their own happiness, that one's wellbeing was ultimately dependent on themselves. I prayed that Gigi would some day come to these same realizations. And of course, this applied to myself, as well.

To put this in practice in daily life, especially when Gigi pushed my buttons, triggering a surge of rage or judgment, I would force myself to breathe, take walks in nature, or smell the salt air by the ocean. These simple physical acts became powerful antidotes to the emotional poison of guilt, anger, and grief. Nature was proving time and again to be my great healer.

What a test to forgive Gigi, and, in the face of my own failures, forgive myself. It was already challenging for me to understand these new principles, but to *live* them from my heart required a whole new level of vigilance. I kept telling myself that Gigi, at her essence, was a beautiful, loving person who made me want to marry her. With this perspective, hopefully, I could minimize her grim determination to drive me to financial ruin and tear me away from my children. To these ends, she refused to honor the court order about my visitation rights with them, and instilled in them the notion that if they saw me, they would be betraying their own mother. When I *was* able to have my precious time with them, she would insist that they keep calling back home to check in with her. Or, frequently, they were simply "not available." What a master she was at touching my sore spots. *Breathe. Take a walk…*

But still, the attack was on. Whether I wanted it or not, I was forced into an intense battle. She hired a very expensive forensic accountant who pored over my records in detail. Her lawyers even confided in me, "Your wife, she's very clever…"

But after many pricey hours of research, they found nothing to incriminate me. Then she called one of my business associates, Steve, and berated him, "Why are you doing business with this crook? Don't you know he's stealing from me, his own wife?"

I was so filled with frustration at her shameless tactics that driving down the freeway, I exploded in rage, yelling and screaming, screaming and yelling at seventy miles an hour. Out came my despair, righteous indignation, anger, and tears. Afterwards, I felt a profound sadness for my predicament, my poor kids, and even… for Gigi. What pain *she* must be going through because of our family upheaval. The world had changed, and she was caught unaware. To protect her sweet feminine side that allowed us to fall in love so many years ago, all she knew to do was to recoil into a hard, tough, fighting stance and release the attack dogs

Recently I had read the timeless classic, *The Art of War,* and decided to apply some of its strategies to my predicament: "Non-engagement," "Practice Invisibility," "Move laterally, not directly." I would make myself invisible to Gigi's attacks, to be off her radar. As a consequence, no matter how damning her letters or statements, I would take it upon myself to *not* react to her accusations, and respond only to direct questions. In her frequent late-night calls, for instance, what was posed as an urgent question, was simply an excuse for her to vent. My practice was to answer her questions directly and side-step her accusations.

"Adam, it's the second of the month!" she spat out. "Where's my money? You haven't paid me my money. Don't you care about your own kids?"

"I sent it yesterday, so you should receive…"

SLAM! She would hang up on me, leaving me flushed with indignation. But I would remind myself to breathe, calm down, remain on center…and it would work!

How sad that Gigi was beating up no one but herself, how sad to watch her tail spinning down to her own demise. This pattern she would continue all the way through our court case, and even after all our legal conflicts were well settled, she would continue her wild attacks for years. I gave credit for my sense of centeredness all through this ordeal on the tactic of "Invisibility" from *The Art of War;* it greatly reduced the conflict and wore her out.

Before going to bed one night at my beach cottage, I dropped into the "Meditation Garden" where Lila often appeared, when, to my pleasant surprise, she was there.

"Adam, how does it feel to reclaim yourself?"

I waited for her to continue, but, quite typically, she didn't say more. *What does that really mean, "reclaim yourself?"* But, trusting my intuition, I let my thoughts unravel their way to insight. Plagued so much of my adult life with feelings of "separation," I could see that I had been separated not only from my family, but from Spirit. Now in the process of reclaiming the connection to my true self in Spirit, I was "reclaiming myself." *So, dear Lila, to answer your question, I feel great! I'm beginning to feel open to love again. But just what is Love? There's that question again!*

After Lila left that night, I still felt her presence, brief as it was, hovering around me like a soft comforter. How reassuring and warm. I received an insight about who she is, not in terms of a definition for my intellect, but more about how she feels to me in my heart—inner grace, inner beauty, a reflection of the feminine within me that honors values, relationship, and the meaning of things, rather than conquest, self-importance, and definitions. A deep gratitude to Spirit began to well up from within for letting me be aware of all this. The Vision Quest was beginning to pay dividends in ways I couldn't have ever imagined.

New Love

I decided to call Lizanne. Something powerful had continued to stay with me ever since we ran into each other at the junior high school graduation of our kids. Was it her natural beauty, or eyes that reflected loving spirit, or her light and carefree attitude? During my Vision Quest, just the thought of her entering my beach cottage to water my plants felt incredibly intimate. It kept alive for me her loving presence in my heart.

Then in that bookstore in Sedona, the rose quartz heart that seemed to belong to her appeared. At that time, I wanted to give it to her, but I didn't want to give it to her. It seemed to imply a degree of intimacy that made me feel afraid, vulnerable, and open to possible rejection. Anyway, I reasoned, I was in no way ready to start up a new relationship. *So, should I get it or not?* I couldn't decide. The last time we had spoken was at the end of my Vision Quest when I was in Santa Fe, but it felt like ages ago.

Back in Malibu, we went out for dinner at Moonshadows, a quaint seafood place perched on the edge of the Pacific. Sharing a bottle of wine, we got caught up with each other's lives. Minutes of conversation covered months, hours spanned years. She told me how meaningful it was for her that I had called from Santa Fe. Ostensibly, on my part, it was to check up on the plants and cottage, but I had really wanted to connect with her.

She told me that she could feel my expansion from the Vision Quest, how excited I was, and the kind of character it took to even go on such a trip. It revealed to her a deeper side of me...and of herself. She wanted this deepening for herself as well. *Secretly, perhaps all humans do?*

I was deeply moved by her surprising heart-felt expression. I glowed as I watched her sparkling eyes across the dancing flames of the candles on our table. We were on the same path. Her face was filled with warmth and empathy. Playfully, I offered her a taste of the rich sauce from my wild-caught fish, and watched her savor it. After all I had gone through with Gigi, I didn't feel I'd be capable of such easy, open communication with a woman again, but here it was happening, and it felt surprisingly natural.

After dinner, I suggested that we take a stroll on the beach. A pale moon had long replaced the sun. Minutes later we were heading towards the water, feeling the cool sand beneath our feet. I took in the clean ocean air. By the water's edge, we stopped, and I reached into my pocket and took out the precious object I had been carrying with me all through my Vision Quest. It was the rose crystal heart from Sedona, and ceremoniously, I handed it to her. Her eyes lit up. She held it next to her heart and inhaled deeply, cherishing it. I might as well have given her a ring. *Open yourself. See, you can love again*, I heard a voice whisper to me from within.

How my path in life turned and twisted. After having isolated myself since my separation, I was genuinely comfortable with another human being, who offered compassion when I felt misunderstood, who remained open hearted when I felt so wounded, and who looked upon me without judgment when all I felt was guilt and self-loathing.

After timeless minutes, we headed back to the car where I caught sight beneath a street light her light-hearted and open face. Before I knew what I was doing, I folded her into my arms and embraced her for what seemed like an eternity. Neither of us moved, as I felt the ground give way beneath me. I felt safe and complete; I felt the perfection of the moment. When we finally pulled apart, there were tears in my eyes.

"You okay?" she asked.

"I just wanted to thank you."

"But I didn't do..."

There was a long silence. I gazed into her eyes, struggling with what I wanted to say.

"It was hard for me to call you," I told her. "It's a strange time in my life. I'm determined to transform myself, and yet it's such a struggle. You could say it's a selfish time, but until I'm healed, I'm not sure I can offer much to anybody."

"I'm not looking for anything. But if I can help you in any way..."

"You help just by being here."

Her expression grew thoughtful. Later, I would find out how appreciative she was that I allowed myself to be so forthright and vulnerable. She took my hand and led me away from my car, and we headed back down to the beach. After a few moments, she broke away with carefree abandon and ran a short distance along the shore, laughing. I caught up to her, and we again embraced as we sank down to the sand. She began massaging my shoulders. When I tried to stop her, she gently pushed my arm away, saying, "I'm not sure I understand everything you're going through, but I want to help. I'm here for you."

"And I am here for you," I said. Playfully, I grabbed her hand and started to splash into the water, "Let's go into the water."

"No!" she said and pulled back. The mood suddenly changed. Apprehension. Fear.

We sat down by the water, and after an uneasy silence, she quietly shared a story about her beloved little brother, Danny. When she was fourteen, she was shaken by his sudden death. Coincidentally, a few days later, she saw the movie *Jaws*, and ever since, she equated the ocean with terrifying sharks and with death—Danny's death, *her* death...death. To swim in the ocean was to die.

Tears rolled down her face, which brought tears to me as well. For a long time, I held her as we sat in silence and watched the waves roll in and roll out along the shore. We looked at each other and smiled without the need for more words.

Self-study

Despite my busy routine, Lizanne was beginning to inspire a feeling of restlessness in me. I wanted to reengage with life in a new way. Thanks to her, my heart was re-opening, and I wanted to re-design my life. But how, and to what end?

I continued to take yoga classes, remained vigilant about meditating every day, and read *A Course in Miracles* as daily practice. The thoughts were subtle, so I read them slowly, one passage at a time, and let them sink in to become a living experience in my daily life. For example, "Love holds no grievances" I found relevant to my ever-challenging situation with Gigi. "Heaven is the decision I must make" kept me positive no matter what predicament I found myself in. And "I am one Self united with my Creator" gave me faith to completely re-design my life.

Sometimes I even found myself adapting the passages in the *Course* to my own understanding and needs. As an example of the Divine Feminine, I would change *Father* to *Mother*, and *Him* to *Her*, as a means to develop the feminine within me. Or, on other occasions, I felt that *Father* was fine, since I wanted to work on the relationship with my own father who still had much to teach me about life.

Every day I felt I was learning something profound, and another piece of the puzzle of my new life would fall in place. But over and over, the text seemed to stress certain tenets that led to a great truth, as if all the rivers would eventually lead to the same ocean, and that ocean was… forgiveness.

One night, I awoke feeling the need to take a leak. As I stumbled into the bathroom, I found myself staring at the mirror. After a few moments, I unexpectedly blurted out, "I forgive you, Adam."

Staring at myself in the looking glass for what seemed like an eternity, I studied my flesh and saw how it hung over my skull, how my hair grew and oozed out my scalp. How bizarre, the expression in my eyes seemed so primordial. It was a look of innocence, of awe. *Who is this creature staring back at me? Do I even know him?*

While the arrogant part of my ego had always dismissed my failures and wrongdoings, another part of me saw my guilt and self-loathing, and took it one step further by repeating over and over again, "I forgive you, Adam."

This was not the way I talk. It was as if I were speaking to a stranger. A bit dazed, I left the bathroom and got back in bed, wondering what it was all about. *What was I forgiving myself for?* I sank back into the comfort of my bed, enveloped in stillness and peace. I felt I was in "Lila's Garden," and then I heard her gentle voice.

"Yes, forgive yourself. Move past judgment into feeling. Forgiving is 'for giving' not only to others, but also for giving to yourself."

I liked that, "forgiving is for giving." It took away the guilt and judgment. With Lila not saying more, I mused on all the implications of "forgiving." So easy to say, so difficult to practice. My stubborn ego always seemed to hold on to a past affront to punish the perpetrator, when in fact, the exact opposite occurs. What a joke on myself. The only person suffering when I held on to some past misdeed is…myself. Forgiveness releases emotional poison from within oneself.

What should I do about Gigi? I asked myself. To forgive Gigi, now that's a challenge. If I were to react to any of her antics with anger, judgment, or bitterness, then it would be a sign that I had not completely forgiven her.

Even more difficult, forgive myself—my self-centered thoughts, my weaknesses, my affair, my anger, my lies. I must keep in mind that everything that has happened, traumatic as it might be, is all part of the journey, part of the divine plan to help me wake up and see that all suffering began with my separation from Spirit.

For a long time, I lay in bed with such thoughts. On impulse, I jumped out of bed and went back to the mirror for another look. Gazing deep into my own eyes, I found that this time, they didn't look "bizarre," but forgiving, loving, understanding. Again, words came out of my mouth:

"I forgive you, Adam. I forgive you for the times when you did harm to Gigi, I forgive you for ignoring your precious kids by constantly being on the cell phone. I forgive you for the harsh treatment you dished out to business associates. I forgive you for turning away from God..." As I went on with the litany of my misdeeds, tears welled up in my eyes. Staring into the mirror, I was transforming myself from the inside out through shifting fundamental thoughts in the deepest seat of my consciousness. By the time I went back to bed, I felt peaceful, and...sparkly! That night, I had a dream:

I am running through a dark tunnel into a stadium staging a fireworks show.

I saw this dream as a confirmation of how the old barriers of my life have been pushed away—from out of the dark tunnel, I was entering a celebration of light, of Spirit.

Atonement

My daily practice now, besides meditation and yoga, was reading *A Course in Miracles*, which resonated even more profoundly than before. After my Vision Quest, the *Course* gave words and language for me to help understand my transcendent experiences, and opened me up to deeper truths. For example, the *Course* spoke about atonement, which it saw as the release of shame and guilt so one could live more freely in the moment. Atonement equals at-one-ment. To live in the present, one becomes "at one" with Spirit, which is the end of separation...and of death, for Spirit never dies. With such study, I gradually identified more and more with myself as Spirit, rather than the physical body, personality, and ego.

As old fears of mortality began to dissolve away, all my perceptions of life began to shift accordingly. Once again, I could see how Gigi's vindictive acts were coming from fear, so understandable since life as she knew it was crumbling right before her eyes. When I met my children, I could see all their accusations of me actually came from their mother, and so I could simply love them as best as I could with no inclination to defend myself or to decide who's right or wrong. My empathy with All That Is extended not only to Gigi, but also to her entire family, to the homeless, and to the victims of terrorists and natural disasters. I could feel the plight of the trees and our beloved Mother Earth.

Confronting "Team Gigi"

On the way up in an elevator of a West L.A. high-rise, I smiled at the irony I found myself in. While attempting to live in accordance with my higher angels, my face was shoved back into the mire of bitterness and rancor that arose dealing with "Team Gigi," the group of expensive law-yers Gigi had engaged to deal with our pending divorce. While I wasn't really contesting anything or fighting for custody of the children, Gigi was accusing me of abandonment, of abuse, of "touching myself inappro-priately in front of the kids" (*that again!*), and whatever more her lawyers could articulate on paper.

At times I would explode in rage, "Screw them!" and prepare to put up a fight. My chest would tense up, cynicism would rise, and I'd work myself up with righteous indignation, "To not confront these lies is to tacitly admit they're true!" But ultimately, I would breathe deeply, regain my center by walks in nature, and use all my willpower to control my feelings and practice the *Art of War*. Instead of reacting, I would become strategic; instead of engaging in conflict, I would be invisible, mobile, acquiescing.

When I arrived at Gigi's lawyer's office for the first time, I was shocked. Massive piles and piles of paperwork were stacked practically to the ceiling! How could they not fall over? And how much money do these stacks of papers represent?

I introduced myself to Jim, a grouchy old man in his sixties who was charging Gigi $550 per hour! The high price of revenge! He began sniff-ing the air in concern, "Did somebody die in here?"

"What?" I asked in bewilderment. It turned out he was responding to the patchouli oil I had on. "Look, Jim, why don't we just meditate… I mean, no, I mean mediate…?"

"Gigi doesn't want to mediate anything."

"C'mon, Jim, let's get this over with. Our family can't afford this."

"Let me talk to her, but it won't do any good."

Leaving his office, I felt dejected to see him so pessimistic about any form of amiable settlement, but still, I tried to remain hopeful. A few days later, my hopes for a graceful resolution were soundly dashed to bits when he served me papers demanding an increase in my monthly payments to Gigi. I sighed deeply and braced myself for a long, big battle. After deep consideration, I decided that even though I had an attorney, I would represent myself. I had no such experience, so it was a big risk and commitment on my part, but I had no money to do otherwise.

Represent yourself? What are you thinking? This is the world of lawyers who can tear you apart with legalese and fine print. In spite of such contrary thoughts, I felt committed to represent myself and kept my spirits up with the conviction that truth does not have to be proved; sooner or later, it will come out. Wasn't it in the Bible, "know the truth, and the truth shall set you free"?

Since I felt my truths were self-evident, the best course for me to take was to be "invisible" again and not react to caustic accusations from Gigi. On a deeper level, to remain invisible meant that I would be in the invisible world of Spirit, a realm based on faith, peace, and love, as I was fast learning from the *Course*. If so, then *I* had to be centered on faith, peace, and love as well.

I told my attorney to make a generous settlement in hopes of resolving the conflict. I just wanted it over. Unfortunately, Gigi didn't accept any offer and continued with the intensity of her hostility. She just wanted to fight. As a consequence, I now saw in legal terms her usual charges against me—I stole from our joint account, I was a liar and a cheat, I abandoned and neglected the family, etc. It made me shudder to see all these accusations in black and white. Quite accurately, I had to admit that I did lie, did cheat, did neglect the family, and the list goes on and on. But that was then and this is now.

On weekends, I was still able to see my children, but I could tell that their brainwashing to view me as the enemy had deepened, that to be friendly to me meant betrayal of their mother. Over and over again, I would hear charges from them, "You stole from Mom...You're not taking care of us...Mom started your business, and then you cheated her..."

Finally, I received my day in court where I could present my own statement to the judge. Just to appear represented hours and hours of study and research to learn the protocol of the legal profession. For months, it was all-consuming, with me devoting fifteen hours a week to respond properly to legal forms, subpoenas, financial statements, and more. Guided by *The Art of War*, I became patient, non-reactive, and co-operative. Guided by the *Course*, I took full responsibility for my predicament and tried to meet every challenge from a spiritual perspective.

Before the judge, I presented my thoughts to the court about concern for my children, which focused on a statement I had written and passed out, "Children's Bill of Rights." It declared that all children have the right to have their physical and emotional needs met, the right to have an education, the right to be free of their parents' problems, and the right to have both parents—mother and father—to love and tend to their needs.

By representing myself, demanding as it was, I felt I could make a strong case direct from the heart about my love for my children (and all children) without having it diluted by lawyers and legal manipulation. After finishing my statement, I felt relieved to have my say, and felt it had made a positive impression on the judge. In any case, I did my best and just kept the faith for a positive outcome.

Shortly thereafter, during one of my visits, my youngest daughter mentioned that Gigi had flown to Utah where her dad and sister lived to look for houses. I was shocked. What was she up to? What was she planning to do with my kids? And without telling me? When I called Gigi later, she didn't deny it.

"Yes, we're moving," she spat out.

"When were you going to tell me?" I demanded.

"I didn't think you really cared anymore."

"Of course I care! I care that you planned to move my kids out of state without telling me."

"My lawyers are drafting up something."

"We can't talk without the lawyers?"

"Look, I don't want to live here anymore. After what you did with your affairs, it's humiliating. I want to get my children away from here, protect them from you."

"You know you can't do it without my permission."

"Are you going to fight me?"

"Gigi, I offered you a generous settlement. Why didn't you accept it?"

"It's not enough."

"What would be enough?"

Gigi remained silent.

"If we go to court, it's going to cost us both a lot more money, and I can guarantee you, you won't get any more."

"Your guarantees mean squat to me. I'm taking the kids out of here to safety."

I was devastated by the turn of events. "Look," I stammered, "I have to think about it. If you really want to move right now, I will…I have to think about it."

I sought advice from Jon and my parents, who all suggested that I let them go. Lizanne's observation was a great help:

"Just because they're moving away doesn't mean they're gone from your life. It's still up to you to decide how much you want to participate in their lives. Don't fall into being a victim."

And then I heard from my daughters:

"Dad, you must let us go. We'll be fine. If you don't, we'll never talk to you again."

That was the last straw. For my beloved kids to reject me was more than I could bear. I meditated and sought advice from Spirit, while trying to work through my lament. It seemed that the best thing to do for the sake of the children was to let them go. *But what about me! I am going to be all alone.* The wounded child in me felt sad and terrified all at once.

Pondering all these heavy thoughts, I didn't hear from Gigi for weeks. My biggest comfort was from Lizanne, who was always there for understanding and support. Though we were not yet involved romantically, we had fallen into each other's lives in an ever-deepening friendship. It was all I could handle at this point.

Agony and Ecstasy of Children

Finally, the dreaded letter arrived, delivered by certified mail. It stated that Gigi was to take the children to live in Utah. The only thing that could stop this move was a last-minute refusal on my part to sign the document. I stared at the signature line as images of my beloved children floated around and around my head like smiley yellow ducks swirling around their bathtub.

I thought of all the wonderful memories I had with them, teaching them to ride bicycles, taking them into the ocean, watching their soccer games, and seeing their expressions when the Tooth Fairy left a silver dollar beneath their pillows. I remembered their exuberant greetings when I walked through the door after work, how they would rush towards me all smiles and hugs.

In view of all these poignant memories, I was torn: Should I sign them away, or should I not? Yes or no? Do it, or not? I was filled with the same anxiety I had when I was fifteen, contemplating whether I should jump off the Malibu Pier into the crashing waves below. I'll do it, no I won't, yes I will, nah, let's not.

As the war raged inside me, I thought of the magical moments of how they came into the world. The first two births had gone so smoothly that Gigi and I felt truly blessed with our perfect family with two beautiful children. How they enriched our lives.

But then, a few years later, we were both inspired to have one more. By this time, Gigi was already in her mid-thirties, and when she became pregnant, the doctors recommended extra tests just in case. When the results came back, the doctor calmly informed us that the baby had a genetic defect, and recommended discontinuing the pregnancy. I was stunned. Mindlessly, I tried futilely to pronounce the name of the genetic syndrome.

That termination, like the one Gigi had when she was a teenager, proved devastating to our relationship. The complex repercussions forced Gigi to devote all her time to the children, while I threw myself back into my work. Emotionally, we were so estranged that our marriage was at stake. Six months later, Gigi got pregnant again, and we both felt a reprieve as if God were giving us another chance. We were overjoyed, and glad that we had stuck it out with our marriage. All's well that ends well!

Five months into this pregnancy, Gigi woke up thinking something was wrong. She said she couldn't "feel" the baby. I assumed she was being paranoid, but when we went to the doctor, our worst nightmare came true. The baby had wrapped itself in the umbilical cord and died, just like that.

Something within me died that day as well. I pleaded to God for some form of understanding, some explanation for these terrible tragedies. No answers came. The depth of my sorrow prompted me to ponder the precious and fragile nature of life itself. A deep lament that was inconsolable surrounded our entire household as a strange, uneasy silence descended over everything. It gnawed at my soul. Any of my feeble attempts to connect with Gigi were met with chilly reception. Communication between us was frozen. At dinner, we each talked to the kids separately, but not to each other. Separately we slept. Gigi began to let herself go physically, as did I. I put on an extra ten pounds myself. I felt lost in the wind, aimlessly going through the motions of life.

But as the cycles of life revolve, somehow Gigi and I soldiered on through that frigid period of mourning and despair long enough to take a vacation to Australia and New Zealand. It gave a temporary respite from our doldrums, allowing our emotions to flow towards each other once again. For a moment, we were loving human beings to each other again.

But once back home, the old patterns returned. She completely focused on parenting, and I threw myself back into sixty-hour weeks of narcissistic business. But alas, our moment of connection during the vacation resulted in another pregnancy. What joy! What apprehension. Will fate disappoint us again? Do I dare get my hopes up? Month by month, I toed the line between celebration and despair, month by month I kept faith and positive thoughts until the ninth month when, lo and behold, everything went smoothly all the way through the birth of our third little girl, who we always considered our "miracle child," Morgan.

Surrounded by four "girls" with all that feminine energy, I had many wonderful memories. In spite of the fact that Gigi and I had returned to living like roommates, speaking only when necessary, careful not to touch as we went about our routines, my children were the light of my life. Just the sounds of their voices would bring joy to my heart.

And now, in a reversal of fortune, I was asked to surrender my precious jewels. I stared at the official letter, at the three inches of black line to which I was supposed to affix my signature that would sacrifice everything that was most dear to me. I couldn't sign it. I couldn't eat. I couldn't work. I couldn't think. I felt sick.

I couldn't even visit Lizanne, my pillar of support. Painful as it was, I knew I had to decide this on my own. Thoughts tumbled through my head in a constant stream.

I thought about Gigi's role in all this, of the time my mom called late at night demanding to know what's going on.

"What're you talking about?" I asked.

"It's Gigi. She showed up banging at our door in the middle of the night."

"She did? Why? What did you she want?"

"To blame us for the 'failure of your son.'"

"Oh no," I said sadly, "I'm so sorry this happened, Mom, I really am."

"Don't worry about me. I'm so sorry for the children," she replied.

If this was all part of Gigi's plan to get back at me, she's doing a great job of it, I thought. *I'm in utter despair.* But was she really looking out for the children's best interests? *Stop it right there, no judgment, no self-pity,* I scolded myself.

I thought of my girls, what would really be best for them? Because of our separation, they had been thrown into tremendous pain and fear through no fault of their own. Everything considered, they'd be fine in either household, and if anything, they'd be better off with their mother at this time of their lives. At least I knew that Gigi loved them every bit as much as I did. The only worry that constantly plagued me was that she would create a condition of torn loyalties that would set up a permanent wedge between me and my kids.

After two days of misery, contemplating every possibility of an alternative resolution to this most pivotal point in my life—the day-to-day loss of my children—I stared out all alone into the ocean from the balcony of my beach cottage and listened mindlessly to the waves crashing.

With tears rolling down my face, I scrawled out my signature at the end of a short, two-page affair, and signed away my children.

Two weeks later, I had a chance to say a last goodbye to them. At Gigi's parents' house, they only let me in as far as the driveway. One by one, they came out, and evenly, putting on a good face, I hugged them farewell. Goodbye, Maya, fifteen. Goodbye, Sophia, thirteen. Goodbye, "miracle child" Morgan, eight. Goodbye, my beloved angels.

They were all very quiet and had no idea of the deep implications of the moment, nor the agonizing pain I was going through. I reassured each of them that in two weeks, I would go out to visit them in Utah. With Gigi's indoctrination, I didn't know if they even considered that a good thing.

The next month the children moved away. It plunged me into a profound lament. I felt hollow, empty. It was by far the most agonizing thing I had ever done. Though I would still be able to visit them, I knew it would never be the same. They would grow older, get caught up in their own lives, and find new friends, all without me. I got drunk, but no amount of alcohol could fill my emptiness. The only relief from my sorrows was to read *A Course in Miracles*. And with it, I intensified my yoga and meditation. With dogged determination, I was determined to focus on the positive and design a new life for myself.

Life Without the Children

That night after the children left, Lizanne held me in her arms as I wept for hours, sobbing into the pillow, the sheets, her shoulders. I was numb with what felt like the death of my children, the death of my own childhood, the death of the most beautiful, precious accomplishments of my life, my children.

Lizanne ended up staying over for the first time as she cradled me in her arms all night long. Few words were spoken, just subtle touches and comforting embraces. Although I felt desolate beyond measure, at least I was not alone. Her presence kept me from permanently plummeting into the abyss.

For a period of time afterwards, I went about the motions of my life like a robot on autopilot with little emotion. I'd get through one day and night only to arrive upon the next. Small moments of uplift would occur when I saw Lizanne, who encouraged me to go on and showed by example that life was worth living.

In ways not fully logical, my shamanic experiences helped me get through this period, resonating in my heart and body more than the intellect. I stepped up my meditation routine and yoga practice, and carried on my daily reading of *A Course in Miracles,* which fed my mind, as Lizanne continued to feed my heart. A couple days a week, to feed my pocketbook, I went to the office to keep up with some investments and to ensure that my business didn't collapse, something I could ill afford. With little enthusiasm, I soon found myself embroiled on the "Student Housing Project" that turned out to be a complex mess, and proved to be the death knell for me of doing business along values of the "old order."

Student Housing Project

I was a co-developer of a student housing project at the University of California, a sizable venture valued at $54 million upon completion. The lead developer, Mike, was someone who I had worked with before, and with whom I had made a few very profitable deals. Here and there, I learned that he had had a number of lawsuits and accusations against him, but in view of those profitable deals, I turned a blind eye and passed them off as honest mistakes. This denial on my part would end up costing me plenty.

Mike had "borrowed" money from another one of his projects to fund the construction of the student housing, and in due time, he was caught doing "payoffs" to some officials of the City of El Monte. Now, with the Feds investigating him and tightening the noose, the pressure on Mike grew so intense that he crashed with a nervous breakdown. It was all out in the open—my partner was a bona fide crook! What a rude awakening for me. With him unable to finish the job, I had to take over, and all his misdeeds were now thrown into my face. Deciding to move forward, I had a plan of how it could all be resolved. After raising the funds to close the loan, I was ready to present my ideas to the other partners.

In my sleek conference room overlooking the palms and the ocean beyond, I was optimistic that my plan could save the student housing project, and centered myself just as the partners walked in.

"Hi, Peter, hi, Ron, it's nice to see you both. Please sit down."

Without much ceremony, Peter got down to business, "Adam, you and Mike have totally fucked up this project. You've put our shopping center at risk." In his sixties, he looked like a short curmudgeon, sharp and caustic, an alpha dog with a narrow face that accentuated his aggressive nature.

"Whoa, Peter, please calm down. I invited you guys here today to discuss some ideas on how to get this project back on track. I spoke with the bank and they're ready to proceed."

"Yeah, sure they are," Ron replied sarcastically in his relaxed, soft-spoken manner. His words and tone were in sharp contrast to his appearance as a tall, handsome man who looked like an elder statesman.

"They'll have to cough up at least three million in cash to get this loan closed," Peter added.

"They do, I know, and guess what?" I answered triumphantly. "I've been able to put together an investor group who will come up with the three million! We can get this closed in the next week or two." I handed them a few sheets of the prospectus, and they devoured it in seconds.

"This is a bunch of bull shit," Peter exclaimed, dismissing the proposal with a gesture. "Mike has taken millions out of the shopping center and diverted it to the student housing project, and now you want to take over the deal with your investors?" he retorted, cynically.

"Nobody is trying to take over the deal. I'm just trying to salvage this mess, so please don't shoot me! I'm not the bad guy."

"Adam, you just don't get it. *Your* group will now control the majority of the deal, and reap all the rewards."

"But, Ron, it's business. It's not uncommon for money partners to get a preferred return and a portion of the profits," I replied.

"Yeah, but sixty percent? That leaves Mike with most of the rest, and nothing for Peter and me."

I breathed deeply, trying to calm myself before I went on. "Ron, please tell me why you and Peter should get a piece of this deal?"

"Because we are Mike's partners in the shopping center, and being that Mike borrowed funds from *our* project and put them into the student housing project we are entitled to *our* share of those funds. And don't forget, the project is being built on land owned by *our* partnership."

"You're right, Ron. For that, you guys are entitled to a bigger piece of this deal, and we'll work that out later. But the main problem here is that you guys need to get things worked out with Mike. He's the one who diverted funds from your deal into the housing project in the first place. So, first, work things out with Mike, and then get back with me so we can salvage this deal."

Inside, I was seething. Of course a fair and balanced solution was required, but Ron and Peter, who knowingly participated in putting this deal together, were now trying to weasel a much bigger piece of the pie. What blatant greed! I was more than willing to do my share, but the blind avarice of these two was nothing I wanted to be involved with. How I wished I had listened to my instincts at the very beginning instead of turning a blind eye to the character of those with whom I was dealing. It made me think of a past incident that threw light on who I was dealing with: Peter in a previous meeting had asked me to secretly give him a piece of my profits if I wanted him to go along with the deal. He was trying to bribe me! I had categorically refused, and he has remained angry at me to this day.

"Adam, you think about what we said," Peter went on. "Mike has had a mental breakdown, the FBI is investigating him for his payoffs to the city of El Monte, and you are his partner, so it's going to be up to you to get Ron and me our fair share, or else."

Having had enough of this shakedown, I called an end to the meeting. "Gentlemen, I have to run, but let me emphasize that my investors are ready to go, and we *can* save this deal. Something is better than nothing!" I began folding up my papers, and stood up. "Here, let me walk you out to the elevator."

The walk and wait for the elevator was excruciating. I so wanted to be free of their toxicity. "Peter, Ron, thanks for coming, and let's get this resolved. I see the light at the end of the tunnel..."

"Adam," Peter cut in, puffing himself up like King Kong, "the light you see at the end of your goddamn tunnel might just be a giant gorilla with a flashlight ready to smash you into pieces!" The door opened, they stepped in sneering, and the elevator swallowed them up for their descent.

The next time I saw those two was in court. They chose to take another route to resolve the project, and I was left embroiled in a legal battle to recover the $200,000 I had invested in the project. It dragged on and on, and after two years and $130,000 for lawyers' fees, I decided to cut my losses and walk away from the battle.

With the new perspective from my shamanic practice, I had to take responsibility for this debacle. My ego and greed had led me to overlook the nefarious character of my partners, which in turn led to this entanglement.

After letting go of the money and battle, I felt strangely empowered. It was the last of doing business for greed, the end of an old order. I could let it all pass, and eventually, could even forgive myself for my own stupidity and avarice. I was determined to forge a new life not only personally with relationships, but also professionally in business. I swore to myself that from now on, I would be involved only with business that mattered, and partners that I respected and enjoyed being with.

Initiation into the Yellow Road

I arrived in St. George, Utah, in a fog of emotions. I was beside myself with anticipation. It was my first visit with the kids since I signed away my rights to keep them in L.A. Gigi had conveniently decided to take an extended holiday in Asia with girlfriends, so I went to see the kids at her parents' house situated in what can best be described as small-town America. Here, at least, I knew the kids would be safe.

How often we had all enjoyed our trips into nature, so I had planned to take them for a two-day visit to beautiful Zion National Park. I loved that "Zion" means a place of refuge, of peace. To my disappointment, Maya, my oldest, was so mad at me that she refused to go. No amount of persuasion could make her change her mind, so Sophia, Morgan, and I went driving off to Zion, just an hour away, without her.

Once there, we stayed in the rustic, big-timbered Zion Lodge set right in the park amidst spectacular natural scenery of towering formations of red rock, colorful trees, and wildlife. The hiking, how could it not be great? And then we went horseback riding. It was nothing like my wild mustang ride, but it didn't matter; I now felt communion with all horses at any speed. To see my kids enthralled, perched on their saddles like little cowgirls poking through the majestic scenery, made my heart sing. I couldn't stop snapping photos, trying to capture the moments. It was like old times with my kids and I having fun so naturally. Lizanne was right, it's up to me to find ways to continue the connection with my kids.

That night when Sophia and Morgan had drifted off to sleep, I became restless. The lodge was full since spring was the best time of year to visit Zion. Perhaps there would be some special events going on tonight. As I lay in bed wondering what to do with myself, I kept hearing a nagging voice telling me, "Get up! Go out for a walk!" It would not stop. I propped myself up onto my elbows to listen more carefully. Was I hearing things again? "Get up. Take a walk out in nature."

My mind started to wander through past tidbits of information. For example, Jon's teacher, Alberto, talked about practices in Peru where shamanic initiations involved walking in the jungle alone at night. I saw them as walks into the dark spaces of one's psyche. And then I thought about what I had read in *The Sacred Path* where very similar ideas were discussed of solitary "night walks" in nature as essential aspects of initiation. This was my initiation into the Yellow Road.

With these thoughts running around my head, I heeded the cry and got up and went out for a walk. A sliver of a moon gave a pale light, and a cool north wind gently brushed over the trees. Following my intuition, I walked to the nearby creek and crossed the bridge to begin climbing the trail up the canyon, but a sign barred my way:

"STOP! Do not Proceed. Trail Closed. DANGER!"

Without much thought, I ignored the sign and proceeded up the steep trail. The thin moonlight was barely enough to light my way, and often I had to slow down to tiny baby steps. After a few hundred yards, I had climbed well off the canyon floor to see the lodge in the distance way below. As I moved around a bend in the trail, I slipped and barely caught myself from sliding off a cliff. The trail had completely washed out!

It sobered me up to the reality of what I was doing—walking in the middle of the night in darkness over unpredictable cliffs with washed-out trails. Still, I felt compelled to continue on, but my hands had become sweaty, and my heart pounded audibly.

After about half a mile, I came to a brush-filled, semi-wooded area. My eyes had adjusted, but I could only see darkness. I shuffled on, blindly, inch-by-inch, proceeding along what I hoped was the path. A crackling sound! I froze. All my senses keenly aware. I was like an animal. Was something stalking me? In the pitch-blackness, my imagination began to go on overdrive. A lion? A bear? *Why are you doing this? Perhaps I was the one doing the stalking? Stalking for what?* After long moments, I continued on. Whatever my thoughts, my body kept moving me forward past my fear. After a few more minutes, I rounded a bend and heard the full downpour of a waterfall.

It was magnificent. With only the dim sliver of moon to give off light, I could see the water cascading down the cliff. As I walked on, I was led step by step *behind* the falls. Water sprayed all around as I breathed in the negative ions and absorbed the rushing sound of falling water.

The trail led me from behind the waterfall, and after a few minutes, using what dim light was available, I could barely perceive that the trail led into a rock formation that was cave-like in nature. I stared into the cave and saw utter blackness. The sheer darkness again inflamed my imagination as I went wild with apprehension. *What if it's a lion's den? Or I accidently shuffle over a sleeping bear?* I could feel the throbbing in my chest. Sweat went down my armpits. Still, a strange power kept me moving forward. *Move through*, a voice inside me demanded.

Step by step, I shuffled forward, extremely sensitive to any sensations. Nothing escaped my attention. Unable to see anything whatsoever, I was forced to surrender to my situation, and after a few minutes, I felt a strange comfort to be so embraced by blackness. *You're moving beyond the physical to enter the spiritual*, I heard the voice say. I felt as if power was flowing into me. Goose bumps. Slowly, inching forward, trusting my instincts, I felt as if I were entering the womb of Mother Earth, and that without any visual distraction, I was able to connect with All That Is. With the void. The unmanifest.

In the utter darkness, another form of sight kicked in that froze me in my tracks. I perceived a soft glow from my own arm! And the cavern walls. Everything seemed to have its own luminosity. I could perceive different degrees of blackness. There was no such thing as complete darkness because as a living being, I was giving off my own light! Playing by the rules of pure Spirit, I could "see" in ways other than through the eyes. For long moments, I felt incredibly safe.

Eventually, I shuffled on, acutely attuned to every step, sound, or whisper whether from animals or trees, wondering when I would reach the back of the cave. Way ahead, I saw a patch of moonlit sky. I was so relieved. I was not in a cave, but in a tunnel, and now I could see the other end.

Coming back out into the open, I could still "see" a soft glow from the entire canyon—a milky white light that emanated from everything. It was surreally beautiful and provoked feelings of gratitude and awe for being part of nature with so many hidden wonders.

Soon, the trail looped back out onto a road, and feeling that I had had enough, I took the road and began to make my way the mile or so down the canyon back to the Lodge. My midnight jaunt had taken an hour and a half.

I returned safely to the room. The kids were sound asleep. As I turned on the light I noticed the park paper on the nightstand. There on the cover was a photo of a very large, mature mountain lion snapped with night photography on the very trail I had just shuffled through! If I had seen this before my hike, I most certainly would not have gone out at night, much less hiked up the trail alone.

I stared at the photo, mesmerized by the power of this animal, pondering why on earth I would do such a crazy thing. On one hand, it was so stupid, even irresponsible with respect to my kids, and at the same time, I felt that I was called to do it, and having answered the call, I was in the protective hands of some greater power.

For two hours, I lay awake, staring blindly at the ceiling, digesting what I had just done. I felt that a crack between the worlds had been opened during my Vision Quest, and with this midnight jaunt, I had slipped into that crack into the mysterious world of Spirit, that I had been initiated into the Yellow Road.

9

THE BLUE ROAD

A Greater Cycle

Reflecting on my recent night-walk in Zion National Park, which I saw as a portal into the Spiritual, I became excited to ground the experience graphically on my ever-growing Life Map. Already I had the Red Road of the physical, the Yellow Road of the emotional/psychological realm, and now I could add the Blue Road of the Spiritual. On the Map, I drew a curved line from the westernmost point of my diagram to the north, the direction of the Spiritual. This I accented with a star. *Oh my god! I am heading northward to discover my North Star!*

As I worked on my map, I remembered having read another variation of my midnight jaunt in Zion. In Native American tradition, young braves were sent out into the night as part of a transformational initiation to help them overcome fears and to discover that great secrets can be revealed in the blackness of night. "Night Stalking," as this ritual was called, forced one to move beyond all normal perceptions—when someone cannot see with their eyes, one is forced to see with his or her "spiritual sight." If my jaunt were an initiation, then, I felt I had passed! It was exactly what had happened to me when I overcame fear and experienced that inner light. I felt a sense of accomplishment and increased faith that I was expanding my life to a whole new level that included the Spiritual. Someone once said, "that deep dark places hold the greatest potential for light."

And how utterly grateful I was to Spirit to let me know, symbolically and literally, that no matter how dark our lives may seem, we always have illumination from the light of our own Being. The magic of all this experience only increased when I found out that "Zion," in the Kabbalah tradition, means "being in the spiritual point from which reality emerges."

Past Lives

After returning from Zion, I felt so exhilarated, I kept wondering, *What's the next thing that Spirit will put on my path?* From then on, thanks to that "Night Stalking" experience, I became inspired to surrender my ego desires to higher authorities. Whatever "they" wanted was what I wanted. Of the incalculable possibilities in the Universe, what could be my next adventure?

Continue to explore your past lives, I intuitively answered myself, loud and clear. As a result, I arranged for another "soul retrieval" session with Jon, my shaman friend. I couldn't wait to ask him a question that had been smoldering inside me since our last session in Carmel.

By this time, I had moved from my beach cottage to a larger house on the hillside of Malibu that overlooked the ocean. It gave me an overview of the landscape, but also, so it seemed, my life. A fitting location for our next session. As soon as Jon showed up, my burning question burst out of my mouth.

"Last time you mentioned something about my tendency towards violence. You saw it in one of my past lives. What was that all about?"

"Good question," he answered smoothly. "Let's get in sacred space and find out."

He did an invocation to the Four Directions, called in the spirit guides, and laid out his "mesa," an antique tan cloth on which he placed a dozen stones and a few crystals.

"Pick one."

Intuitively, I selected a craggy rock about an inch and a half in length that was in the "western" direction on his cloth. He had me lie down, took back the stone, and without a word, conducted an "illumination," a monitoring of my energy body. With a crystal, he passed over my *chakras* (energy centers within the body), first to open them, and then to rebalance them. With my eyes closed, I could feel energy that seemed to hover over me. After twenty minutes, he finally broke the silence.

"Let's look at this life where you suffered the most."

"Uh, okay." That wasn't exactly what I wanted to hear; I felt a little nervous. *More suffering? Why?*

"Who suffered the most?" he asked. "Your mother or your father?"

"My mother." Though a part of me balked, *What kind of question is that?* I had no time to think and answered off the top of my head.

"What about *her* parents?" Jon pushed on.

Immediately, an image popped into view. Grammie and I. In my twenties, I'm eating ice cream as she plays pop songs on the piano. Suddenly, she stops in the midst of the song and, out of the blue, tells me, "Adam, life can be all that you want so long as you have a relationship with God."

"But…but Grammie, I don't know God, so how am I to have a relationship?"

"Listen to your heart."

Grammie planted a seed that took years to blossom, but blossom it did. She also inspired me to take note of my cultural roots. She had grown up near an Indian reservation in Oklahoma where she would sit on the steps of the country store and watch all the Native Americans come and go. Their plight and sufferings had touched her deeply, and this heart-felt empathy was one of the main sources of whatever compassion I had. How appropriate that she was born on Valentine's Day, the holiday of love and matters of the heart.

While thoughts about Grammie floated around my head, I felt a profound sense of peace that was connected to a familiar garden, Lila's garden. Her silent presence was palpable like a gentle breeze. The quiet was abruptly broken by Jon's voice.

"Call the Gatekeeper," he told me. "Where are you now, who is the Gatekeeper?"

In my mind's eye, I could see my pathway leading directly into a huge stone about twenty feet high blocking my progress. "I can't go forward," I replied out loud.

"Ask for permission. Let the Gatekeeper know your intent. You want to find your 'original wound.'"

A Life of Suffering

I did as told, and noticed to the left of the huge stone a pond.

"Jump into the pond," I heard the Gatekeeper say without words. I plunged into the water, and soon saw myself moving through Mother Earth past bulbs and roots, soil and rock, until I found myself in a cave beside a clear pool of water. It was pitch black, but I could "see" just as I had experienced on my Night Stalking in Zion.

Again, I asked the Gatekeeper, "Please let me see my original wound." After a few minutes, images came into view…

I am moving over cobblestones through a bleak, colorless town of bricks under a gloomy sky. It is in England, perhaps in the 1300s. I spring aside from a horse-drawn carriage that nearly ran over my foot, and see on the side of an old church a penniless, emaciated woman wearing tattered clothing. Going through a body-wrenching coughing fit, she reveals a few crooked yellow teeth with each lurch. It starts to drizzle as I gaze into her vacant, yet vaguely familiar eyes. Suddenly I know—this pathetic homeless woman is *me* in a past life. I'm observing the past life where I had suffered the most.

I can't take my eyes off of her, and as an impersonal witness, I watch objectively with no feeling or judgment how she is suffering. Pedestrians all around ignore her, and many cover their nose and look at her with disgust. One man spits at her, shouting something about her being a "blight to society." Sympathy is completely absent, except for one man, an older priest who made it a point to feed her every day, and during the cold, cruel nights of winter, provide her with a blanket. As that impartial witness, I see how victimized by society she feels.

Meanwhile, through another coughing fit, I watch as that poor homeless woman staggers from her makeshift shelter to the entry to the church. With her thin, fragile hands, she tries to open the door, but it's locked. "Save me," she gasps to no one in particular, and collapses, striking her head against a stone.

After a few minutes, the door swings open. It's the priest, who peers out into the dim light of dusk, and sees the woman's inert mass trimmed with a gentle halo of blood growing around her head. Gently, he picks her up, listens for any sign of life, and shakes his head. Looking up to the heavens, he mumbles something of a last rite.

At the gravesite, I hear a dull thud as her body is dumped into a pauper's grave. When shovelfuls of dirt are thrown over her chest, in spite of my detachment, I feel heartbroken. No one should suffer like that with no family, no hope, all alone in the world with nothing but pain and despair until the bitter end.

"Now is the time to forgive." Startled by Jon's prompt, I intuitively used my breath to send from my heart love, understanding, and blessings for that poor woman. It would be a gesture I would repeat many times whenever I thought about her.

After a few more minutes, Jon brought me out of my meditative state back into normal reality. I must've "been under" for about forty minutes. He gave me some instructions on how to process and heal this past-life regression, and left.

The Homeless Woman

After this poignant session, my mind percolated with questions and insights. So *that* was the life in which I had suffered the most. No joy, no accomplishment, no peace, no hope. If "you create your own reality," as the sages remind us, then I must've been convinced that I was unworthy for even the tiniest amount of love or happiness in that life. Can that be true?

In a moment of insight, I knew that her plight had formed a grim determination in me of *never be a victim*. These were the seeds of the "eat or be eaten" mentality that had so driven me in my business life. Often, I had so over-reacted to avoid becoming victimized that in my obsessed need to be in control, I turned into a tyrant filled with explosive anger.

A complete victim, that homeless woman had no faith, courage, or wisdom to take initiative to better her situation. How pathetic! But that precious word *forgiveness* kept coming up, just as Jon had prompted me. I had to forgive her—*myself*—for how she had sold herself short her entire life. If this were true, there was a lot to forgive, but that was exactly what was called for if I were truly determined to transcend this vicious cycle that has bled through centuries all the way into my present life.

I learned how our original wounding could lodge itself so deeply into our psyche that, unconsciously, we keep recreating the pattern over many lifetimes. One such "bleed-through" happened to me when I was a student in Berkeley.

I was riding my bike to class, a route that took me through a parking lot behind a church. Many times, I would pass a smelly homeless woman who would routinely be ignored. But one time, without warning, she lunged in front of me as I jammed on the brakes to avoid hitting her.

"I know you! I know you!" she shouted, knowingly.

Trying to get the hell out of there, I maneuvered my bike as best I could, as I shouted out a desperate reply, "I know you, too!" With a stench that felt toxic, she personified suffering and the complete lack of self-worth. For years, I had passed off this incident as just another weird experience of life, but now I saw this "bleed-through" as an opportunity for me to look at deep-seated patterns within myself.

Four Steps to Heal

To be willing to come face-to-face with my "original wounding," I had accomplished, according to Jon, the first of four steps for true healing: *acknowledge its existence.* The next step was to see what was the "original contract" that allowed this wounding to occur. Third, I was to "rewrite the contract" by forgiving all parties involved (myself included), so that finally, for the last step, we could bring the treasure back into the present life.

This process to heal the "original wound" through *soul retrieval* would go on for months. Spontaneously, all along, I would receive insights, which I found exhilarating, like finding pieces of a complex puzzle that would yield new levels of awareness and wholeness.

I chuckled at myself for how my views on past lives had changed. It was not too long ago that I had proclaimed to someone, "Past lives, what a bunch of nonsense! I don't believe in it. How could it help since it does not even exist?"

This was my knee-jerk response from watching commercial TV that often scorned such metaphysical thought. But now I knew that everything is possible, "reasonable" or not. After all, love is "unreasonable," but it surely exists. So now I had come to understand that with past lives, it's not whether it is factually true or not, but rather "does this information enhance my life now?" Many people are inspired by *Star Wars* and "the force," let's say, but it's all fiction.

But then, another powerful antagonist challenged my involvement with past-life regressions.

"*Past* lives? Ha! I thought you were big on there being *no time*, that time is an illusion, like you had read in *The Power of Now*? With no time, there's no *past* lives. So what gives?"

So proclaimed my reason, trying to undermine my newfound discoveries. It was a good question, and it had a good answer: Yes, ultimately, there is no time. We are multi-dimensional beings, and all our so-called "past lives" are all going on at the same time. Some lives, however, are dominant (like my present one as a businessman and father of three), and some are in the background (like my life as a poor homeless woman). So, if we use the term "past life," it is only a language of convenience so as to communicate better in a society beholden to time. With this answer, my inner critic sneaked away.

After a few weeks digesting and forgiving my past life as that pathetic woman, I felt ready for the final step in healing the psychological wound—"rewrite the contract." How symbolic, the homeless woman lived just outside the church, i.e., outside Spirit. So close, but so far. This must have been the pattern that I endured for many lifetimes, including this one where I always felt separated from family, from happiness, and most importantly, from Spirit.

To "rewrite the contract," I got into a meditative state, entered a deep calm, and revisited the moment when the priest gave the woman her last rites. With the power of imagination, I re-created the moment to my liking with a most favorable ending. I saw the priest looking upon the face of the homeless woman, and repeating over and over again, "You are forgiven. It's not your fault. All is forgiven. God loves you, always has, and always will. You are loved, you are so worthy of love..."

Then the priest lifted her up in his arms and took her body inside the church. It was a beautiful, grand edifice with very high ceilings and intricate stained-glass windows. A sea of candles, all aglow, gave off a warm illumination. I was an invisible witness standing right next to the pulpit, watching the proceedings as dozens of parishioners, their eyes glistening with the reflection of the candles, watched the ceremony and sent love and compassion to that homeless woman, a complete stranger, *me*. It was *me* they were blessing with their love. Their concern was so heart-felt I could feel a shift within myself even though I was but a witness. No longer feeling "separated," I belonged to a loving community.

In rewriting the scenario, I saw and felt how darkness and despair could be transformed into a scenario of love, forgiveness, and resurrection. I was "creating my reality." The "contract" had been rewritten, and it is this image that I now carry with me about that life. Yes, even complete strangers are capable of giving love and understanding through the kindness of their hearts.

This new "contract" reminded me of an evening after yet another round of fighting with Gigi when I stepped out of the shower feeling despondent and unloved. Tears rolled out of my eyes. In my mind I heard echoing inside my head, "*What is love?*" I cleared the steam off the mirror, and catching my reflection, I suddenly heard clearly from some unknown source, "Adam, *you* are love." Though initially caught off guard, I realized from that moment on that the truest, most significant love did not come from outside, but from within.

Soon after this past-life regression, I found a heart-shaped stone while hiking, and decided that it would be the fourth stone in my ever-growing *Map of Life*. I placed it on my new Blue Road of the spiritual. How gratifying after all my profound, but abstract, revelations to express my findings through something as physical as a stone. This sacred stone would come to represent and honor the homeless women and my beloved Grammie.

After processing that sad, dismal life of suffering for a month, I was poised to embark upon my next Soul Retrieval. This time, I wanted something upbeat. Jon had mentioned a past where "life was the fullest," so I called him, and he came over to my hillside home to guide me through my next adventure.

A Full Life

Once again I went through a similar routine—I picked a stone, lay down, and followed his instructions until I was in a deep meditative state. I could feel Lila's strong presence that seemed to envelope me with a cushiony feeling of love. I felt so protected with Jon on the outside and Lila on the inside that I could easily let myself go, and found myself on a path through a lush garden.

"Look for the Gatekeeper," Jon said. "Where's the Gatekeeper?"

I looked around and saw beside the path a small, crystal clear pond. In it, I saw my own reflection when I heard Lila prompt me silently, "Ask."

"May I have permission to see my past life that was the fullest?" I said.

"What is your intention?" the Gatekeeper inquired, invisibly.

"To heal myself and become whole."

The pond turned clear and alive, and with no hesitation, I dove in. Similar to my last regression, I went through water, through earth, through moist soil, along roots until I found myself sitting by a pool in a dark underground cave with no light. I saw in the pool a wavering of green color that turned into lush, tropical palms...

I am in a Polynesian village, no specific time, but it feels like a few centuries back, when life was simple and natives lived close to the land and grew their own food. The island is a banquet for the eyes, with magenta, pink, lilac, yellow, and periwinkle blue blossoms, all harmoniously interwoven with vibrant emerald green leaves. Palms sway in the gentle breeze with plump, ripe fruit like mangos and papayas, and the surrounding mountains are gentle and green. I inhale the fragrance in the air, which makes me feel as if I were home, and relax completely.

I am part of a large extended family. Rarely is there a time when I am not surrounded by children, grandchildren, and great grandchildren.

What innocence and joy. As a respected and wise elder, I am frequently approached by members of my clan for advice.

To get away, I retreat to my favorite private spot overlooking the ocean of cerulean blue where I could see my grandchildren frolicking in the waves.

Jon's voice cuts in, "You are in the midst of all this feminine energy—children, family, Mother Earth. How does it make you feel as a man?"

With that prompt, I now see that this wise elder has a heavy look on his face. A private worry. Trouble in paradise. A child, horsing around, runs up to him, disturbing his thoughts. He explodes in rage, scolding him for interrupting his thoughts. The wise elder has a hidden mean streak. The child stops dead in his tracks, and after a few moments, runs off crying, as the elder returns to his troubled thoughts.

As the witness, I see everything. Deep down, he feels separated from this loving tribe because his heart is closed. Is his wise counsel performed out of duty instead of love? Filled with an over-abundance of the Divine Feminine, his "masculine" qualities have not been challenged nor fully developed, hence his anger and mean streak. Somewhere in the shadow of his psyche, his self-worth as a "real man" is missing, though he has no means to explore the issue. After all, he is the wise elder. This unresolved balance between his masculine and feminine principles is the original wound in this life.

The scene changes. As the witness, I am in the midst of a tribal celebration. Members of the extended family are holding hands in a circle. Around them, the community is in a larger circle, holding hands. Flowers and garlands are everywhere. Love and reverence is being poured onto the one in the very center. It is the wise elder lying on a pallet. It is his funeral…*my* funeral! I have mixed feelings, gratitude for all the love and respect being showered on him, and regret for not having lived life to the fullest as a man in the midst of all this abundance…

My eyes popped open, and I found myself on my living room floor with Jon watching over me. After a few parting remarks, he parted, leaving me with plenty of homework to gain full value out of this session. At the center of my work would be to find a new balance between the masculine and feminine aspects within me.

Through the next few weeks, I lived my daily life, of course, but these past-life regressions occupied front and center stage. I could not help but think of how so much of the so-called masculine qualities in my life—maintaining leadership, order, control, independence, assertiveness, and success in the world—had gone astray. Though I did have innate qualities of leadership and assertive focus towards success, they were not tempered by the feminine—meaning, value, and balance—to include loving relationships into the equation.

In my business, for instance, I wince to remember how utterly ruthless and self-centered I was in my blind drive for success, and how I was brain-washed into thinking that it's a "dog eat dog, eat or be eaten" world that I was party to. This attitude required so many layers of armor, lawyers, and mistrust that it was impossible to be intimate with anyone. Don't dare be vulnerable; they may stick it to you. Even when I had success, it was impossible to really enjoy it. How could I since I didn't ever dare let my guard down? As a consequence, my abundance in material possessions proved to be nothing but a fancy facade hiding the fundamental emptiness inside.

Death Stalks Me

With masculine principles out of balance through lifetimes, including this one, the consequences could be crucial. In one instance, it almost cost me my life. It happened years ago as a student in Berkeley. Being late to a morning class, I had jumped on my bike and took a shortcut by racing the wrong way down a one-way street. Somebody in a Chevy came straight at me, honking furiously. Without missing a beat, I flipped him off and kept going. Burning rubber in the process, the Chevy did a screeching 180-degree turn and chased after me. The Chevy was now going the wrong way on a one-way street. *This guy is nuts!*

Not being able to pedal fast enough, I jumped off my bike in terror and ran off to hide in some bushes in the Bank of America parking lot. I could see his blue Chevy Nova shoot by looking for me. The rumbling of the hot rod engine shook me to my bones. After several minutes, I heaved a sigh of relief and left my hiding spot only to feel hard metal against my head!

"Don't move, asshole." A click of a pistol. I froze in terror. He had a deep voice, with red pupils for eyes. "You flipped me the bird, mother fucker. Nobody flips me the bird."

"I am so sorry," I stammered. "I… I was caught off guard when you came around the turn so fast."

"Next time we meet, you'll be at the end of a bullet!"

"I'm sorry… I am."

After a long moment, he took the gun off my head, walked back to his car, and drove off. I was so shaken—*a gun to my head!* —that I skipped class and went straight to bed, trembling. The image of his demonic-looking red eyes haunted me for years.

Now, thanks to these past-life regressions, I could see how the issue of my unbalanced masculine energy had almost gotten me killed even in this life. Luckily, the soft feminine side allowed me to apologize and save my life.

Reminiscing about this incident made me recall other times that death had so stalked me—car crashes, setting myself on fire, and having that gun to my head—that I promised myself that an out-of-control ego with an unbalanced masculine/feminine qualities would no longer be tolerated as I moved on with my quest.

The Divine Feminine

Understanding how past-life patterns can transfer over lifetimes, I thought of a wonderful trip I took to Tahiti when I was 23 that echoed the lush comforts of a past life on that island. It seemed to be another "bleed-through" from a past life to this one, this time a pleasant experience.

In Tahiti, I relished the exquisite sensation of my bare feet squiggling into fine white sand with turquoise water lapping right before me. The balmy weather wrapped its arms around like a loving mother when I saw a perfect focal point for this tropical paradise—a beautiful native of the island with mocha skin, long hair, and soft curves.

Her name was Laylonnie, and she was part of a large family with grandparents, grandchildren, aunts, and uncles, a tribe as much as a family. They all lived near each other and celebrated life together in harmony with ocean and land.

My first night on the island, Laylonnie and I went out dancing and later fell asleep on the beach in each other's arms. Waking at sunrise, I felt I had come alive at the morning of the world, a new day in the Garden of Eden.

"I was with you before I am with you now," Laylonnie whispered. "I cannot wait to be with you again."

Even though I only knew her briefly, our days together felt timeless. She made me feel that my heart was alive and well, and that all's right with the world. The experience of the "Divine Feminine" seemed to have bled through from my past island life into this one.

Triggered by this memory, my thoughts began to drift through all the women in my present life—mother, wife, three daughters, and Lizanne—which had often made me feel like a masculine flower in a feminine garden. Perhaps it was a way to rebalance my excess of masculine energy.

The relationship with my mom wasn't always pleasant, but she *did* allow me to find my own way. To explore life as a great adventure was one of her most important legacies for me. On the other hand, I always felt that her love was conditional, that I had to measure up in some way before she would truly love me whole-heartedly.

But then, triggered by these past-life observations, I thought, *What about my having conditional love for her?* I always had assumptions of how a mother should act, and if she didn't measure up to my expectations, I would become sullen and withdraw my love for her. As a matter of fact, I could often be downright disrespectful. Oh, how my homework kept piling up.

Then there were my three lovely daughters. To nurture them called for me to draw upon feminine aspects within myself—an open ear, compassion, and tender loving care—so I could help them nurture a balance of masculine and feminine qualities within themselves. Though I had done the best I could, many times I felt I had failed miserably, especially when I became obsessed with my work. I didn't know any better. But just as I was about to beat myself up, I would be consoled by remembering how my youngest once told me, "I love you to infinity and beyond."

Gigi was my biggest "teacher," or as Castaneda would say, a "petty tyrant." All her vindictive acts of recent years forced me to take a spiritual perspective, or else drown in anger and bitterness. As I opened my heart, I could see life from *her* viewpoint and feel her pain. Her life, self-identity, and purpose of living were completely disrupted over things she didn't understand. Though I would have liked to see her open up to other ways to be, and to have made different choices in trying to assuage her fears and sorrows from our break-up, I knew everyone must live their own lives. With Gigi, I could only remain vigilant, centered, and free of judgment, and pray for her that she finds her own peace.

In "rewriting the contract" of the elder in the tropical island, I drew upon the powers of the feminine to give compassion and kindness to all concerned. Without denying the wonderful feminine qualities that he exhibited, I could still see with compassion his blind spots, his anger and meanness. I could sense how it came from some unfulfilled yearning, a private sorrow that he had no way of resolving. It gave me a basis for true forgiveness for his shortcomings. In the "rewriting of his contract," I could see what he needed, an opportunity to have camaraderie with other powerful men so that he could continue to hone his masculinity in the domain of men.

The consequence of this work yielded a fortuitous result. I could attract and cultivate a deep relationship with a woman who maintained a harmonious balance with her own masculine energy, her "animus"— the love of my life, my personal goddess, Lizanne. She was testimony to where I was within myself. We *do* create our reality—as without, so within.

The past life on that tropical island had another "bleed-through" aspect on a whole other level. With such fulfilling connection with the land, that life must've cast seeds of love for Mother Earth that blew over the centuries, because in this life I have such a great respect of our beloved planet.

A Squandered Life

About a month later, I was ready for my next past-life regression, so Jon again came by and repeated the protocol that allowed me to come face-to-face with the life where "I had everything, but threw it all away." It seemed heavy, so I braced myself for anything.

As I went deep into meditation under Jon's guidance, I wondered, *The life I had everything and threw it all away? Why in the world would I throw away what's so perfect? Could I be so blind as to engage in self-sabotage?* I continued to meditate and could feel Lila's silent presence, but for some reason, I was having trouble concentrating. Fear of the subject? Fleeting images with violent energy would flash by, but nothing seemed to stabilize.

"Where is the Gatekeeper? Look for the Gatekeeper," Jon's voice intruded, which helped me focus.

Now I saw roaring flames before me, and recoiled instantly. I could never forget how I had once set myself on fire that caused me such terrible fear and pain.

"Ask the Gatekeeper for permission," Jon said.

Permission? I do not want to go into that fire, I thought to myself. But then, I asked the Gatekeeper, "Show me the life where I had everything and threw it all away," and I jumped into the flames. I surrendered to the feeling of total annihilation, and for a moment, totally disappeared. The next moment...

...more flames, but as if I am hovering over a crackling bonfire below. Through the smoke, I see dozens of Native American tribesmen seated around the fire.

Once again I am in the distant past at a time well before the white men had come to this land. I am the son of the Chief, a highly respected, powerful leader of a peaceful, loving, and prosperous tribe—the very same Chief that had appeared in Sedona during my vision quest! My role as son of the Chief is that of a protector, and taking my job seriously, I am concerned about a neighboring tribe who has begun to encroach onto our territory. My father, keeping a watchful eye on the situation, lets it play out so as to avoid conflict. As of now, he does not find the trespassing serious.

I find that intolerable and weak. I demand that we do battle immediately, fight them off and teach them a lesson. But I am forced to heed my father's advice and attack only when he says so. He is determined to maintain the peace as long as possible. Outwardly, I abide by his decision, but inside I seethe with rage to be continuously thwarted and under the thumb of my father. Inside, I scream, *What about my power, my will, my knowledge?*

Stealthily, I sneak off in the middle of the night with a handful of renegades to launch an attack on that neighboring tribe. My strategy is to surprise them all before dawn, plunder, destroy, and massacre all trespassers with no mercy. They should not encroach on our land!

By arrow, by tomahawk, by knife, we throw ourselves into battle, killing indiscriminately women, children, and anyone in our path. In a mad blur, everyone is slaughtered. With arms covered in blood, I feel a strange exhilaration of power-lust and accomplishment.

It is morning, and everyone is in shock. Like wildfire, the news had spread, and the whole region knows about the massacre. Other tribes become wary of our clan filled with "cold-hearted killers." My father is beside himself with rage. The betrayal, the unnecessary deaths, the needless suffering, the loss of honor and their good name.

I am ostracized and banished from the tribe. In a flash, I lose everything and become separated from all I love. *What had I done?* I indeed had it all—family, prestige, power—but threw it all away. I'm all alone, filled with confusion. *What had I done?*

After the session, Jon departed, leaving me on my own to contemplate my terrifying past. There was no denying the horror of that life. What hubris I had! What cold-heartedness! These qualities were the source of my demise, not only in that life, but in my current one as well, especially in the way I used to handle my business transactions. Add to this my tendency towards anger and violence, and I could see it was a volatile mix.

Could one of my great issues in this life of "feeling separated" be rooted with the banishment by my own father from the tribe? Though my exile was utterly justifiable, I could still see the agony and despair that that son of the Chief had to suffer through.

In a flash of insight, I now knew why, as a kid in this life, I would get a strange uneasiness when I picked up something as common as a kitchen knife or a hatchet. My body would feel queasy, but not having the slightest clue as to why, I was forced to ignore my trembling and confusion.

I could also see how in this life, a similar pattern had emerged. I had gained prosperity, family, and respect in my community, but it didn't make me happy—"Everything is nothing"—and I "threw it all away." Although, this time around, I did not throw it all away because of the arrogance of ego, but rather because of humility to Spirit. This time around, I was not on a path towards destruction, but towards self-realization.

To this end, I had to take full responsibility for my wrongdoing, admit flaws in my emotional/psychological make-up, practice forgiveness, and "rewrite the contract." I had to follow what Jon had outlined for me with the four steps for healing. A tall order, but I was dedicated to this process. But how? Especially with this murderous past of mine.

I decided that *on my own*, I would revisit my life as a violent killer to try and heal my "masculine" that had gone amuck. With techniques gathered from Jon and my spirit guide, Lila, I was confident that I could do it by myself.

So one evening, sitting cross-legged on my couch, I began meditating. I felt the space between my thoughts, observed as my "monkey mind" slowed down into a zone of tranquility. I could feel Lila's presence encouraging me.

"Be clear in your intent. Hold it in your heart. Then let go…" After a few minutes, I find myself walking down a busy urban street, Fifth Avenue in New York. I enter a door that leads into a circular staircase winding around a powerful "vortex," a forceful column of energy. I go down, counter-clockwise to enter the Underworld that I intuitively know contains, among other things, everything of my past. At the bottom, the vortex comes to a point, and the stairwell ends at a dark windy shore next to a turbulent ocean. On a table, an antique sign-in book.

Understanding that the book is another variation of the Gatekeeper, I sign in, and a dinghy appears. I begin paddling in the dinghy, the ocean calms down, and intuitively, I head west, the direction of the setting sun, the direction of endings that allow rebirthing. The sky begins to lighten as the sun rises from the east. I land at an island and climb to the top of a nearby peak. There, I see an eagle fly by. I'm in touch with the "elementals." I begin to drift off into a deep state of stillness. My brain waves are slowing to a near standstill.

I walk into the fire; it's the entry point back to that violent killer, and...I turn into fire. Crackling with life and heat, I look out through flames, and see slumped before the bonfire a Native American warrior as broken and depressed as I have ever seen. Banished from his tribe and everything he loved by his own father, he reflects on his unconscionable deeds. He has absolutely nowhere to turn. All alone by the fire at night, his shame and remorse is so unbearable that he is considering suicide.

As fire, I witness his agony—another expression of the "original wounding" I've been seeking.

"What's to be done?" I ask Spirit. "If it be Thy will, come through me to help bring healing to that man." Suddenly, a power courses through me, and I feel an authority to not just be a passive witness, but to take action to help that sorrowful man. As fire, I reach out with forgiveness and unconditional love, which comes out in the form of light and warmth.

"Come, warm yourself. Feel the light. Bask in it," I say to him without words.

Unconsciously, he moves closer to the fire. Though he is wrapped in darkness, I can see the imperishable light hidden deep within him that is his true Self.

"You may have lived this life in darkness, you may have done heinous deeds, but still, your truthful essence is light. Take a stick. Blow into it all your darkness—remorse, fears, anger, violence, judgments, despair. Blow it all into the stick. Do it as many times as you need with full conviction. Then throw it into the fire."

The warrior stares at the flames for a while, then picks up a small branch. After a long moment of concentration, he blows fiercely into the stick. After another moment he blows again. Three times he does this, and then throws the branch into the fire. Mesmerized, he watches the stick being engulfed in flames. When it finally turns to ash, he rises to his full height, looks to the heavens with tears in his eyes, and lets out a powerful roar. It is a release of all his "darkness," and also a plaintive call to Spirit that the broken warrior of old is ready to die.

The sun reappears, the morning of a new day. Instead of wearing the tough leather breechcloth and leggings of someone on the warpath, he is now dressed in a light robe.

My eyes popped open, and I found myself back in normal reality on my couch. After a moment readjusting, I wept to have made such a strong connection with that wounded warrior, my sorrowful self in a past life. I felt lighter, as if a deep and open sore that had gone untended for lifetimes had finally been dressed so it could heal.

I knew that the sorrows, angers, and sufferings I had caused would still come back to haunt me as a natural reaction to my horrendous deed. Action and reaction, it's natural law, or *karma*, as they say in the East. This reaction I was fully prepared to take full responsibility for. (For all I knew, much of my sufferings in this life may have been some of this reaction playing itself out.) But the good news was that through forgiveness, no *new* negativity would be created. From this point forward, as far as this incident was concerned, I would be clean in thought, word, and deed.

A New Balance

After this session, I felt a profound sense of accomplishment. I had successfully completed the last step in these past-life regressions, "Bringing home the treasure." I felt raw and vulnerable, and much more in touch with my feelings. When I saw Lizanne, I could only look at her with a new level of gentleness and warmth. She must've picked up on it when she remarked, "Wow, what happened to you in there? You look... so much lighter."

With my daughters, too, I had no more inclination to defend myself if they came out with accusations, but just radiated unconditional love to them. At first, they seemed caught off guard, but gradually I noticed a return to the original purity and innocence of our times together as father and daughters. And with my mother, she still felt a bit impersonal, but she seemed to look at me with more loving eyes. After "rewriting the contract," I could more than ever observe things deeply, *just as they are,* with no judgment or desire.

During this period of digestion, I had a dream involving a tribe that settled by the St. Lawrence River known by the name Algonquin. I felt it referred to the tribe of my past life, especially when I found out that "Algonquin" means "to belong to" or "they are our relatives." How fitting, since one of my big issues of this lifetime has been the lonely feeling of "separation."

As I assimilated my "soul retrievals," the issue at the core seemed to be finding a balance of masculine and feminine qualities. My thoughts drifted over the women who were the strongest influences on me—my three beloved daughters, a most compassionate grandmother, a stern but loving mother who ran a lot of masculine energy, and a wife who gave a clear example of someone who seemed to have lost her precious feminine attributes. And, of course, Lizanne.

Likewise, to gain insight on a balanced masculine, I mused on the influential men in my life—a most compassionate priest from my life as a homeless woman, the elder from the life on that tropical island, my father in the Native American life, and in this life, my father.

Preferring to keep to himself, my father seldom acknowledged me, which made me feel a sense of rejection for the longest time. But, deep down, I knew he was there for me, and I've remained forever grateful. When we almost got into a head-on collision that shook me up terribly, he had stopped the car and just held me with the greatest tenderness, telling me over and over again that everything would be all right until, finally, I calmed down. Similarly, like the peace-loving father in my Native American incarnation (although I didn't heed his wisdom), he gave me a living example of equanimity and calm when under duress.

In the midst of walking the Blue Road, I had been led to my first experiences in the vast, ineffable spiritual realm through soul retrieval and past lives. Finally, as *A Course in Miracles* has urged, I was becoming a *co-creator with Spirit* by setting aside my ego to make room for Spirit to guide, heal, and inspire me on all my undertakings.

Following Spirit, I was led to soul retrieval so I could understand my past, which in turn allowed me to create a new blueprint for my life that included a harmonious balance between masculine and feminine qualities. With my new blueprint, I will harbor no separation ever again from family, earth, or Spirit.

10

PERU

Listening

On the path of the Blue Road, I had finally learned to *listen*. What does Spirit want from me? Or for me? Who am I to meet, where am I to go, what am I to do? The answers could come from anywhere—an accidental meeting, a tweet from a bird, an uprush of adversity. All could be signals from the Universe if I listened and remained available. This open-minded awareness had washed into my cell memory ever since the Vision Quest, and it had only continued to bury deeper ever since. All I needed to do was show up and listen.

During one of the sessions of soul retrieval with Jon, he had told me, "Do one of these trips. If you really want to expand, go to Peru. Between the mountains, jungle and *ayahuasca*"—a natural power plant brewed into a tea that is drunk for the purpose of self-transformation—"your perception of everything will forever be altered!"

I was intrigued. Listening to a tape by Jon's mentor, Alberto Villoldo—a shaman with a doctorate in psychology and a medical anthropologist who had been leading expeditions for years to Peru and the Amazon—I was struck by a statement he had made, "We can dwell on our healing picking at the sores one by one, or go on the hero's journey and shift our total consciousness." I knew I had to go. Onward to Peru with Alberto. I was on a roll, and *listening* to what was being offered to me, I saw a great opportunity to expand, to step into a greater truth of who I am and what the world is. My "seeking" was over. I had found what I wanted, Peru, and I most definitely intended to show up for it.

To help digest this decision, I worked on my Life Map, which had evolved into a Medicine Wheel. Taking a stone from the west sector of the Wheel, the direction of the setting sun, I blew my intent to release all beliefs, habits, and thoughts that no longer served me. Into a stone taken from the east, I blew my intent to expand my heart and mind. I was seizing the moment to rewrite the blueprint of my life. I was discovering how every point on this map was connected. Nothing was separate.

Talking it over with Lizanne, she was at first quite skeptical about Jon, his suggestion to go to Peru, and all he had to offer. We had just started dating that January, so things were moving fast personally and spiritually for her. Regarding psychics, she had run across too many "fakes," but after one session with Jon, who conducted an "illumination" that balanced her energy body, she was convinced of his authenticity. Only a day after I had brought up the idea of her going to Peru with me, she agreed. "If I'm to be with this man, I want to have this experience, too," she told me later. So, six months after returning from my Vision Quest, after starting our relationship, we were both in a plane on the way from L.A. to Miami, the first stop to Peru. Within a few days the summer solstice would arrive. We were going from the longest days and shortest nights in North America to the shortest days and longest nights in South America. *We were turning our world upside down.*

Taking Flight

In Miami, we spent a couple days sunbathing by the pool and dining on gourmet cuisine in fine restaurants. After my Vision Quest, I sensed what ordeals could lie ahead, so I chose to have a moment of hedonism, indulgence, and relaxation so Lizanne and I could relax in preparation for what might lay ahead.

Sufficiently pampered after a few days, we returned to the Miami airport, teeming with excitement to catch our flight to Peru. In the

American Airline Club, a private lounge for business class passengers, Lizanne pointed out a man with an "Indiana Jones" hat.

"That's our guide, Alberto, right over there?" She recognized him from his picture in his book, *Shaman, Healer, Sage.*

"Where?" I asked.

"He's got his back to us…he's walking up to the bar."

I quickly got up and headed up to the bar, "Hi, Alberto, I'm Adam." Pointing to Lizanne, I told him, "We're to join you in Peru."

"Great, let's have a glass of wine together," he replied.

We found a table, and immediately felt relaxed around him and sensed his integrity. Looking me in the eye in a light-hearted spirit, he took a sip of his wine and smiled in relief.

"So glad this is not like the cheap stuff I was recently served by this priest." He shook his head with the memory. "Me, I like good California wine." We chuckled as he relished another sip. "So, I hope you're ready to shed your skin. This trip could radically transform your lives."

"That's why we're here," I replied.

On the plane to Lima, the capitol of Peru, we ended up sitting across the aisle from each other. I saw this as a good omen of our connection together, which in time, proved to be true. We are now like brothers, friends, companions on the path.

On the plane, letting my mind roam free, I thought of how I now saw that everything of the visible world was an illusion, everything comes and goes, all temporary and ever-changing. And yet, here I was, excited about another adventure that will come and go. No choice but to enjoy the moment.

Peru

When we deplaned in Lima, we had to change planes to catch a short flight to the Incan capital, Cusco. Upon arrival Lizanne and I, along with about twenty others, climbed onto a local bus, freely painted in bright red and white colors with bold graphics everywhere. It looked wild and beat-up, and full of character. On the way, as the scenery bounced past our windows, we soaked in the mountains towering above the hills and valleys, the landscape unfurling before us like a vibrant, crumpled carpet.

In Cusco, in southeastern Peru near the Urubamba Valley of the Andes, we stepped out of the bus and immediately were hit with the timelessness of this ancient city. With worn stone pathways and the famous Incan walls that have been there since it was the capital of the Incan Empire centuries ago, it has survived earthquakes, the conquistadors, and the onslaught of contemporary tourists. The magic of the place was palpable.

Down a cobblestone roadway we went to enter the Novotel Hotel, a 4-Star hotel inside a 16th century building in the Spanish style. Located in the historic center of Cusco, it featured stonework, arched colonnades and a sumptuous courtyard under a giant skylight, and proved to be a perfect base for exploring the Incan civilization. We were served hot cocoa tea, which added to the sense of homey comfort after all the traveling we had done. After settling into our rooms, I began to notice how the 10,000-foot elevation affected me, and reminded Lizanne and myself to take it easy until we acclimatized. (As for me, it would take a few days before I could sleep soundly.)

That evening, about a hundred of us participants from all over the world gathered in the hotel conference room, along with various staff members, for an orientation meeting. Standing out in the throng were six local shamans, male and female, looking fabulous in their traditional clothing filled with exotic designs and rich colors of vermilion red, cobalt blue, and yellow.

Alberto outlined the itinerary and schedule for the next ten days and explained how we could choose various options to personalize our journey. He introduced each shaman, who spoke in *Quechuan*, one of the ancient languages of Peru. Through translators, we got a sense of their specialties for more individual needs—healing, energy balancing, entering the spirit world. We could choose one of four rituals conducted in each of the four directions—east, for what you intend to illuminate, for instance, or south for "serpent work to shed old skin."

Sacred Valley of the Incas

The first major phase of the trip took us to Urubamba Valley, the Sacred Valley of the Incas situated below Machu Picchu. Very dramatic, the flat, narrow valley is lined with high mountains on both sides, some of which were terraced, making the mountains look like man-made sculptures.

Here in the barren valley, we explored archeological remains located in the vicinity of villages. Over gentle green hills, there were what looked like outcroppings of rock, but they were the ruins of temples more ancient than the Incas. You could tell by contrasting the Incan stonework with the much more eroded remains of those ancient temples, some parts of which were cut into solid rock. *What possibly could be the look of these structures of so long ago?* I wondered.

In the midst of this area, one power spot was the *Amaru Machay*, the Serpent Cave, a place of death and rebirth. Three broad steps hewn out of solid rock brought us down into a narrow and dark cave where there were remnants of a much-eroded serpent carved into the stone that led into the interior. In the main chamber, perhaps ten feet by fifteen in size, was a smoothly finished block of stone that contrasted dramatically with the pockmarked texture of the natural cave. An opening in the roof of the cave gave enough illumination to move about. With that finished block of stone serving as an altar, it was obvious that this space had been used for sacred ceremonies for centuries. I sensed, filling the area, a powerful, but indefinable energy.

Instructions from the shaman were kept abstract, "As you go down the spine of the snake into the cave, what do you feel? If the snake is running through you, what does it mean?"

Such instructions forced us to rely on our own instincts rather than ruminating on an intellectual level. Seeing the snake as an animal that regularly shed its skin, I performed a silent ceremony to release habitual thoughts dominated by fears and ego. Over and over again, I chose to purify, surrender, and release all my old patterns. Then I declared my intent to further open and receive Spirit into my life.

Machu Picchu

A few days later, our group huddled in a train that took us up a steep climb out of Cusco, then descended into the Sacred Valley through lush fields to the town of Aguas Calientes, the town closest to Machu Picchu. About 8000 feet above sea level, this famous Incan site with its smooth stone walls was one of the highlights of the trip. My first sight of it seemed surreal. A sophisticated culture, prosperous, with masterful architecture, was once thriving here in the middle of what is now nothing but wild nature. Sitting in a saddle between two mountain ranges with a commanding view over two valleys and a nearly impassable mountain at its back, Machu Picchu still holds commanding authority over the whole region.

In the grounds of Machu Picchu, we were turned loose to explore the ruins on our own. Most of us in our group kept to ourselves, involved with our own processes. Having adjusted to the altitude with no more headaches and shortness of breath, I could tune in to the sacred geometry of the architecture, the aliveness of the stones, and the majesty all around.

I had seen pictures, of course, but to slap my palm against the huge smooth stones, each so exquisitely fitted to its neighbor that the walls have survived centuries of earthquakes with no mortar, made my perceptions shift. They'd been there for hundreds of years, but why? How? What can one say? *No point in getting into my head about such things.*

With such immense power intertwined with such beauty, the walls were beyond my scope of expression, except to caress them and gasp in awe and wonder. Who had placed their hands there before me? What were they thinking when they did? My mind kept wanting to bring the mystery of the place down to the level of human intellect, but I surrendered my need to know and focused on how it made me feel. Here, with a balance of masculine and feminine energy, I yearned to commune with the ancients who walked these grounds.

With such exquisite sights all around, all beyond understanding, I felt like I was in a dream as I floated around the Temple of the Sun, the Room of the Three Windows, and the Intihuatana Stone ("Hitching Post of the Sun"), a sculptured stone altar believed to be an astronomical clock by the Incans. Soaring over the ruins as if it were a great protector was the pillar of rock, Huayna Picchu, that towered a hundred feet above, which enhanced the beauty of the ruins huddled below. Seeing Lizanne wander close, we were both so speechless we could only hug each other.

Later, with my back against one of these magnificent stones over eight feet high, I imagined what life could have been like here centuries ago. Then I remembered Alberto's instructions before we went off on our own, "Stay attuned to your breath. Notice where you are hit by the sun, what you feel when you look at the ruins. If you can attune to the energy of the site, healing is possible." Taking note of all this, I closed my eyes, meditated to open myself to the invisible powers of the Incans.

When, finally, I opened my eyes, I looked up to the brilliant blue sky. As if on cue, a condor flew overhead. It triggered the thought of wanting to be like the bird, and fly between the worlds with a vantage point that would allow me to see an overview perspective of my life. If so, *what would I see?*

Later, as I continued my wandering through the grounds, I felt as if I could melt into the various temples, that I was in a waking dream that allowed me to, now and then, commune with the original builders. Over and over again, I would gain poignant experiences that defied reason, and that could barely be expressed through words. As the power of the place permeated into my psyche, I felt I *was* in communion with those ancients. *Is this true? Can I prove it? Do I care?* I was way past having to justify, defend, or verify anything with my reason.

After Machu Picchu, we hiked up into the mountains and were joined by local shamans, the Q'ero, who lived in the area up to 14,000 feet above sea level. How commanding they looked in their indigenous clothing filled with bright embroidery in reds, blues, and yellow set against the subdued hues of the mountains. One of the shamans, Don Francisco, walked with us playing a reed flute. With sparkly eyes, he was our pied piper leading us ever onward up the mountain.

Once, one of the shamans in his colorful raiment walked right behind me, step by step, as we made our way up the mountain. Not three minutes later, I noticed his bright outfit a hundred feet above me. It was him! What happened? How did he do that? But, again, with no need to appease my reason or justify my experiences, I simply accepted it as part of the usual magic of these Incans. These "high mountain" shamans were considered "altomayseoks," or EarthKeepers, and known for their "gift of sight" and other powers.

A Ritual with "Prayer Bundles"

"Think about your personal myth. How has this changed?" said Alberto to all of us as he set us up for a *Despacio Ritual*. This was a ceremony that we would perform every day, usually at a power spot. Following Incan tradition, we gathered around a Medicine Woman, and all together, we made a "prayer bundle." On a piece of paper maybe 24 by 36 inches, we placed fresh flowers, candy, sprinkled wine, llama fat, and other offerings while the shaman called upon the forces of the universe. Among other things, I added a message to my children and placed it on the paper. Then it was folded up to form the prayer bundle.

That evening, in sacred space, it was placed into a bonfire. All twenty or thirty of us were instructed to turn away from the fire as it burned, to effect a better release to Spirit. For me, the act of offering prayers with so many others gave our intent a special force. It was the last thing we would do before going to sleep.

Prompted by Alberto as I went to bed, I *did* think about my personal myth, and how it had been changing. With such simple but profound questions, we were constantly guided to look within and rely on our powers of intuition to effect our own healing. Once again, I reminded myself that, "No more do I have to seek; I need only show up to receive what was offered."

As usual at the end of the day, I was physically exhausted, but inside, I was churning with so much released power that my "energy body" felt much larger than my physical one. Lizanne couldn't help but notice.

"What's going on? What're you feeling?" she asked.

"Hard to explain, all this energy. Been building since we got here."

"I kind of know what you mean," she replied. "I'm still trying to get used to all of this. I feel like a fish out of water."

"You'll get used to it," I reassured her. "Just stay with it. Experiences you seek often come in waves. Get ready to ride a few big ones."

That night, I had a dream:

I am flying directly over the mountains, over the wide expanse of the valley containing Machu Picchu as it was in the distant past. I see workers bowing down to pray before one of the temples being constructed with its sturdy foundation of stone.

When I woke, I had the thought that *I* was that temple, that I was seeing the construction of a new me. The temple was built with a solid foundation that grounded me for the purpose of a balanced communion with Spirit.

Here and there, Lizanne and I had precious moments with our chief guide, Alberto, a reflective, thoughtful soul who offered up a mix of inspiration, wisdom, and dry humor. His exotic and beautiful girlfriend, Marcela, also accompanied us.

"Why, finally after I got divorced," he once told us, "I turned right around, fell in love, and got married to another woman just like the first." He shook his head, amused at his own folly. "Makes you wonder, how do you see your own repeating patterns?"

Other times, he would offer cryptic instructions, "Sit by the river, or by a rock. Be that river. Be that rock." A strong proponent of flowing along with life, he allowed participants to experience the moment with minimal intellectual discourse, repeatedly encouraging them to trust their own intuitive knowing. One must dig deeply into one's personal mythology. "To bury the hatchet one must first dig it up." *It was a deep hole that I had been digging. When will the hatchet appear?*

Heart Lake

One of the extra options on the trip was to take an all-day hike up the Pachatusan Mountain outside Cusco. If Machu Picchu was down valley, then this mountain was considered "up valley." When one reached the pinnacle at 16,000 feet, it was said that one could truly experience being on top of the world.

Not knowing what to expect, Lizanne and I decided to go for it. The meaning of its name sounded cool, "One that Sustains the Earth." So, at the crack of dawn along with about fifteen others, we were ripe and ready to go. It was sunny and cool, perfect for such a climb. Marcela, a powerful shaman (and Alberto's partner) was going to be one of the guides. All together, we walked through fields and a village to the base point where the ascent was to begin. Just then, the rising sun threw light that hit the mountains, turning them aglow.

Following a circuitous route, we began full of energy and enthusiasm, but soon, the heat began to have its effect. After a half-hour or so when we paused for a short visit into a local landmark, I was relieved to have a chance to catch my breath. A little house known as the "Shaman's Lair" was the landmark, which had a great site that overlooked the valley. The owner was the well-known and powerful shaman, Don Martin. Supposedly he had dealt with black magic, but now had turned to the light. Marcela commented that the line between positive and negative magic, between power for the general good and for self-aggrandizement, was tenuous and thin. Be careful.

I made my way to the basement where he had set up an altar for his sorcery. The darkness was illuminated by a few candles. I was immediately struck by a very heavy and unpleasant vibe. It had a dirt floor and a full condor mask complete with two full wings that had a span of ten feet. One of the other shaman guides, Pasquito, a seer, came in, looked around everywhere with a scowl, and left. I stayed only five minutes before I had had enough.

As we continued, the hike for me began to be unusually grueling as we climbed another five miles of a steep ascent. About a quarter of the way up, there was a donkey corral, and everyone could choose to take donkeys. Lizanne and I decided not to, turning out to be the only ones who chose to go up all the way by foot. Speaking for myself, I didn't feel I needed help, and my decision felt heroic and liberating—*I don't have to rely on anything outside of myself.* Soon, I would see it as arrogance and false pride, but that would come later. Unbeknownst to me, another initiation was about to unfold.

As we ascended higher, the views became more spectacular with each step until everything seemed surreally perfect. A picture postcard. A fantasy movie set. Abstract stone outcroppings were set against rich earth tones. In my increasing altered state, I had new eyes that could see the raw vitality of every living thing. The play of shadows shifted as the sun slowly climbed higher into the sky, and all colors looked unusually vibrant.

After another couple of hours, I felt totally beaten down. Weak, with no strength, no energy. I was fast going through my gallon of water, but still, with all the water I had taken in, I felt increasingly dehydrated. *What's going on?* It wasn't like me, who usually could power through any physical challenge. Luckily, Lizanne felt strong as ever and seemed to be smoothly gliding up the mountain.

Though feeling compromised physically, I was totally committed mentally. Utterly determined that I was going to prevail, I silently called upon Spirit for help, surrendered to what is, and fed off...the love of Lizanne. Her encouragement and support was becoming crucial. Lizanne later joked that it was during this time of my ordeal that we really fell in love, and I agreed. Her presence propelled me to soldier on. I was in for a marathon, and no way was I going to quit, so step by step, in spite of feeling wobbly, weak, and fuzzy in the head, I made my way upwards.

Philosopher's Stone

After two grueling hours or so into the journey, we reached a stone mono-lith called the Philosopher's Stone. This was a common stopping point for a lunch break. Thank God, I could rest my weary bones. Between the natural beauty of the surroundings and the utter fatigue inside, I was beside myself. I felt mesmerized and "heard" the stone call out to me to come closer. With no strength for resistance, I ambled over to the massive rock and embraced one of its protrusions so I could place my ear right against the smooth, cold slab and listen.

"What do you hear?" I heard Marcela ask.

"Listen to the voice within," I heard the stone tell me, "and you will hear of hidden treasures." Immediately, I thought of the "Philosopher's Stone" of divine alchemy, of changing base metal into gold. In the manner of free-association, I thought of my father's eighty-eighth birthday party that we had recently celebrated, and how he had toasted us with a statement that was out of character. It seemed that a spiritual wisdom from deep within his psyche could no longer be hidden.

"You are all so golden," he told us all with eyes shining. "Find that within yourself. Know that you are golden."

After lunch, our long climb continued, now ascending to 13,000 feet. At one point, we peered down into a valley below and saw a lake in the midst of a flat terrace of natural rock that was shaped like a perfect heart. Was I hallucinating? It was a perfect valentine in symmetry and proportion in an enchanted landscape. I had to take a picture just to prove to friends that I wasn't imagining things. In my "listening" mode, I took it as a sign for Lizanne and me, a reflection of our blossoming love for one another. Our eyes swept from the heart below to each other.

"I feel so blessed to be in your presence, and to be taking this journey together."

Caught off guard from this unabashed statement of love, she replied, "I'm right with you."

After another three hours of, for me, a laborious, punishing climb, I finally reached the top, the last one to do so. Pushing my body beyond its limits, it had taken me all day for this momentous achievement. Now, perched on top of the mountain, I half expected that some hidden portal to another dimension would suddenly open up. My eyes met Lizanne's. Silently, we embraced, and let our bodies, exhausted as they were, express this exhilarating moment that was beyond the power of words.

After only five minutes with such lofty musings, perched as we were on the pinnacle, I knew it was time to catch up with the others, who had already begun their descent. By this time, 4:30 p.m., the sun was starting to retire for the night, being winter south of the equator. I didn't want to be forced to hike down in the dark, especially arduous with my body so weakened. I noticed that the temperature had dropped ten degrees within half an hour. We had better get going.

But then, a flash of hope: I will take a donkey down! I had been secretly beating myself up for not riding up like all the others had—oh, my foolish pride!—but now I'll gladly ride back home. However, I found out that nobody rides down. The path to descend is so steep that no donkey can carry anyone on their back. I had to go it by myself.

Dusk set in soon after we began our descent. Before long, my legs were not working, and my eyesight became a bit fuzzy. Finished with my gallon of water, dehydration had started to have its effect. Lizanne kept offering me hers, but after a while, I insisted that she keep it for herself.

For another hour, I toiled on. By then, it was difficult to see. Luckily, one of the shamans, Chino, had a flashlight, and along with Lizanne, helped me down, step by step, foot by foot. Having to show my weakness, ask for help, and become totally vulnerable, I got cranky, testy. With a few miles yet to go, I was in a surly mood. And yet, another part of me was seeing my ordeal from the viewpoint of a witness—another rite of passage to push me beyond my limits not only physically, but also psychologically—I'm not Superman; I have limitations, and sometimes I need help.

Later, I would find out how Lizanne relished this incident. I was supposed to be the experienced one with my Vision Quest and all, and now her ascent was effortless, and mine, a grueling ordeal. So touching it was for her to see me so vulnerable and in need of help. I laughed along with her. She was right. I needed help, and she was a life-saver. Apparently, she had night vision!

In the dark, perhaps nine in the evening, I finally caught sight of my salvation, the bus. I was almost at the bottom, the last one in. Everyone was patiently waiting for me. At the base, there was a simple, unmemorable church where I wanted to go in to thank Spirit for allowing me to make it down alive, but it was out of the question with everyone ready to go home.

That night, I fell fast asleep and almost immediately dropped into a powerful dream that proved to be more vivid than usual, with me especially aware and purposeful.

Dream of the Wailing Wall

I am in Jerusalem. Careful and deliberate, I am walking softly towards the Wailing Wall, passing several podiums and stands, some with sacred texts. A sprinkling of people, some rabbis, some laymen, are also present, conducting prayers with great reverence.

As I kneel at the foot of the wall, I hear the beating of my own heart, and then a voice strong and clear, "Come closer." I look around thinking it is one of the others, but no one is around me. I know it is the wall speaking to me.

I inch forward until my nose nearly touches the limestone. Myriad questions dance inside my head, but one comes to the fore.

"How do I get through to the other side?"

"You must be in a relationship."

"Relationship?"

"What do you see?" the wall responds.

"Stone, the color of pale cream, beige, the color of sand," I answer, though these colors are more felt than seen.

"What else?" the voice asks.

I run my fingers over the stone and notice gradations of colors, textures from smooth to rough, and streaks running randomly through the wall in every direction. "I see veins," I finally answer.

"Follow one of the veins. Circle back."

Circle back? I wonder. I see how the veins meander, how beautiful they are, and how strong the stone is, porous in places, and…regal in its purpose. My thoughts quiet as perceptions change from visual and sensory to those of feeling. I feel as if I am the stone, a tangible energy force, powerful and consistent. I love this wall, I think to myself. I am the wall.

Without warning, I am no longer standing where I was. No others are around me any longer. I am alone on the other side of the wall. I had moved through the seemingly impenetrable wall. I am momentarily stunned. All rules of matter as I understand it no longer apply. Strangely, I take it all in stride.

When I woke to bright morning light, the first thought I had about this dream was that in stepping through the wall, I could break through all barriers, both seen and unseen, by embracing them.

The Eagle Has Landed

After the previous day of such an arduous hike, Lizanne and I decided to take a day off, hang out by the pool, get a massage, and enjoy the rustic charm of our hotel. All day, we took it easy, and at dinner, we did have a few light conversations with others, but mostly, like the others, we were deep in our own processes.

Over a bottle of wine, Lizanne and I both realized how incredible it was to be spending our first adventure/vacation together in such a mystical place with such transformational purposes. I thought about how this trip was forcing me to experience a breakthrough physically, emotionally, and mentally, and that it was "grounding" my knowledge with the Blue Road of the spiritual realm.

"The eagle has landed," I told Lizanne, to summarize my observations.

"It sure has for me, too," she replied, knowing exactly what I meant.

What a blessing to have found the perfect person to share not only my spiritual journey, but also my life. She inspired me, cared about me, and loved me as I loved her. Through her, I was rediscovering myself. Emotionally available, I could now give and receive love, beginning with the ability to embrace myself, and, thus, break through my longtime sense of separation and loneliness. Lizanne was a reflection of my own inner transformation, and a sign that I was in a whole new ballgame. I felt, for example, my love and connectedness now extended to trees, mountains, and walls!

The next leg of our Peru excursion entailed a trip down a river, heading deeper into the Amazon jungle. *Wow, I'm getting into the Heart of Darkness or Appocalypse Now territory,* I said to myself. Alberto had deliberately scheduled this portion last, knowing that many might not be able to handle what was the most powerful phase of the journey. Having gathered us all together to set us up for this phase, he stressed how important it was for all of us to keep balanced, that we're here to keep grounded no matter how high our transcendent experiences have been. In this way, "we can learn from the eagle that flies high, but still knows to come back to earth. For us, then, the eagle has landed."

My jaw dropped, and I looked at Lizanne and laughed. It was the exact same phrase that she and I had used. With my increasing awareness that everything is a sign, it made me feel once again that we were especially attuned to Alberto and his teachings.

That night, right before we were scheduled to go on to the plane, I became violently ill. From 3:00 to 8:00 a.m., I was painfully sick. Food poisoning? Yet Lizanne ate everything I ate, and she wasn't sick. Another omen? But of what? Between the vomiting and diarrhea, I chose to see it as a form of purging, of purification.

While throwing up repeatedly, I spotted a spider as big as my hand crawling inside the bathtub. I was blown away by the size of the critter, black against stark white, which helped distract me from my agony. Partially hidden behind the sink basin, I noticed silken threads of her web. Another sign: I, too, for most of my life was caught up in an intricate web of illusions, often stunningly beautiful, but still illusion. Seeing it as a portent that I am breaking through the web of my own illusions, I let the spider be, and chose to experience my sickness with no self-pity, but as a wave of energy that I had to ride for my own purification.

Exhausted from a sleepless night of vomiting, I had second thoughts about going on the jungle excursion, but with Lizanne's encouragement, I decided to forge ahead.

"Mother of God" River

The next day was a travel day, beginning with a bus ride, although I hired a separate taxi for Lizanne and me so that others on the bus wouldn't be disturbed should I have to throw up. Then we flew south an hour from Cusco to Puerto Maldonado, a jungle town on the "Mother of God River" (how I love the name!).

From the airport, we headed south straight to the jungle near the Bolivian border. Both of us were so struck by the intensity of the stunning landscape, we didn't know where to set our gaze first. The colors, the air, the sounds. The weather was comfortably warm. Being south of the equator, we were in "winter," the best time to travel because it had the least bugs and rain. Still, we came prepared, and took vitamin B, slathered insect repellent on our skin, and wore "Bug-Off" shirts, specially designed to ward off insects and still be breathable.

At the edge of the jungle, we boarded wooden motor boats with two long benches along the sides that together seated twenty of us. Another boat carried ten more participants, plus all the luggage. Everyone chatted away in high spirits as we pushed off and headed downriver to what would be a two-hour ride. Though I still felt a touch queasy and a little dizzy, I could appreciate the exotic sights and sounds as we made our way deeper and deeper into the jungle—a tree limb bounced up and down from the weight of a falcon that had just landed, a squadron of red and blue parrots chatted away as we passed by, a troop of wild monkeys scampered around in glee and mischief...

We were headed to an area that remained in a pristine state, a place where all of nature worked harmoniously and in balance, Mother Nature at her most fertile. Abundant trees brimming with clumps of jade growth supported dense leaves way above to create an overhead canopy of dappled green. I felt we were in a womb of vegetation. Though I felt no danger, I did feel vulnerable and got ready to be vigilant against the raw elements of nature, whether they were poisonous snakes, jaguars, piranhas, alligators, falcons, or giant spiders. The cycle of death and rebirth surrounding us was palpable. It brought to mind my Night Stalking in Zion, which taught me a deep respect for the unseen powers of nature.

As we motored on down the river, Alberto began preparing us for our upcoming work with *ayahuasca*, a tea brewed from two different natural power plants that, when combined, possesses psychoactive properties for visions and healing (*aya* means healing; *huasca* means vine).

"All initiations involve a death of sorts," he told us on the boat. "Intention is most important. You will be working with a power plant we call the Doctor of Death—death of the old order—so embrace it with love and forgiveness to move beyond into the new order."

His statement was a bit cryptic, but it didn't matter. I trusted my intuition to do the right thing when the time came. In any case, I felt so ready for this adventure, whatever it was exactly. *The jungle is a great place to let the old me "die," and to transform into a new version of myself,* I thought. The idea of death brought no apprehension; I've had enough recent experiences, beginning with my Vision Quest and Night Stalking, to know that the greatest opportunity often comes under the guise of the greatest danger.

The Blue Road Initiation

As we continued to move downriver, I soaked in the sights of the trees and an occasional turtle, alligator, or gang of monkeys scampering along the riverbank, and felt blessed to be entering such a sacred world. Spread out before me was the rainforest, so rich, interconnected, and true.

Finally, our boat landed in the middle of the afternoon. By then, the nausea from my "food poisoning" had subsided, and a feeling of serenity washed over me; I was totally at peace in the moment. A short walk from the riverbank brought us up to our jungle lodge, the Eco Amazonia. With thatched roofs, wood construction, and a pool, the lodge had a series of separate bungalows that were simple, organic to their surroundings, and full of character. Our hut was called The Falcon, and proved to be perfectly comfortable.

Butterflies fluttered about with wingspans of a foot wide, their needle-like tongues sipping nectar from huge blossoms. To be part of this rich fabric of life made me feel "high," while, with no contradiction, I never felt so grounded and connected to the earth.

Lizanne and I joined everyone for a very light meal of salad, rice, and tea. We were instructed to eat little to prepare for our ayahuasca session that evening. While we ate, Alberto gave a short, fifteen-minute talk to prep us for what was coming.

"A rare opportunity to connect with Mother Earth. Tap into the energy of the jungle, tap into how it makes you feel. You may be like a serpent, belly to the ground, that inspires you with feelings about the physical. Or maybe you're like a jaguar, and resonate with the world of the emotions that are stalking the true you. Then again, you may relate to the hummingbird for the joyous sweetness of life, or perhaps the eagle for the overview and spiritual perspective. Work with these archetypes. The spirit of the jungle is as powerful and intense as its overlapping mass of vegetation, so you definitely want to work with it, not against it."

After the talk, Lizanne and I strolled the lush grounds of the lodge. I thought about simply letting the creative powers of Mother Nature come through me. In the midst of this overwhelming bounty of life in its myriad forms, I could only conclude that real power had nothing to do with me, that it was not my will, but the will of the universe that was in charge—let Thy will be done.

Wandering through the brush, I experienced every boy's dream with monkeys frolicking in the trees, a huge jaguar footprint in the mud, and the most majestic of butterflies with cerulean blue wings flirting with blossoms of every color from sunshine yellow to scarlet red.

Each creature from the tiniest of ants to the largest of cats had a position in the complex interweave of the jungle, with nothing more important than anything else. Watching some insects working on a dead rodent, I could see how nothing "dies," nothing is wasted, that nature recycles everything in a cosmic harmony. Even the dead tree gave life to the termites that were devouring it, one mini-bite at a time. As I strolled along with my thoughts, a blue streak slithered to the side, maybe four feet away. Later I would find out that it was one of the most poisonous of snakes. Another omen? I was in a world where one unlucky step could turn you into someone's meal.

Right then and there, I was determined to change my basic interpretation of the jungle.

Dominating much of my professional life back in the cement jungle of Los Angeles, the so-called "law of the jungle" meant a world that was threatening, wild, and predatory. Eat or be eaten. It had made me wake at the crack of dawn braced for a vicious fight because everyone and everything was threatening. This was the "survival of the fittest" at its worst.

How I had maligned the precious jungle. Now I saw it as a place of profound harmonious interaction where plants, animals, and insects all worked together to create a place of fertility, beauty, and inspiration. From now on, *this* would be my basic understanding of the jungle, and all of nature for that matter. *I began to feel that living in harmony was innate in every man, woman, and child walking this planet.*

We were warned not to walk in the jungle at night. Understandably, they were concerned about liability. But "boys will be boys," so my shaman friend Jon and I decided to do just that. Around 9:30 in the evening, we headed into the jungle. After just a few minutes, it got drastically darker because of the density of the foliage, and as we looked around, we saw that the trail had virtually disappeared into the thicket of plants. We decided to leave sign posts for our return, and hung a piece of napkin on a branch here, and broke a limb at a strategic spot there. Pretty meager, considering the darkness, but we did what we could.

My heart was beating faster than normal. Why? Excitement? Fear? I figured both, which put all of my senses into high gear. How I could smell the soil. We decided to find a place to sit still and listen to the pulse of the earth. We turned off the flashlight, which plunged us into utter blackness. *Perhaps the predator of old needed to know how it felt to be prey?*

With no moonlight, the darkness brought out an acute sense of hearing—drops of moisture falling onto broad leaves, exotic whistling, whirring of wings that flashed by, and scampering of little feet. I sensed the earth moving around my feet. *Am I hallucinating?* I had to turn on the flashlight for just a brief moment to alleviate my fears, and saw insects and spiders everywhere doing their business. Turning off the flashlight, we were once again immersed in a blackness that opened my senses to the rich orchestra of jungle sounds. Everything was teeming with life! Everything played its role in the complex ecosystem.

Including me. I was part of this mysterious fabric of life, but it depended on me utilizing my perceptions beyond the five senses, otherwise the jungle could be a fearful place indeed. Perhaps my night walk in Zion a few months back was a training ground so that I could learn to trust my sixth sense and really embrace the womb of this jungle. I was beginning to see that beyond the cycle of life and death—does death even really exist?—there lies the all-pervading reality of Spirit.

Jon and I were only a foot apart, but as we sat in complete darkness, it was as if we had melted into the jungle itself. And then gently, it happened again with me and with Jon! We both saw a soft glow of light that permeated ourselves and every living thing that surrounded us. With our sixth sense, we were "seeing" the life-force energy that emits from every living thing. The soft radiance of light overlapped and mixed, giving visual testimony that yes, we, too, are of the jungle and interconnected.

OOOOoooo! OOoooo! A chill went up my spine. *What was that? Something out of a horror movie?* It was so perfectly scary, we laughed nervously as if somebody were trying to give us a fright. They were howler monkeys. We both took it as a signal to get out of there, and immediately started to retrace our steps. After about twenty minutes, we found our way back to our huts and tucked in for the night.

The next morning in the meeting room of the Lodge, we all gathered to be introduced to the three *ayahuasceros* (the shamans that would be administering the ayahuasca) and told what their specialties were. They were a blaze of color that illuminated the whole meeting room with their colorful garments hand-woven with bold patterns in red, yellow, and greens and blues. We could choose between Ignacio, in his late seventies, who, through translators, stressed with a laugh how, "Everybody thinks that I know more because I'm older, but the more I know, the less I know." That was disarming. Though I've heard such pronouncements before, his statement at that time resonated with me because as I have been expanding and learning, I felt my growing portion of knowledge only enlarged the size of the Mystery.

Then there was Pundero, in his fifties, stocky, about 5'7", who looked strong and immovable, and whose specialty was traditional, indigenous healing. And finally, there was Javier, also in his fifties, who spoke about "the oneness of everything." They all talked about the balance and flow of life, how all healing could be achieved not just by the physical herbs, but by utilizing the "medicine of the jungle," energy patterns of the jungle itself. We just had to know how to access them. All of the *ayahuasceros* had such a lightness of being that it was hard to choose between them. Each of them was dedicated to the well-being of humanity.

The shamans taught from an oral tradition that had been passed down for generations. Assessing one's energy, they could see energetic imbalances and perform healing acts accordingly. It was easy to feel self-conscious around them because they had such pure hearts and saw things with such keen, unfettered clarity, I felt as if I were standing naked before strangers.

After some deliberation, Lizanne and I chose to work with Pundero because I wanted to be outside with the ceremonies, and his station was to be on an island in the middle of the river. Their gentleness belied their power. At one point later during the ceremony, for instance, a Swedish girl had gotten "possessed," her voice transformed into something masculine as she began blabbering loudly in Swedish in an ominous tone. We all found it extremely disconcerting, until Pundero, who had had enough, made a decisive move as if he were lassoing her. Suddenly, she clutched her throat, became still, and, accompanied by the screeching of howler monkeys, quickly left for more purging through vomiting.

Alberto gave a few more pointers for those of us who chose to use ayahuasca, and told us how important it is to know where the plant comes from and how it is made. He explained that in the mix of the two plants, the element that causes hallucinations was kept to a minimum—"We don't want you to be distracted by a Disneyland experience"—and stressed clarity of intent on "why you are here." The shamans would hold the space to allow the magic of this mystical plant to work, but all participants had been instructed to not eat for eight hours prior to the ceremony and to come with a "clear intention" beforehand.

For those who did not choose ayahuasca, Alberto offered homeopathic rituals. By offering us a choice, he helped each of us find the inner angels that would guide us into the spirit realm.

My intention was to have the "powers that be" show me anything that blocked my connection with Spirit. While many of my fellow travelers seemed apprehensive, I was excited. I knew that all that I had experienced before was a preparation for this moment.

The Ceremony

Beneath the nighttime sky filled with glittery stars, on the island at the river's edge, twenty of us—men and women, young and old, from Europe and America—sat on a sand bar in a big circle, excited and apprehensive as the ceremony began.

Counter clockwise, Pundero worked his way around the circle. When he came up to me, he did for me as he did for the others, and muttered in some Incan dialect a soft prayer. Then he handed me a small metal cup about the size of an espresso demitasse and filled it up with a dark brew from a plastic half-gallon bottle. Gingerly, I tested the syrupy brew; it was room temperature and intense, as could be expected from something that had been brewed for hours. In two gulps, I drank it down. It tasted somewhat like a cross between raw roots and medicinal syrup, and it had a force to it. It did not go down easy, and my body involuntarily recoiled and shivered. I sat there, observing my body's reaction. And waited...and waited.

After another ten minutes, Panduro, having made his way around the circle, came to perhaps a third of us and offered a large pipe. Fiercely, he blew on it a few times, and then handed it to me. The "jungle tobacco" as well as the pipe itself had been soaked and cured in the ayahuasca brew. I took in one puff, gagged, and repeatedly tried to clear my throat. Heat and energy moved down my gullet, and I began feeling a little dizzy. After another few minutes, my stomach began gurgling, my whole body tingled, and my heart began beating noticeably faster.

After a while, I noticed that Pundero had been singing, "Ayahuasco, ayahuasco, medico..."

This would go on for hours. Now and then, he'd vary the singing by whistling the same tune while shaking a rattle. His voice was magnificent. He sang to my soul. *I love this man!*

After about forty-five minutes I began to feel nauseated and uncomfortable. Small beads of sweat dotted my forehead, and then with no warning, I lost control of my stomach, spun around, and threw up with no restraint onto the sand behind me. Wild-eyed, I vomited a few more times, with the retching wracking my entire body. Weakened, I got down on my hands and knees, stooping close to the ground. Others were beginning to throw up as well, some into plastic bags, but I barely noticed.

This vomiting was of another order, and made my throwing up from "food poisoning" seem light. It was violent and seemed to pull from below my stomach down to my guts. Soon, my stomach felt on fire, I sweated profusely and could barely breathe. Exhausted from the expulsion, both physical and emotional, I attempted to relax and regain my bearings. I saw this ordeal as a release of age-old angers and resentments. It left my mind with tremendous clarity.

As if to punctuate the drama of that moment, Mother Nature took part with a special contribution: in the only spot free of the jungle foliage all around us, I thought I saw downriver a flash of light. Did I see what I saw? Then a tremendous boom! An electrical storm was working its way towards us. Another flash! I could see the energy go up the river, and then, within a few seconds, WHAM, it hit us! The thunder was deafening! A sheer force of wind howled all around as a deluge of rain poured down, drenching all of us. More blinding lightning, followed by rumbling right over our heads. Bolts of lightning turned black night into azure blue, shapes of trees appeared and disappeared like a wild, haphazard cosmic shadow play. Oh, the chaotic dance of life all around us, whirling around in such magnificence with no rhyme or reason but for the Creator's amusement.

After an intense twenty minutes, the storm blew over, leaving us all soaked and cold. Everyone seemed to have different reactions to this storm, from deep sadness, to irritation, to euphoric bursts of joy. Me, I thought of it as more of the untamed play of the Great Mother. All through this, Pundero whistled or sang his hypnotic tune that helped everyone refocus on their ayahuasca process.

By this time, after the purging, a new phase began for me. For the next hour, my own senses were of no use, upstaged by "the doctor" (the medicine) to whom I surrendered. Squares, diamonds, pyramids, and hexagrams morphed into one another, forming "sacred geometry" of all kinds and all colors. The hues were so intense, they came alive and emblazoned their existence onto my perception in an overwhelming montage that was beyond comprehension. Streams of ether—carmine red, black, viridian green, bright yellow—pulsed on and off like strobes and acted like living beings with their own will and metabolism. The never-ending dance of atoms and molecules mingled and merged in ever-changing combinations. A Technicolor light show! I was seeing through God's eyes. Time slowed, time quickened…time revealed itself to be an illusion.

My closely held thoughts about the physical world got blown out of the water—it's but one of many realities. My reason balked, but I didn't care. Not when I was so honored and privileged to see the secret existence of alternative realities. It was all I could do to drink in the phantasmagoria of color and shapes that flooded my perceptions.

After a while, the experience shifted from what Alberto had called the "Disneyland" phase to clarity of perception for self-transformation. My intent had been to remove all obstacles from my connection to Spirit, and I began reviewing my relationships.

Very lovingly, I saw my parents and my own family, seeing and feeling their essence, their Godhood, and what they were looking to do for their own evolution. Sadness surrounded my observations, and I wept for the loss of my children, and for my own childhood filled with conflicts and disappointments that took me away from my own essence. Still, I could perceive how each of my kids had her own destiny, her own karmic path that I could best help by *not* playing the role of father, but rather by being a loving help mate for her own transformation to fulfill her destiny. I saw how their sense of loss and separation with their father had begun well before me, that it was a loss carried over from past lives.

With Gigi, I wondered, *Why was Gigi in my life?* Then I saw a clear image of myself as a vibrant young man and knew that I had gotten my answer: to become a fully realized man, filled with vitality and free of age. From my thinking mind, my perceptions had drifted into seeing with my heart, and, applied to Gigi, the best I could do was to honor all her attempts to move forward, to have compassion for her trials, but to not take on her *karma*. I needed to cut loose from her, release myself from our entanglement, for I had outgrown our time together. Perhaps without her I would have drifted into the abyss.

Blue Hole

Visions of Gigi coursed through my mind as I recalled a day early on in our marriage.

"It's so great to be here with you," I shared, looking into Gigi's eyes.

"Good to hang with you," she shared with a touch of emotion.

A perfect day to go for a dive in the famous "Blue Hole" of Belize.

The Hole, as it was known, got its name because it is a sinkhole, 1,000 feet across, in the Lighthouse Reef. They say the bottom can be found about 400 feet from the surface. A virtual abyss!

We gathered our gear and headed out to the pier to meet the dive boat. The hotel was just a few steps from the light green and blue Caribbean water. It was a playground for all, especially scuba divers.

It did take long to launch the boat. The ride to Blue Hole was a short twenty minutes.

"Let me check your gear, honey," I said in a matter-of-fact tone.

"Sure, is my weight belt on tight enough?" she asked.

"All good," I said.

"Let me check your equipment," she said.

"Ok, Capitan," I said in jest.

"Is your air on?" she asked.

As I checked the BC, no air came out!

Embarrassed and feeling foolish, I turned the air on.

She smiled, giggled in her charming way.

Soon we were in the water, descending to a maximum depth for the dive, 70 feet.

Schools of colorful fish roamed these 90-degree waters. I had enjoyed diving for many years. After each dive I felt a sense that I had just adventured to another world. Diving was another world…an underworld that required my utmost respect and admiration.

As we dropped below 40 feet on our way down, suddenly my mouth piece broke off from the hose to the air tanks. I was breathing water in an instant. Gigi was 20 feet away. I had no extra line to grab on my tank, the so-called third stage. I quickly darted toward her. She begin to swim to a deep depth. I found her leg and pulled on it. She was startled. Instantly she knew that I needed air and began to share her respirator. The buddy breathing skills we learned in dive school were now being put to great use. We gained our composure and slowly began to surface.

Now on top of the ocean, I breathed a sigh of relief.

"You saved my life," I shouted, trying to catch my breath.

"I told you not to swim so far away from me," she said sternly.

As we got back on the boat I realized that it could have gone either way. Was I to sink or was I to be saved? God and Gigi had the answer.

The ayahuasca was taking me on a ride of gratitude, and I was apparently front and center. The journey continued.

I saw my violent life as the Native-American son of the chief and had great compassion for the ordeals of that misguided man. I could truly forgive him. Though I might still suffer consequences from that life, I knew that I could finally let go of that trauma, and with that, I perceived light surrounding everything. I was a witness seeing everything with innocence and love.

With my heart open, I became overwhelmed with euphoria and love, and felt the desire to hug myself. I did, and wept tears of joy knowing that I was a part of everything, that I could never be separated from the universe because all the threads of the universe and those of my body and soul were so intertwined.

My heart was the true source of vision, not my eyes. Fortunately, ayahuasca seemed to allow me to slowly absorb the changes in perception to match what I was seeing. I connected with reality at deeper and deeper levels. As the shaman sang in the background, I morphed into the rhythm of the chant itself. My beating heart became the center of the universe. I lost my sense of time and relinquished all fear. I knew that there was no death because I was pure consciousness swimming in the power and the glory of my true nature...

"Finished... Time to go... Finished..." My reverie stopped abruptly. It was about 1 a.m., and Pundero had stopped the music and was walking around repeating to everyone, "Over... Finished... Time to go home... Finished..."

With the end of the ceremony, many seemed spacey, others delirious. Me, I felt light and airy, and took a few minutes before I could gain full coordination of my body to even walk. A few needed help to make their way to the boat, and eventually, we were taken across the river back to our Lodge.

After showering, Lizanne and I went straight to bed. We could barely speak. She felt totally spent and fell right to sleep, but I was buzzing all night. How wonderful to have a body and warm blankets. The pleasures of physical comfort! All night in a hypnogogic state between dreaming and waking, I felt in awe to have experienced all that happened, an expansion into the essence of my being.

The Download

Around 9 or 10 in the morning, we woke to the sound of jungle birds and a whole new world.

"You are God," I said to Lizanne, spontaneously.

"And you are as well," she replied.

"What imposters we are," I told her, shaking my head. "We are all Gods, but we insist on masquerading as mere mortals!" We laughed, ate a light breakfast, and took a stroll through the morning jungle. Sharing our adventures, she, too, had powerful experiences involving, among other things, meeting her "celestial mother and father." I so admired her courage in taking this trip, and told her so. Looking into each other's eyes, I knew without having to say it that our intimacy had deepened immeasurably.

The shaman had said before the session that we could choose to leave behind normal time-space reality, and move through a portal to another dimension. I must have done this because the nature of normal "reality" was never quite the same after. There was no longer any question that life could, and should, be experienced beyond the mere physical, emotional, and mental realms with which I had been so embroiled. The strange other world I had entered was no longer disturbing at all, but rather it held a great wondrous allure because it was so filled with peace and love. It was—is—the source of everything.

With absolute certainty, I knew that, as spirit, I had soared beyond my body, free of the material world, and at the same time, thanks to my body, I could return to enjoy the rich flavors in the realm of the senses. The eagle had taken off, and the eagle had landed. I was a free bird.

The Four Roads

On the trip home, I had plenty of time to reflect on my experiences. Coming to Peru and taking ayahuasca enabled me to see my journey from the condor's vantage point, which encompassed different levels of reality from the broadest of perspectives.

I had shifted away from being a goal-oriented person. The process is at one with the goal. Material possessions were of secondary importance. Knowing that thoughts could change one's reality, in the blink of a new intention, I could be in a different world, and in one of my own choosing. What freedom in being able to co-create with Spirit!

When I got home, the first chance I could, I climbed up the Santa Monica Mountains to get the condor's perspective and took in the grand panorama of the mountains, the city beyond, and the vast Pacific ocean. With utter clarity, I saw the overview of my life, and recent endeavors as delineated by the four roads:

First, I had delved into the "Red Road" of the physical life, which included setting myself on fire, the various traffic accidents, my mortality, and obsession with the material aspects of life.

Second, I saw behind the visible world the "Yellow Road" of the emotional/psychological aspect of life, including love, sorrows, angers, fears, and belief-structures both positive and negative.

Third, I became aware that the first two roads were rooted in the "Blue Road" of the spiritual, which was revealed to me when I was kneeling in the shadow side of Mitten, during sessions of my past lives, and my nightwalk in nature.

Finally, I had a new road, the "Silver Road" of being a witness, an impartial observer of my own life with no fear or desire. This happened during the wild ride on the mustang with thunderbolts hurling down; my soul retrieval sessions when I saw myself as that homeless woman or knew the utter despair of that chief's son; and most recently on ayahuasca, witnessing all the members of my family, including myself, and seeing all our destinies.

These are the four roads that I knew could help map out the parameters of my life. I worked it into my "Life Map," and the exercise made me feel whole and grounded. That night, Lizanne and I went out for dinner, and as I sipped a nice glass of wine with her enjoying the moment—the only moment—I felt that life was perfect.

"Wow, what's going on?" Lizanne asked. "You're…radiant."

"What can I say?" I smiled, "you're so right."

11

THE SILVER ROAD

Old World, New Eyes

Suffice it to say, it took me a while to re-adjust to Malibu after the intensity of Peru.

With my heart so open, I felt raw and vital, and came out with a completely new outfit to reflect the new me. Proudly strutting my stuff to impress Lizanne, I asked her what she thought. She looked me over.

"Going to a funeral? Looks awfully dark. Like the way my dad dresses."

I was dismayed; *that takes care of this combination!*

Deep down, however, I cherished how candid we had become with each other. Naked and vulnerable, we could easily express "negative" opinions and feelings with no offense being taken. It would come out in the simplest details of daily life:

"You never take me out anymore," she once complained.

"Never? Where do you think we went Tuesday? And Wednesday?"

"But I'm sick and tired of cleaning up the kitchen after you. Let's just go out."

Fighting guilt and the life-long need to have it my way, I answered, begrudgingly, "Alright, already. Have it your way."

"I don't want to go if you're like that!"

"C'mon, we'll just go," I groaned. Inside, I was determined to break through my old patterns of winning arguments and maintaining control.

"Boy, after all our profound experiences," I muttered, "We still have our own shit to deal with."

"Uh, speak for yourself, why don't you?"

"I am," I quipped. "That's why I always carry a little plastic doggie bag for myself."

She looked at me an instant, then laughed. The tension was broken, and we went out in high spirits. Ah, our honeymoon period may have been over, but I felt great in our deeper connection and in how effective my "new eyes" were for old situations. Though neither of us had any intention of getting married, I had complete trust in Spirit for wherever our relationship would take us.

This also applied to all my relationships—husband, father, son, friend, and lover—which had always been clearly defined, and separated. But now, I let all my personas float free, merge, separate, and merge again. I just had to keep everything in balance, fulfill my day-to-day responsibilities, and simply appeal to Spirit, "Spend me now, I'm at your service. What do you want me to do?" I had no idea that this idea could be so liberating.

After Peru, I felt more comfortable with myself, and more open-hearted with people at large. "How are you?" I could say easily to the clerk at the airport, or to a homeless peddler. Or to the great spiritual teacher and author, Eckhart Tolle, at a restaurant; I felt very comfortable going up to him, introducing myself, and telling him how his books had been so helpful on my quest to reclaim my own divinity.

The Life Map

However, one of the most powerful activities to help me digest the otherworld enchantments of Peru was through the use of my "Life Map," a continually evolving blueprint of my soul's journey. It helped me to digest and ground the airy, transcendent experiences I had gone through, and to become *consciously aware* of who I am.

Over a few months, I had carefully gathered three stones for each of the four corners of my Map, knowing that each stone was a storehouse of transpersonal energy. For example, in the Red Road of the physical, a key stone had an image of a lightning bolt epitomizing the spark of creation for birth into the world.

For the Yellow Road of one's emotional-psychological life, those three stones represented the patriarchal line of ancestors, including my life as that murderous Native American warrior. For the Blue Road of the soul, there was a mysterious one signifying the "keeper of secrets." During a ritual, I was given a brief glimpse of some of those "secrets," but then, just as easily, I was made to forget.

As for the Silver Road, all I knew was that it had to do with being a "witness," but more than that I didn't know. So, surrounded by mystery, I continued to work on my Life Map to deepen and ground my understanding of the various layers of consciousness I had experienced.

Complementing all this mental effort, I continued to meditate, practice yoga, and hike through the mountains. Through the sights, smells, and sounds of Mother Nature, which continued to keep me balanced, I grew increasingly appreciative of her magnificence. The earth in all her fragility, power, and beauty had become my beloved.

Old Business, New Eyes

As for my work situation, I had already closed two of my three offices to keep my overhead low. While co-developing a project involving affordable housing for seniors, I realized that in spite of the bureaucratic grind of legalities, demands from the Building Department, and all the usual complications of real estate development, I was actually *enjoying* this project. This was something new! I sensed its worthiness—affordable housing for seniors—and realized that there is much more to the business of business than just making money. How long it has taken me to understand this basic truth!

I continued with other development projects for several years, when, as fate would have it, the whole economy tanked. The old me would have screamed, "Failure is *not* an option," and blamed, shouted, and railroaded people to try to force the situation to bend to my will. But now, I had a whole new *modus operandi*. Instead, I accepted the reality of the market, and surrendered to *what is*.

With no loans possible, and everyone hunkered down to survive the financial debacle, we were forced to return the remaining portions of a housing project to the bank. The investor and I both suffered significant financial losses, but remaining centered, we were both cool about it and ended the project on good terms.

After the project ended, I closed this last office in Brentwood. It triggered some serious questions for myself. "Now what do I do with myself? How do I utilize my skill-set as an entrepreneur cultivated over a period of 24 years? Do I junk it all, and reinvent myself completely by going into another profession? Or do I stay in the industry, but in a different capacity? If I were to stay in real estate, should I focus on brokerage or finance, development or direct investment? Hmm. Most importantly, how could I best serve the greater good?" Since I had lost much of my financial wealth, it was a real challenge for me to find a new balance between profits and social good.

Running through my head, I kept thinking of a famous athlete who had once declared to a journalist, "Golf is what I do, not who I am." That comment triggered my own response to that theme: "What I do expresses who I am." As a result, after some more soul searching, I decided to stay in the industry, but not just for the money; those days were gone forever. I would stay in real estate, but get involved only with meaningful projects...but what?

Right before the financial debacle, I had closed a deal involving a large tract of land in Big Sur right on the ocean. The way it all fell in place so effortlessly I saw as a good omen of my new and better ways of getting things done, and my new values of developing projects for the general good. It would eventually prove to be a huge breakthrough in helping me see my new calling.

Southeast Asia

Six months after Peru, I was itching to go on a trip, one that wasn't so intense like Peru or my Vision Quest. Rather, I wanted a relaxing, comfortable journey to recharge my batteries. My brother Peter had spoken highly of Thailand, where neither Lizanne nor I had ever been.

Increasingly interested in Buddhism the last few years, Lizanne and I, before we knew it, were in the air on the way to Cambodia and Thailand.

We flew over on Thai Airlines into Bangkok, a big, polluted industrial city like so many others in the world. The air was as thick and heavy as the airport was crowded. But soon, after an hour and a half on a connecting flight, we found ourselves in the airport in Siem Reap, the gateway city for visitors of the famous temple of Angkor Wat in Cambodia. Military police were swarming around everywhere, but hovering slightly over all the heads, we spotted a sign over the crowd, "Mr. Adarn Hall." That must be me. *At least I went from Mr. A. Hole to Adarn,* I thought to myself as Lizanne and I worked our way to meet the sign carrier.

"My name is Kim. I will be your driver for the next few days," he told us with a warm smile. He turned out to be a most beautiful, gentle man.

Once out of the airport, working our way through the city, we were overrun by motorbikes that swarmed over us like giant mosquitoes. In the midst of the traffic, a commotion. Some motorbike had hit a pedestrian. A messy accident. "Better watch your step here," I told Lizanne.

As we rode on, Kim told us about his brother, father, and grandfather, and the Khmer Rouge.

"My grandfather. He had education. He was of upper class, so he would be killed. Or sent to countryside and work as slave labor."

"So what did he do?" Lizanne asked.

"My grandmother, she hid him under the floorboards. But still, they got him and he died."

"What about your father?" I asked.

Kim shook his head. After a while, he said, "All dead."

His story gave me chills, and I didn't feel like pursuing it. Approximately 2 million out of a population of 7 million were slaughtered. Going by percentage, it was the most devastating genocide in the 20th century.

Along the Siem Reap River on the outskirts of the city, we drove by the slums—acres of shanties with falling tin roofs, muddy pathways, and trash heaps right on the river bank. A group of women was gathered around a water pump, desperate for potable water, as children scampered over trash heaps looking for recyclables or played on them, shouting and laughing. I was so moved to see them like kids anywhere in spite of their dire predicament.

"Here," Kim commented, gesturing to the slums, "this is where those who don't have much live." How I felt for those poor kids. What hope have they? What future? Although, inside, another part of me was beginning to wonder whether this was still going to be the relaxing, easy trip Lizanne and I had wanted.

After a few minutes, those slums gave way to a beautiful part of town with lush, exotic plants setting a verdant background for elegant wood structures, all elaborately carved. Turning around, Kim told us with a smile, "And here, this is where live those who have much belongings. You would think them living here would be happy. But no, those back there with no belongings, they are the happy ones."

Driving on, we saw peeping above the buildings and trees statues of the Buddha in a great variety of sizes and materials. They reminded me of how the Buddha overcame suffering by knowing himself. And by realizing the profound connection he had with "all sentient beings," it gave rise to one of the fundamental tenets of Buddhism, compassion.

Finally, before a nondescript 3-Star hotel, we stopped. Kim helped us with our bags, and when we were settled in, told us, "Get rest. Tomorrow, we look at temples."

Exhausted after a long day of traveling, we went straight to bed. The last thing I remembered before sleep took over were the words from Buddhism rolling around my head, "You are not your thought. You are what thinks the thought…"

In the morning over tea, Kim outlined the agenda for the next two days.

"We'll be busy. Weather looks good. Let's get started."

"But, Kim," Lizanne said, "we also want to visit some orphanages." He looked at us in surprise. What he didn't know was that Lizanne and I wanted to do something, however small, to help. "Giving is receiving," we had both agreed. We ended up bringing over with us four duffel bags stuffed with toys, pens, paper, balloons, and soccer balls for the kids in the orphanages.

Kim finally answered.

"For orphanages, over there where we passed. Where they have no belongings. By the lake, there is a schoolhouse for the orphanage. Don't tell my boss, and I take you there. Tomorrow, we skip a few temples, so later today, we go to the lake."

Angkor Wat

Kim took us first to Angkor Wat, where we traveled through heavily wooded terrain and began to see, peeping out of lush undergrowth, old temple ruins with elaborate stone carvings that announced the ruins of Angkor Wat. What a breath-taking sight! Like a dream we saw, presiding over a lake, a dozen towers dominating the skyline, the main temple, 190 feet high, exquisitely decorated with 300 heavenly nymphs, a bas relief on a long wall of over 2400 yards depicting Heaven and Hell, Churning of the Ocean of Milk, the Elephant Gate, and the Battle of the Gods and Demons.

Overall, I was struck with the sense of great intelligence, divinely guided. With all the depictions of their history and battles, they still seemed to be able to carve gods and celestial beings and maintain a balance between the mundane and the spiritual, time and eternity. It inspired me to further soften my masculine armor to bring out the feminine.

After the temples, we found ourselves walking through the slums with no electricity, no running water, no sewers, and trash everywhere. At the shore of a polluted lake, a pig was asleep, and next to it, a shanty building on the shore that served as the schoolhouse. Upon entering, we saw an elderly man, maybe 70 or 80, teaching the kids. Kim spoke to him, telling him that since Christmas was next week, we wanted to give out some gifts. He looked at us and smiled.

A few minutes later with my Santa hat on, Lizanne and I were handing out pens, hair clips, toys, and much more. The children were thrilled beyond belief, yet remained very well-behaved and waited patiently until they received their gift. My heart could have burst to see their smiles light up the whole schoolroom. From their dark almond eyes, nothing but joy and enthusiasm radiated out.

I saw that in spite of the seriousness of the adults (so understandable, having endured the Khmer Rouge), all the children were filled with joy and smiles everywhere. What a strong contrast to many of the kids I had seen in Malibu, who have every material advantage, yet seemed to be filled with incessant worries, envy, and competition. After this experience, I promised myself I would never take anything I had for granted. It made me question the meaning of wealth, which, through all I had seen recently, kept steering me back to spiritual abundance of kindness and compassion as much closer to true wealth.

Thailand

After Cambodia we ventured to Thailand, where the people were soft, gentle, and feminine, a culture of love and kindness. *Now we could catch up on the ease and comfort we sought,* I told myself. With fine white sand for beaches and turquoise water, all complemented with cool wine and succulent shrimp, we could now truly relax.

We climbed mountains, rode elephants, swam in the ocean, and visited the hilltop tribes of the *Karen* and the Long-Necked Tribes where the women wear brass rings that make their necks seem stretched. Everywhere we went, we saw turtles in rock formations, paintings, sculptures, and live in the ocean. They were revered and symbolized the celebration of life. *Celebrate! That's what I need to do in my life,* I told myself.

How fast time goes by when you're having fun. After three weeks, our adventure came to a close, and we headed home thoroughly rejuvenated.

Back Home

As I sat meditating one morning, I unexpectedly heard Lila's voice.

"You are no longer controlled by fear."

Though it was an observation that I was beginning to know, I was delighted with her confirmation. "So, where do I go from here?" I asked.

"Love guides you now."

Why, I asked myself, *do I keep asking the same questions, when deep down I know the answer.* It was my old habit of getting stuck in my head and refusing to embrace my newfound wisdom. Something else to work on.

Alberto's Proposition

As the bright sun played with the ocean swells in Malibu, Lizanne and I, along with our house-guest, Alberto, my guide from Peru, sat outside on our wood deck sipping tea and munching on fresh fruit.

"Look!" I exclaimed, pointing to the ocean. Everyone strained their eyes to where I was pointing. After a few moments, a small group of dolphins leapt out of the water in unison into the glittering sunlight. What is it about the magic of dolphins? The mere sight of them uplifts everyone's spirit. We all took it as a good omen, a blessing for the perfection of the moment.

Since Peru, I had invited Alberto to stay at my place in Malibu whenever he was in town. To spend time with him informally I found especially rewarding. Studying his face, I couldn't help but notice how alive and radiant he looked, and told him so. He thanked me with a smile and then asked, coyly, "What do you guys think of the following? In our lineage, there are nine ancient rites of passage. A series of initiations that will transform *homo sapiens* into *Homo Luminous.*"

"*Homo Luminous?*" I remarked, "Sounds great, but what does that mean?"

"That's when we can step out of a time-space reality and defeat death. We can then realize that we are spiritual rather than physical bodies, and become a person of wisdom and power."

"Where do these rites come from?" asked Lizanne.

"They're from the Laika, medicine men and women who went through the Bering Straits some 30,000 years ago. And since then, they've been handed down generation to generation, and kept safe until humankind is, once again, ready to receive them."

"So now it's time?" I asked.

"Now, it's time. The people are ready. So I'm releasing the Nine Initiation Rites in Peru this summer, and I would like you and Lizanne to be a part of it."

"Really?" I exclaimed. "We're honored, but how can we really help?"

"We're just *releasing* these rites. Each person is still responsible for integrating them into their own lives. We're planting seeds that will help someone remember who he or she really is," he explained.

"I would be honored, truly honored." I looked at Lizanne, and in a glance, we knew we were intrigued, but of what exactly, I didn't know.

"Great. These Rites are called the Munay-Ki."

"Which means…"

"Many interpretations, but the one I like best is, *Be as Thou Art.*"

Then we launched into an in-depth conversation about how the Munay, being of pure light and love, reside at the source of all living things. Though I didn't know exactly what they were, I knew they could deepen my experience in the spiritual realms. Alberto shared a long, rich story, too much to go into at this point, but here are the highlights:

The First Rite is about healing ancestral wounds, of past lives and past traumas.

"Alberto," I said, "I've had some experience with past-life regressions and with Soul Retrieval, and the healing that they had inspired. So is this First Rite connected with Soul Retrieval in any way?"

"Yes, most certainly. The human journey requires life-long healing of issues that sometimes have gone on over many lifetimes, so this initiation embraces the on-going healing process with love and forgiveness."

The Second Rite is about spiritual sight. Intuition. Heart centered.

"You mean love, then?" asked Lizanne.

"Yes, most definitely. Seeing from your heart."

The Third Rite balances the spiritual with the physical, while the Fourth Rite is about energy bands of power—earth, water, fire, air, and the rainbow bridge and golden thread of pure light.

"They protect your luminous body. Real important if you recall that we are *Homo Luminous,*" Alberto explained.

"What about protection from…ourselves?" I asked.

"You mean those boogie men from within," he laughed. "It takes care of them, too."

The Fifth Rite is called the "Day Keeper," which concerns the Great Mother.

"It rules the feminine energy that heals and balances the world, and the rising of the sun to keep us all warm," Alberto said.

"Rising of the sun? Don't know about you guys," Lizanne quipped, "but I haven't seen a sunrise since I was seven."

The Sixth Rite is that of the "Wisdom Keeper."

"…those men or women who have been able to step out of time and defeat death," Alberto explained.

"Really?" I asked. "How do you do that?"

"Come to Peru next year," he replied, "and when you are on the Holy Mountain, you can ask the Wisdom Keeper yourself."

After a few bites of fruit, Alberto went on, "The Seventh Rite is that of the 'Earth Keeper.' Here, one becomes a steward of the earth, a guardian of the planet."

"Wow," I muttered. "How this one resonates with me! But I feel torn. I have enough problems dealing with the 'earth' within me, so how can I even begin to extend myself to include the whole planet?"

"But to be a good Earth Keeper, you *must* begin with yourself," Alberto explained.

All my apprehensions evaporated, and I felt totally in sync with his comment. This rite would have tremendous significance for me, but it would not be revealed until my second trip to Peru.

The Eighth Rite is that of the "Star Keeper," which cultivates the relationship not only with our own sun, but other Star Nations.

"Real important, especially now, for protection and changes coming with 2012," Alberto said.

Finally, he told us about the Ninth and last Rite, the *Titanchie*, or the "God Rite," the union of your soul with Source. For a long moment, we were silent, with me trying to take in all he said.

"Yeah, go on," I finally asked. "Is there more?"

"Ahh, the answers are in Peru. You must go back to Peru," he replied with a smile.

I looked at Lizanne, she looked at me, and we knew. In our minds, we had just booked our tickets to Peru.

After this conversation, we all took a walk up in the Santa Monica Mountains. How nice to be physical after all that intense mental activity. Nine months for human birth, nine rites, and nine months from now we will be back in Peru, I mused. How natural and fitting.

That night, after Alberto went to sleep, I sat down with Lizanne to digest all our new input and prospective plans. My head was spinning.

"You want to talk about it?" she asked.

"It's all happening so fast. Back to Peru, already?"

"But you've been preparing for this moment your whole life," Lizanne pointed out. "Maybe it'll set you up so you can find a way to start giving back, like the way you've helped me."

"No, we'll do this together," I whispered. Grateful for her encouragement, I held up my wine glass, "To our lives unfolding, to happiness, to love, and to us!"

As the second trip to Peru approached, I read through material that Alberto had given me and hiked to keep myself in good shape. I felt electric with enthusiasm.

Father

One day, after dinner with my parents, I told my father about our plans to return to Peru and a bit about the Munay. While he didn't fully grasp what it was about, he was completely supportive of what I was doing.

"I hope you find what you're looking for," he said.

"Thanks, Dad. I have. And I have you to thank."

"Me? For what?"

"For everything. For raising me to be independent, for encouraging me to search for my true purpose in life."

"By the looks of it, you've found it."

"More like, it found me!" I exclaimed.

"Look at you, you're glowing like a light bulb, all golden and everything."

My father's encouragement meant a lot to me. With his strong Christian beliefs, it felt so heart-warming to have his blessings on what I was doing, especially at 88 when he was becoming frail and reaching the end of his days. After a little more conversation, he excused himself and went to bed early, as was his habit nowadays.

This was the moment that I had been waiting for. After an hour, I entered his dark room to have a moment of communion with him when he was sound asleep. The light from a candle I had set on his nightstand washed over his face with a soft golden glow and made me feel as if we were together spirit to spirit. I could feel my heart beating strongly with his.

Silently, I thanked him and let him know that as far as I was concerned, his work with me was complete, and that he had fulfilled his role magnificently. Standing over him, I opened my arms to embrace his "energy body." My intent was to help him release any leftover regrets, angers, or sorrows he might have, although I knew that they would be minor, such as not spending enough time with *his* father. Still, I knew that it was a good thing to be as clean as possible, considering how close he was to making his transition. I offered a prayer that his passing would be sweet and gentle. After about fifteen minutes, I was done, took my candle, and silently stole away, feeling complete with my father.

Filled with deep sense of well-being, I received a phone call from my mother about a month later. My father had fallen and broken his hip. Rushing to the hospital, I saw immediately that he was soon to make his transition.

A few days later, I went to see him again. He had been in pain and had stopped eating. From my collection of powerful medicine stones from my "Mesa," I had brought a red one, attuned to the patriarchal line of the ancestors, and a "portal stone" that facilitated movement into other dimensions.

Decisively, I put one stone in each of my father's hands. Though he was fast asleep, I was heartened to see how, subconsciously, he took to the stones and held them both firmly. I said my goodbyes, and watched for a few moments as he uttered a few last words, "Jesus...[mumbling]... Jesus." Peacefully, he died the next day.

He had chosen to be cremated. I was called by Spirit to be present with him as he entered into the fire, and was the only member of the family to come to this last moment of his on earth. Waking at sunrise, I began the day in meditation and prayer, feeling strongly my father's presence. Ending my meditation, I saw outside my window two hummingbirds dancing around a bright red flower, relishing the nectar of a morning feast. *A sweet sign of closure between my father and me,* I thought.

It inspired me to formally commemorate my gratitude for him. Picking up a pad of paper and pen, I wrote out a note that I planned to leave with him as he went into the fire.

Lizanne, bless her soul, drove with me to the crematorium. We rode in silence much of the way. Time seemed to stand still. After an hour or so, we arrived with me relishing every second of these final moments with my father.

Lizanne and I were shown the way to the back of the cemetery into a nondescript concrete building that looked like a tomb. There we met the undertaker (who looked like a ghost himself with an outdated black suit and utterly pale skin) and were shown into the furnace room. Directed to a plain wood box wherein rested my father, I asked to have it opened and was gently surprised that his big blue eyes were still open. But he seemed to radiate a peace that filled the room. What a man of grace. I felt honored to be in his presence and blessed to send him on his way in this final moment. Tears rolled off my cheeks as I took out the note, and read:

"My beloved father, you have now begun the ultimate journey. I am grateful for the wisdom you shared. I honor you. Your guidance and grace have shown me the way back to my heart. As you walk into eternity, the light of your love will guide the way. I am with you now and forever, and you are with me always. Bless you, God loves you, I love you. With honor, Adam."

By now, though numb and overwhelmed by the finality of the moment, I was able to place the note on his chest like I had intended. The box was then closed, and the undertaker directed me to the button that would start the conveyer belt to move the box into the roaring fire. With my finger on the button, I froze, bowed my head, and then pushed it firmly. Slowly the coffin moved into the furnace. The door finally shut, and though I couldn't see what was happening, I could hear the fierce roar of the fire that marked the dissolution of his mortal body.

A couple of days later, the family received a metal box of his ashes. The immediate family, including my mother and brothers, and my sister-in-law—no children, no Gigi—met at the beach in Paradise Cove for a ceremony to cast his ashes into the sea. It was a magnificent day. As my brother, Ben, had suggested, we paddled out on surfboards beyond the breakers to release his remains. With the urn on the front of the board, we found a calm spot to cast him to his final resting place. Ben spoke first.

"Dear father, thank you for bringing me into the world…" We shared our tears, held our hearts, and sighed. Then, raising my right arm high into the sky, I spoke.

"To the winds of the north, hummingbird, grandmother, grandfather, ancient ones, and my beloved father: Come and warm your hands by my fire. We have received your gifts; we have been guided by your wisdom and grace. We honor you now and return you to the sea."

We poured his ashes into the sea. As the last of it fell into the cool water, I heard a voice. My father's!

"Thank you!" I heard him say. "After that hot fire of cremation, this cool water feels so good!" I was so caught off guard I practically broke out laughing. The somber mood was broken, and I knew to my core that my father was in a very good place. Paddling back to shore, we embraced the whole family in love, and met back in the house for a final get-together.

Showdown with Gigi

The only lingering toxic factor in my life was clearing up the mess with my ex-wife and finding peace with my children. As I held my kids inside my heart, it brought up old issues connected to my own wounds as a child, such as feeling alone and separated. With my own children, I knew what to do: simply love and nurture them with no expectations whether they called back or not. I would simply always be there for them.

Gigi was another story. A year before, with attorneys and a mediator, we had finally agreed on a resolution. I had offered a generous settlement from the marital estate, in addition to an ample monthly allotment for spousal and child support. All was agreed, but at the last minute, Gigi refused to sign! (Later, her attorney told me that her mother had convinced her not to do it.) *Oh well*, I thought, *just keep moving onward until we reach a resolution, one way or another.*

A year later, on my way to court, I mused how she had insisted on going through these legal proceedings to teach me a lesson. She was out for revenge and more. There wasn't much I could do about that but to take responsibility for my own actions. I promised myself to undergo the entire trial from a place of my heart, to not be reactive, to stay centered. I took a Chinese herb, *Shen*, that April had recommended to keep me calm. Having let my lawyer go so as to represent myself, I had been swimming in legal paperwork for a year and a half, and now, after another couple of months of delays, it was showdown time.

Following a long meditation, I had double-checked that it was right for me to continue to represent myself even in this new phase of actually going to court. Gigi had a very sharp $550-an-hour lawyer, and I had my spiritual tools of understanding, compassion, and composure. The trial took place over the course of five days in a Los Angeles courtroom, with Judge Steinberg presiding.

For an opening statement, I was able to speak from my heart and tell the truth of my love for my children, and gratefulness for the times Gigi and I had shared. Having forgiven Gigi and myself, I was able to face her without any rancor. When she spoke, however, I was a little taken aback by the depth of her hostility spoken out loud in court—I was a liar, I was a cheat. Not only had her rage not mellowed, it had intensified. It made me sad because that anger could wreak serious damage on her health and the well-being of our children.

"Your honor, it is difficult for the kids to visit me in California, and when they do, our visits keep getting interrupted by the petitioner's phone calls, and Gigi's demand that my kids call her every few hours." After hearing our statements to settle these visitation rights, Judge Steinberg made her statement.

"We will expect uninterrupted visitations," she told Gigi. "If not, you will be held to contempt of court." (Later, she would violate the agreement and would be convicted.)

Then we addressed the financial aspect of the settlement. Gigi's forensic attorney spoke out to jack up my earnings as high as possible so as to increase Gigi's settlement.

"Just because you haven't earned a lot the last few years and had to borrow to maintain the lifestyle you are accustomed to, this borrowing should be considered earnings."

Nobody considered this sound logic. Even the attorney himself, looking down with a furrowed brow, didn't seem convinced of this declaration, so I figured he was only mouthing what Gigi had insisted he say.

"If I'm not earning a lot, it's not because I don't want to," I explained to the judge. "It's the ebb and flow of the real estate market. I'm only harming myself and my children if I'm not earning enough. In any case, borrowing is not earning."

"But, your honor, he had been hiding real estate and other assets," the attorney continued, "and had been taking money out of the marital estate. That's how he was able to pay Gigi's expenses."

"There is nothing to hide, your honor. But I did take money out of our joint account to cover the house payments, and I won't do it anymore."

"That's fine," the judge said, "We will restrict any withdrawals from the marital estate."

Since Team Gigi had demanded a tremendous settlement plus $15,000 a month for Gigi's living expenses (including $6,000 a year for beauty and hair), they were intent on convincing the judge of my huge (hidden) earnings that would justify their request.

As they struggled to inflate my income, I had a chance to speak my mind to the judge.

"The record shows that last year, I made zero. Nothing. But, your honor, you could allocate…"—and here I named a six-figure amount—"as my income, because, quite frankly, that's what I should have earned. I'm a bit embarrassed about what I actually brought in. Though I was emotionally distracted by our separation, it's not up to my standards. I could have done better."

And so it went. After four days of this, and after closing arguments, the judge made her final decisions. She accepted my figure for yearly income and allocated living expenses to Gigi based on that figure. She ruled that Gigi had to pay her own attorney fees and accounting fees, which by that time had added up to nearly four hundred thousand dollars.

Finally, the judge ruled that my payments would end when my youngest turned eighteen. This was even better than I had hoped, because I had told the judge that we shouldn't be imprisoned with each other for the rest of our lives, and had suggested that my payments would continue to equal the number of years we were married. But with the judge's ruling, Gigi became enraged. She had expected that the payments go on for life, as had my original attorney.

What irony. If Gigi had accepted my first offering, she could have saved hundreds of thousands in legal fees and received 40% *more* in settlement than what the judge had ruled, and gotten payments for years longer than what the judge had ordered.

Upon hearing the judge's decree, Gigi had slumped in defeat. Bitter to the end, she categorically refused to sign the final divorce papers. Her attorney was forced to act on her behalf and execute the documents.

On the way out, the judge told me with a smile, "Mr. Hall, you did a fine job representing yourself." I thanked her for that, but inside, I felt bittersweet. I was happy for the outcome, much better than I had thought, but saddened by the waste, the rancor, and the inevitable suffering that lay ahead for Gigi. I did not feel victorious, because I felt that the whole "showdown" was unnecessary and ugly.

And yet I felt a profound lift in my spirit because truth had prevailed, "Know the truth, and the truth shall set you free." Faith in the power of my spiritual practices had risen to a new level.

That put an official end to that chapter of my life. Or so I thought. For Gigi, though, it was only the beginning of a new onslaught of vindictive drama, a terrible backlash reaction to what happened in court. Her rage, I could see, began to seep into my children. Morgan, who had often told me, "Dad, I love you to infinity and beyond" and lifted my spirits for weeks, would now say, "Adam, I don't want to talk to you."

Feeling kicked in the chest, I would force myself to not react and answer, "I understand, Morgan. When you *do* feel like talking, I'm here, because I would always love to talk to you."

This flip-flop from loving me one moment to anger the next happened with all my kids. We would have wonderful times together just like old times, and then everything would turn to its opposite. It forced me to take it all in stride and go deeper with the practice of equanimity. Deep down, I was convinced that they loved me, and that when they were a bit older and free of their mother's influence, truth would be revealed, and love would flow freely once again.

The Christmas Meeting

About a year and a half after the court proceedings, and a week before Christmas, I sat in my living room enjoying the warmth of the fire. I chanced upon a quote in a magazine from a seven-year-old boy named Bobby. He was asked, "What is love?" His answer was inspiring, "Love is what's in the room with you on Christmas if you stop opening presents and listen."

His answer got me thinking. Whenever I went to visit my kids, Gigi had never let me into her home, so I would pick them up on the curb. Since the court settlement, the level of hostility was higher than ever. She had even recruited an ally in waging war against me, her brother, Jack, with a black belt in martial arts who over the years had instigated many a fight, including some against the law, for which he had been thrown in jail.

Still, for my upcoming holiday trip, what if I asked Gigi if it were possible to meet with the entire family, all in the spirit of Christmas? Inspired by Bobby, I thought that there was no harm in asking.

So, bracing myself, I called her and told her my idea. "No big deal," I insisted, "just a visit. I come in peace, for the kids. It *is* Christmas, after all." After a long pause, she agreed! I was so pleasantly surprised. Immediately, however, I began to have second thoughts because, knowing her, she always had something up her sleeve. But I refused to dwell on negative thoughts and kept faith that my good intentions would prevail.

A few days later, I was in Utah getting ready for the big meeting. Before I left my hotel at the Courtyard by Marriott, I spent some time just breathing, being still, and meditating. Insights about the best behavior for the meeting would come, "Just listen. Hear what's being said, and do not react nor judge… Keep sending love and light into the room."

Before going to Gigi's house, I went to each corner on the square block and called in the "four directions" for protection, healing, and peace for all. In the south direction, I called in the winds to release all the pain and suffering of the past. In the west direction, I called in the winds to help us go beyond anger into love and joy. In the north direction, I called upon the winds of the ancestors to join us and share their wisdom so that we can taste the sweetness of life. And in the direction of the east, I called in the winds to help fulfill my intent for a new day.

Situated in a very nice neighborhood called St. George, the house was new and had character—Gigi always had good taste in matters of home and décor. While circling the block, I took a few deep breaths, determined to do everything possible to promote a successful outcome. Putting myself once again in sacred space, I drove to the meeting.

At 6 p.m. on the dot, on a Thursday, I arrived at the house, only to find Gigi waiting for me.

"Hello," I said.

"Let's just get started," she replied coolly. *Get started?* Her tone of voice immediately put me on guard. I felt she was up to something.

As I entered the dining room, I was greeted by her brother, Jack, her mom and dad, my three children, and my eldest daughter's fiancé. They all took their seats as if pre-arranged—Gigi's dad, Sid, sat on one end, and her brother, Jack, sat on the other. They pointed out where they wanted me to sit, in the middle, up against the wall. I was fine with that, since it was in the north, the direction of the ancestors who could help resolve old issues. Instinctively, I knew that I would have to come from a place of surrender and not ever be on the offense. Everyone else arranged themselves around the table. *I'm surrounded. Perhaps I'm the feast, and they're going to gobble me up,* a voice inside cried out. But immediately, I squelched the thought and got back on center.

Gigi's father, Sid, broke the awkward moment of silence with a sneer, "Adam, you're a brave man for coming."

He might have just said, "You're a *stupid* man for coming," his attitude was so cynical.

"No, he's just a wimp and an asshole!" Jack interjected.

Involuntarily, my body jumped, but I forced myself to continue being the "witness," and did not react to their taunts. Instead, I calmly managed to meet everyone's eye. *Keep breathing!* I told myself.

"So tell me, Adam, are you involved with organized crime?" Sid demanded.

I did everything to control myself from laughing out loud. "No, sir," I replied.

"Yeah? Because we have reason to believe that you're involved with organized crime related to your partner Ken," he continued.

"Do you mean my partner Ken who I was in business with 19 years ago?"

"Yes."

"I have not had any business with him since then. And if you are concerned about the safety and well-being of Gigi and the kids, I can assure you I have nothing to do with Ken, organized crime, or any other illegal activity," I told him firmly.

"Bull shit! You're a fucking crook!" yelled Jack.

"And a lying, cheating asshole, besides!" Gigi shouted. "Didn't you cheat on me?"

"Yes, Gigi, I did cheat on you at the end of the marriage," I said softly. "As I have said many times, I am deeply sorry for my selfish actions."

"Oh no, you're not! You're just a piece of shit!" Gigi yelled.

Breathe...breathe...This meeting for peace is not going very well, I thought to myself.

"You better make good tonight, Adam, or the ball will be in *my* court," Jack injected. I had no idea what he meant, except that it was threatening.

"So why did you come here tonight?" Sid asked.

Quietly, I took in a deep breath as I glanced around at my kids—Maya directly across from me, Morgan to her right, and Sophia to my left. All my poor kids were in stupefied shock from all the anger and hatred displayed. I knew that they were all secretly terrified by their mother and her vindictive anger. Wincing with heart pain, I fought off tears and answered softly, "It's soon to be Christmas and I came for two reasons. One, I would like to bring the anger, pain, and suffering we've all been undergoing to an end. And two, somehow, help the children, who have suffered enough."

"What hog wash!" Jack yelled.

"You're so full of shit," Gigi added.

Gigi's mom, Carolyn, pulled out a piece of paper. Then I noticed that Morgan had one too. And Gigi. Obviously, they had prepared this meeting designed to crucify me.

"Adam, there is nothing worse than a scorned woman," Carolyn said, as she began reading what she had written. "We have done everything to resolve these problems for the past five years, and you have just been an asshole." Looking up, she added, "You must have gotten that from your mom, too!"

Breathe, breathe... In one cruel sentence, she had debased her own daughter, my mom, and me. *Just keep breathing,* I told myself.

"She didn't care about anybody but herself! Just like you, you asshole!" yelled Gigi.

"Can we cut out the foul language," I cut in, "The children don't need to be subjected to it."

"Fuck you! They don't need to be subjected to *you,* you fucking asshole!" Jack shouted.

"And your dad, how could he have put up with your bullshit all these years?" Carolyn continued. No longer reading from the letter she had written, her rage flared out, unable to be contained by a piece of paper as she spewed out insults, profanity, lies, and sarcasm. I sat upright, determined to keep centered.

"I want to know if you're going to pay Gigi the money you owe her? Her fucking attorney ripped her off, and now you're doing the same!" Jack exclaimed. His face was turning red. Maya got up and left the room, but after a few moments returned. Her fiancé, lanky 23-year-old Wes, was quietly weeping.

"You sure, boy, that you want to be a part of this family?" Sid asked him with a smirk. This quip was his idea of a joke, but Wes continued to sob. Sitting to my right, I put my arm around him, and suggested that he go outside and get a breath of fresh air. He shook his head and just continued to shed his tears.

"Listen, dumb fuck, if you do not pay Gigi more money, I am going to take matters into my own hands." Jack threatened again.

"He's just a little man, Jack, a good-for-nothing…" Gigi started to say, but Jack shouted over her.

"Still, I'm going to …."

"But he's a nothing, a nothing…" Gigi screamed back over her brother. Sid then shouted out something, only to be drowned out by his wife, who got interrupted by Gigi and Jack. It was surreal, everybody yelling over each other, no one listening. I could not get a word in edgewise, which was just as well. For an eternity, it seemed, they exploded with poisonous grenades going at each other, but mostly at me. Finally, Gigi shouted over everybody, and managed to claim the floor.

"Morgan! Morgan, you hear me? It's your turn. Read your letter… Everybody shut up and be quiet! Morgan's going to read her letter."

Morgan, only twelve at the time, took out her letter and began reading. Through a crackly voice, I could see she was trying to be strong, which made me wince in pain for her having to go through this.

"Dad, you are so mean to mom. I do not like what you have done to my family…" Morgan bravely read on, and finally, looked at me.

"I am so sorry, Morgan. I came here to find a way to be peaceful. It's Christmas, and I just wanted to be nice to…"

"BULL SHIT!" Gigi interrupted. "You've done nothing, but screw the children and me out of our due."

"Are you trying to say that you have been victimized by me?" I asked.

"YES!" they all shouted back in unison.

What a mistake to speak out, I told myself. *Don't react. Keep quiet. Just listen.*

"We want to know, what are you going to pay Gigi to end this?" Jack demanded. "'Cause, I'm warning you, if you don't get this resolved tonight, I am going to take matters into my own hands."

Another threat. How many times was he going to say that? It had been over an hour since I walked in the door, and I was not sure why this should continue. No way was it going the way that I had intended.

"Let's call it a night," I said. "We tried, and obviously, it's not working out." I got up from the table and began to walk towards the door, when her mom got up and literally blocked my exit.

"Oh no you're not, you chicken shit," Carolyn spat out, practically right in my face. Inside, I felt invincible, so I sat right back down, wanting to show how I was willing to comply with their wishes.

"So, let's continue," Gigi barked. "Maya, tell your Dad what you have to say to him."

"Dad," Maya began with all the strength she could muster up at 19, "I'm so disappointed in you."

"I'm so sorry," I replied. "Let's find some time to talk about it?" I suggested.

"YOU'RE NOT SORRY!" Gigi suddenly screeched at the top of her lungs. Her face had turned bright red and purple as she began a tirade filled with expletives. This outburst was so venomous, Maya and Morgan left the room, thank God! *How can I, too, escape this insanity?* I wondered. Finally, Gigi got back on point and turned to her middle daughter.

"Sophia! Sophia, I'm talking to you. It's your turn. What do you want to say to your dad?" she demanded.

"Dad, last night after you took my soccer coach and me to dinner, he told me that he would have traveled across the country to see all my games, and you, you could only make a few a year," she read. At 17, she sounded extremely reluctant to be playing out this travesty of a Christmas meeting.

"I would have loved to be here for all your games, sweetheart..." I replied. I was beginning to feel sick at this point. Even though everyone in Gigi's family seemed to be enjoying the drama, all I could think about was, *God please allow this to end.* But I forced myself to stay on track and told myself, *Send love, forgive, be strong, listen.*

"If you don't get this straightened out, Adam, I'm going to take matters into my own hands," Jack repeated for the tenth time.

"You keep saying that, Jack. But this is not about you. It's about the children. And Gigi," I finally retorted. "When you threatened the family a few years ago with physical violence, I forgave you. I knew you were going through a tough time with your divorce, so I forgave you, I forgave you, I forgave you! We all make mistakes."

His head hung low, a moment of guilt. But just for a moment, as he fired back, "So you screwed your family."

"Jack, I have made many mistakes, that's true. But when you broke into your ex-wife's house in the middle of the night and confronted her boyfriend in rage with a knife in his face, was that not a mistake?" I added in a cool firm tone. With Jack, I knew it was best to be forthright and strong. I could see him weakened by some inner conflict within himself. Then, addressing all the adults in the room, I told them, "We all make mistakes." To my surprise, they all remained quiet and only muttered to themselves. Some, in spite of themselves, even nodded in agreement.

Emotionally exhausted, with no hope of peace, I saw in this brief period of quiet my chance to announce that I was leaving. Slowly, calmly, I got up from the table. Jack broke the silence.

"Adam, if you don't take care of Gigi, I am going to take matters into my own hands."

"Jack, I heard you the first ten times. Are you trying to threaten me? What are you going to do, beat me up? Hire someone to kill me?" I asked, incredulously.

"I would not give anyone the pleasure of killing you," Gigi yelled. "I would do it with my own hands!" Suddenly she took a couple of steps to lunge at my face with her fingernails, but I retreated, faced her down, and she retreated.

I called the children back into the room, and said I was going, and told them, "I had come to make peace, but obviously I had not succeeded. That person that your mother and her family described, I'm not that man anymore. That man is dead. Instead, your new father is in a place of love and fun." I then gave them all a group hug, but they were so numb and tired of the whole thing, they could not really respond. With everyone on their feet silently watching, I staggered out the door into the night. I had survived two hours in hell.

I managed to make it back to the hotel, jumped into a hot shower, and for the next thirty minutes with water pouring over me, I wept uncontrollably. I had held to my truth, and that's the best anyone could do, I told myself. As I tucked myself into bed, I immersed myself in the welcoming silence. It brought to mind the silence that Bobby had spoken of in his story of Christmas, which reminded me that we are all always surrounded with love if we would only listen.

I had planned to stay four days, but I only stayed two. All the gifts that I had carefully brought for them I left at the hotel, and told Sophia to pick them up. I couldn't bear to return to Gigi's house.

Back in California, I told Lizanne and my mother everything, and they were so supportive. They knew I had come from a place of love, and gradually, I felt looming up from within a powerful sense of well-being. In spite of my ordeal, I had held to truth and love, and had survived my own crucifixion. Just in time for Christmas, I was reborn with my head high, shoulders back, and heart open. I was a new man.

12

EARTHKEEPER

Coming Home

I couldn't wait to sink into one of those plush chairs at the Country Club, drink in hand, to unwind after a long business meeting. Ever since I was a child around seven, going home was something to do at the last possible moment because with my parents so busy with their careers, coming home meant loneliness. So, as a kid, I'd go out on my bike, find my own friends, and we'd go exploring up in the mountains to amuse ourselves. It was fun.

At the same time, however, a deep hunger for intimacy continued to plague me, which gave rise to my old emotional pain called "separation." Marrying Gigi, I had hoped, would satisfy in me a sense of belonging, but she, too, was always busy with her own affairs and the mothering of our kids, so once again, I felt left out on my own. It was not her fault, of course, because I picked her to marry, thus (unconsciously) repeating a familiar pattern of alienation that had started in my youth.

All these thoughts raced through my head as I was driving to the Club because something felt different. There was a shift in my life-long habits... I didn't want to go to the Club; I wanted to go home!

After our first trip to Peru, Lizanne and I spent more and more time together until we were practically living together. It felt so natural, but it was causing changes to life-long habits. Suddenly, I realized that to go home meant that I would be warmly greeted! If I had problems in my head, just to be with her would make them evaporate. Before I knew it, I was making a U-turn away from the Club. Home was where I belonged.

Once, on a particularly cold evening in the midst of winter, Lizanne and I were having a rare spat. Her sister was going to stay over, which was fine with me, except that she had not checked with me first. The "independence of woman" and "control issues" had come up, and the argument put us both in a funk.

"C'mon, let's do it. Let's connect," Lizanne said, as she came up right in front of me.

"What're you talking about?" I replied in a sour mood.

"You know. It will make us feel better."

I knew exactly what she was referring to. It started a couple of months ago after we had been initiated into the Munay Rites. Inspired by putting our foreheads together with the shaman during those initiations, I had spontaneously suggested to Lizanne a crazy idea.

"Let's put *our* foreheads together, except this would be for our own intimacy," I told her. She looked at me quizzically, and I got defensive. "Is this too weird? I…just an idea. After all, Munay means love," I muttered to myself. She just stared at me another moment.

She finally spoke, "why don't we first take three breaths together? As a matter of fact, why don't I put my hands on your shoulders, like this, and you… put your hands here on my side, like you're holding my heart."

"Okay."

"*Now*, we're ready to put our foreheads together," she said. We closed our eyes, took three slow, deep breaths together, and gently placed our foreheads together. It was as if our third eyes were kissing. I felt a "hum," an electrical vibration that made us feel profoundly connected.

From then on, we adopted this little ritual. Instantly, we would tune into the sacredness of our relationship. Now, in my funk from our spat, I went along with her suggestion, breathed deeply, and put our foreheads together. Sure enough, after a few minutes, all my tensions dissolved.

"I've never felt so connected with anyone," she told me as she looked deep into my eyes.

I nodded in agreement and kissed her head. "Thanks for the suggestion. I feel great now, thanks to you." The solidity of our relationship allowed me to relax into the life I was destined to live.

The Holy Mountain

Before long we were off to Peru to receive the final three initiations into the "High Rites of the Munay-Ki," #7 of the Earth Keeper, #8 of the Star Keeper, and #9, the "God Rite."

With this trip back to Peru, we had a much better sense of what to expect, even as we kept open with no assumptions. Once again we found ourselves in Cusco at the same time of year, June–July. The group consisted mostly of those already experienced with this work, some of whom I recognized from our trip before. For me, it felt like coming home. Along with the Indian Nation, Peru had fast turned into a destination for pilgrimage.

In the morning, we left Cusco and continued on our journey into the expanse of the valley. Then, maneuvering through winding dirt roads, we trudged up and over high mountain passes until we reached a high plain at 13,000 feet elevation. The terrain was barren and rocky, with llamas grouped here and there among a scattering of white snow patches. Finally, after eight bouncy hours, we arrived at our base camp, which consisted of fifteen tents.

We settled in our "lodging," two per tent, and right before nightfall, we gathered outside in the open air for a simple dinner as we marveled at vistas of towering mountain peaks that lost their tips in clouds. When the sun set, we took the cue and retired for the night. For many in our group, as for Lizanne and me, it was challenging to get acclimated to the altitude. Though exhausted, we both had slight headaches and slept badly, but seasoned from our last trip, we took it all in stride.

In the morning, I was again impressed with the rarified air of the Holy Mountain. Alberto gathered us together in a circle to give us an orientation of upcoming events. The optimal environment for these initiations, he remarked, was in the mountains of the Andes at an elevation of over 15,000 feet. He offered the choice for each of us to either ascend the "feminine" mountain of Salkantay, or the "masculine" one of Ausangate.

We chose to go to Ausangate because, for me, I had been working on rebalancing my masculine energy by offering it in service to the Divine Feminine.

Alberto introduced us to the four *alto mesayoks*, master shamans of the high holy mountains who, we were told, were "connected to the stars." Leading the way was the elder of the Q'ero Nation, Don Umberto, who looked especially auspicious dressed in the vibrant reds and yellows of the traditional tunic. Radiant and youthful, he was in his sixties, and exuded a deep kindness. Accompanying him was his wife, Doña Bernadina, a master shaman in her own right.

Our first outing for the day was a short hike from our base camp up the valley towards the mountain. We would climb up only 500 feet maximum to allow us time to acclimate. After the grueling hike last year where I had to be helped down, I felt prepared physically and psychologically for anything.

The next day, clear, warm, and sunny, we were ready for the Initiation. Twenty-five men and women from all around the world gathered around as Alberto presented to us wisdom secrets passed down for generations from the ancient Incans. He had adapted them so that they would be compatible to contemporary life.

"Today marks a new day in our journey. For the first time ever, we are here to receive the first of the 'High Rites' of the Munay-Ki," Alberto said with a sense of joy and pride. "They're designed to be revealed now, during our current period of accelerated change for personal healing and transformation. These rites will upgrade your energetic field and re-inform your DNA, enabling you to grow a new body—one that ages, heals, and dies differently. They will help you transform into the new human, the *Homo Luminous*."

At the mention of that term, a chill went up my back. I looked at Lizanne, but no words needed to be spoken.

"Today, the Seventh Rite, the Rite of Earth Keeper, will be bestowed upon each of you," Alberto continued in his gentle tone. "You will be entrusted with a great responsibility to attend to the needs of mother earth. From a grain of sand to the towering tress, you will tend to the land and well-being of our humanity. The *Pachamama*, our earth mother, speaks to us today."

Alberto looked all around in that pristine landscape, deeply inhaling the crisp air.

"It was not long ago that I could look around these holy mountains and see the great glaciers. Today they are no more. The prophecies long ago spoke that the end of time would follow the melting of the ice. That time is upon us now."

Does this mark the end of life as I know it? I asked myself.

"Today we mark not an ending, but a beginning," said Alberto, as if he had heard my silent question. "The moment has come, now, to shed our past and embrace our destiny."

With Alberto beside him, Don Umberto then stepped forward, and the ceremony began. With all of us around him in a circle, Don Umberto called out in Q'ero the winds of the Four Directions. Then he crouched down and placed both palms firmly on the ground. Following his example, we all did the same. While kneeling, I thanked Mother Earth for holding us on her belly.

Then, back on our feet, we reached for the sky, asking for the love and light of our Heavenly Father to shine upon us now. Soon, Don Umberto came around to face each one of us in the group, and one by one, recited a sacred blessing.

Finally, he leaned forward and gently put his forehead to mine. An intense force shot through me from the base of my backbone, through my spine, and out the top of my head like a lightning bolt! I began to totter. I couldn't remain on my feet and fell back down to the earth on my knees. Dazed, I held the earth, overwhelmed with love, with forces beyond my control, as my whole face, mouth, and nose was planted in the soil.

For a few minutes, I couldn't move and remained motionless, until finally I was able to slowly get back to my feet, at which time Doña Bernadina began gently hitting me all over my body, chest, and head with her "mesa," her medicine bag, that looked like a red embroidered pillow with all her power objects wrapped inside. Following Don Umberto around the circle, she was administering the *Humpe* for giving each of us a blessing and for opening our bodies to receive the transmission of the Earth Keeper energy.

Jaguar Lagoon

The next day was also clear and cool. Without much thought, I began the ascent with the others, knowing only that we were going to climb another 1,500 feet in elevation to a new base camp at 15,500 feet. Here we would find our next destination, the Jaguar Lagoon.

As I climbed, I felt energized, but everything felt surreal and seemed to move in slow motion. Though many of us felt dreamy, we had to stay grounded because the trail with all its switchbacks and crumbly rocks could be treacherous should one slip and fall.

Alberto stopped a few times along the way to allow people to rest, meditate, and take in the awesome scenery. Way below, I could see patches of white…llamas. As we trudged up the trail, Alberto made it clear that we were in no hurry, as our party gradually began to spread out.

As we trekked onwards and upwards, I began counting those key people who had so helped me in my own transformation, my personal "angels." There was Lizanne, my beloved companion through life, who I considered the angel of the heart. Lila, who helped me so much when I was plunged in the dark abyss of "separation," I considered to be an angel of light. Then there was Gigi, who mirrored my own materialistic delusions that had been killing me, and inadvertently forced the death of the "old Adam"; she I saw as the angel of death. Now, on this sacred mountain, there was Alberto who had been opening me up to my own Godhood, and showing me the way to my mission in life as an EarthKeeper; he I saw was the angel of transformation.

The gratitude I felt for my angels! How could I ever repay them? The only way, I mused to myself, was to share my gifts to the world just like they did for me. In this airy terrain, my resolve to do this deepened down to my core. Wistfully, I looked out at the endless expanse of the majestic terrain punctuated with snow-clad peaks and felt how its radiance was a reflection of my own inner radiance. I most certainly will honor the sacred responsibility of being an Earth Keeper, I promised myself.

Finally, towards the end of the day, we had climbed to 15,500 feet, where we set up camp. I was happy to notice that I was breathing like normal; I had acclimated. During a light meal of quinoa, night descended, and everyone retired for the evening. Lizanne and I stepped away from the camp to take in the nighttime view. With no lights for miles, and the high altitude, the presence of the dizzying array of stars felt so close that I could *feel* their vibration. So many stars, so bright, so…alive! For long minutes, we just stood there speechless under the Southern Cross.

"*Chaska*. That's who you are," Lizanne said, breaking the silence.

"What?"

"You know, *Chaska*, the name of that spiritual warrior of the Star Nation," she explained. I smiled.

The next day, we continued our ascent. It became more difficult to breathe with air so pure and thin, and chilly in the low 40s. Thank God that it wasn't in the teens as it was during the night. By now, many hikers were struggling to keep up, but fortunately for Lizanne and me, we were in good physical condition. Fueled by enthusiasm, we were able to keep trudging up the mountain, step by step. Feeling a bit dreamy again, I felt as if we were reaching the outer limits of physical life.

In the afternoon we all reached our destination and embraced in celebration. 16,000 feet! We were "on top of the world," nearly as high as trekkers go in the the Himalayas. What a feeling of accomplishment! We looked out across the panorama all around, and at Ausangate, the place where Heaven and Earth come together. It had taken nearly a day of hiking (not to mention my whole life) to reach this holy destination.

We camped out near the Jaguar Lagoon, fed by an underground glacier-fed stream. Considered by the shamans to be the purest water on the planet, it would be here that we would receive the next rite, that of the Star Keepers.

I made my way down the gentle slope to the lagoon, which was perhaps 150 feet in diameter and filled with turquoise water. Dropping to my knees, I saw my own reflection and was surprised at who was looking back.

He looked so innocent! I had been hunting my own true self, and there, finally, I found an image of him in the reflection, and he looked so pure.

Getting down further, I lay face down on the ground to feel the full impact of Mother Earth, and felt her nurturing love rise out of the rocky surface to permeate every cell in my body. *Wait a minute*, I thought, *isn't this supposed to be a masculine mountain? Yes*, a voice answered, *it's the masculine welcoming the guidance of the feminine so as to serve her better.*

That evening during my meditation, I felt connected to the community of Wisdom Keepers, Earth Keepers, and Star Keepers that have existed throughout millennia. I felt as prepared as ever for receiving the next initiation of the Star Keepers.

The next day, Marcela took us to an even higher pool of water, the Rainbow Lagoon, one of the most elevated bodies of water on earth. Legend has it that the great shamans and the wizards of the Four Winds consider the lagoon as home. We were there to receive its powers as we conducted the Star Keeper Rite. In preparing us for this ceremony, Alberto had told us that, "Star Keepers are the liaison between the earth and the star nations. This rite will keep you safe even after the great planetary changes are upon us, as designated by the Mayan calendar of 2012. When you receive this rite, you begin to evolve from *homo sapiens* to *Homo Luminous*. Your aging process is slowed, and you heal much faster, for you will be working on energetic levels."

In similar fashion as during the last rite, we all received our transmissions of power.

After the initiation, everyone descended, but I remained behind. By myself, I recited an invocation to enter Sacred Space and carefully took out my bag of high-desert sage tobacco that the Indian elder, Gus, had given me a few years back. I had always been deeply moved by the powerful sweat lodge he had guided me through where he had even taken on some of my toxins. To fulfill his request that I smoke the tobacco "beside a body of water," I, having prepared accordingly, brought along his sacred tobacco plus a wood and silver pipe I had gotten from Thailand.

I placed the tobacco into the bowl and lit it gently. Puffs of smoke wafted into the air and blew back into my face. Then I felt a presence floating near me as a most subtle pressure on my face. The smoke seemed to coalesce into an image, a person, someone I recognized.

"Gus?" I said silently. I could see even with my eyes open that it was indeed Gus, looking inscrutable as ever.

"Thank you for bringing my spirit here," he replied, silently, although it was as clear as if he had spoken out loud.

"I didn't know you'd be around."

"I'm here so my spirit can pass on. I am grateful. I am home."

I was surprised to hear him say that *this* was his home, but accepted it.

"This is the place of the rainbow of life," he continued. It made me think of the stunning rainbows that I had experienced at Mitten during my Vision Quest.

"May you continue to walk the path of beauty," he said. "I see your light. There is fullness in your colors. The moment has come. Take your place among the Earth Keepers. Live your life in joy and love."

With that, his image dissolved away like dissipating smoke, and became one with the crisp air. I couldn't help but look around for any visible signs of spirits, and found no one but myself. Alone again, I sat completely still, deeply moved, and reviewed every word he had spoken. He seemed to have become a part of my lineage of ancestral fathers and, thus, a part of me. He, of the red earth, had given me one of the great gifts of my spiritual journey, the richness of blood, soil, and vitality.

I saw Gus as among the great shamans and angels supporting the journey of all souls on the path of transcendence. My heart felt like it could burst with gratitude beyond words. Tears welled as I sat there trying to assimilate the indescribable.

The sun got lower, the clouds swirled, and the temperature dropped. Finally, after twenty minutes, I got myself to my feet to descend to join the others.

"I love you, Gus. May your journey with infinity be ever so sweet."

(Jumping ahead a couple of months later, I learned that at the same moment that I had perceived Gus's image, he had indeed passed on to the spirit world. I had returned to Canyon de Chelly to meet him for another session in his sweat lodge, only to find out that he had died in his sleep.

Though saddened, I knew that death did not really exist, and that he was fine following his destiny in the spiritual domain.)

The Silver Road Initiation

Back at our base camp after we had trekked down from the Rainbow Lagoon, we barely had time to catch our breath before we prepared ourselves for initiation into the ninth, and final, rite, the *Titanchie*, or God Rite. For this, both Alberto and Don Umberto were going to lead.

In the late afternoon, we gathered together for the rite. While waiting in a circle for the ceremony to begin, I consciously breathed deeply to calm myself. Too much excitement was not good for such events. It had been perfectly clear all day, but now, approaching sundown, the temperature seemed to drop fifteen degrees in just a few minutes. The wind began to blow, clouds covered over us, and thunderclouds suddenly rumbled to life. Before we knew it, we found ourselves pelted by hailstones nearly the size of golf balls!

Racing into one of the large tents, we found our refuge and waited to see what would happen. Thud, THUD, thud! Those hailstones hit the tent. We had all been prepared for rain, but this was something else. Luckily, after about ten minutes, the hail stopped as quickly as it had started, and we all scrambled back outside, arranged ourselves in a circle, and waited for the ceremony to begin.

Alberto glanced up at the sky, then urged everyone to keep focused on the mission at hand, and tune in to the energy of Ausangate, the Holy Mountain. His words were accented by distant thunder:

"This ninth rite is the *Titanchie*, God Rite. It will awaken your God-nature. When you receive it, you will share as a caretaker, along with Spirit, all of creation from the smallest grain of sand to the largest galaxy. These rites have been transmitted many times from Spirit to human, but until now, they've never been available to be shared human to human. Though we are here to guide you, open yourself to receive the transmission direct from Spirit. They are God-given, and as such, belong to no one and must be shared freely."

Thunder again rolled in the distance, but we all stood silent, focused on the potency of Alberto's words. There was a special reverence in his voice as he spoke. He exchanged a glance with Don Umberto, who moved to the first person in the circle as Alberto stood there "holding the space."

As I stood awaiting my turn for the initiation, I prayed that I'd be open to its power, and felt deep gratitude for being able to receive this rite. Tears welled up in my eyes, and then... Don Umberto was before me. For a moment, he looked at me with unconditional love and kindness, and then he opened his arms high to the sky. My heart was beating strongly. Speaking softly to himself, Don Umberto blew prayers into the top of my head, placed one hand over his own heart and the other on my belly, and then blew more prayers. This routine he repeated a couple more times.

Finally, he held his hand over the top of my head. I felt as if I were being lifted out of my body like a feather into another realm. In an altered state, I could only surrender to whatever happened because everything thereafter was beyond my conscious awareness. The next thing I knew, our foreheads were pressed together. After a few moments, he moved on to the next person, leaving me in a daze. Silently, I stood there and easily surrendered to whatever happened and was happening.

About an hour after we had started, all the initiations were over, and we all scrambled inside the large mess tent because it had begun to rain in earnest. The temperature had dropped close to freezing.

Inside the tent, everyone was very quiet as we warmed up with our quinoa soup. Seeing Alberto, I walked over and gave him a warm embrace, all in silence; no words needed to be said. After supper, as Lizanne and I went back to our tent, we were again mesmerized by the billions of stars. I felt as if my entire body had been infused with newfound consciousness, and suddenly, I sensed the profundity of the gift of being an Earth Keeper. And the responsibility. *I must share this gift with the world*, I told myself. Afterwards, in our tent, I sat with Lizanne for long, rich minutes, but few words were exchanged. To speak of what happened would do nothing but dilute its power.

The next day, the sun was out, adding to our high spirits. During breakfast, Alberto made an announcement to all of us in a ceremonial manner.

"The time had come, the deed was done. For the first time, human-to-human, the Nine Rites of the Munay-Ki have been released. The leap from *homo sapiens* to *Homo Luminous* has officially begun."

With our mission accomplished, we all gathered our belongings to begin our descent down the mountain. I relished every step and took in the expansive vistas as if I belonged there, which, in a way, I did. At one point, Alberto, walking beside me, said with a grin, "Looks like you're no longer a half-baked human, Adam. You've been fully cooked."

I looked at him with a smile, "Looks like the eagle has landed."

Still smiling, I snaked my way down the trails with all the others. How I appreciated this physical activity after all the transcendent experiences I had undergone. With every step, I could assimilate their power into my body. With every step, I was massaging my beloved Mother Earth, as she in turn, appreciating my love and respect for her, seduced me with her beauty and glory. My role as an Earth Keeper was turning into not only a calling, but also a love affair.

How different it was coming down the mountain compared to the laborious effort it took to go up. Now, I felt as if I were floating downstream with no effort required. With a newfound lightness of being, I followed all the switchbacks through the barren terrain. Rounding a bend, I saw patches of white shining bright against the greenish brown landscape. Some were snow, and some were llamas. We were fast descending. Upon reaching base camp we were greeted by a swarm of children. They all lit up with joy. Their warm hearts touched me deeply. I handed out some candy and shared in the sweetness of life.

Red Tail Ranch, Big Sur

After returning from Peru, I got back to my routine in Malibu, wondering how the Munay-Ki rites would affect my daily life. More to the point, I pondered what specific form my role as an Earth Keeper could take. In dealing with real estate conventions, I knew to use the term "steward"—one who loves, maintains, and cultivates the land—rather than Earth Keeper, which may sound alien to people ("You going back to being a naked Indian?" I could hear them say.) As a "steward" to a piece of land, then, whatever development was necessary would be kept to a minimum so as to preserve pristine nature for the general good.

A while before, I had made the distinction between *fate* and *destiny*. With fate, the "world dreams me," and I would remain somewhat passive in manifesting my aspirations. With destiny, on the other hand, "I dream the world into being, in concert with the force of nature," a much more active role. With destiny, I don't seek, I find. In my reckoning, this required action on my part, and so I began exploring the central California coastline for possible land to steward. Being aligned with Spirit, I reminded myself, allows the impossible to happen.

A broker who knew of my passion for stewardship told me about a ranch in Big Sur. It had been homesteaded since the turn of the last century and had been cared for by the same family for close to a hundred years. But now this family was willing to sell, depending on who the buyer might be.

I went with the broker to check out the land, and I was stunned—the grandeur, the magnificence in every respect! The ranch was situated on 385 acres of pristine beauty, two groves of redwood trees, a 200-degree view of the ocean, 19 natural springs, two natural waterfalls, and an oceanfront of one-and-a-half miles along the Pacific Ocean!

After I saw the ranch, my brain reeled with possibilities, apprehensions, humility, and excitement. It had only been four months since Peru, and already, this came into my life. Is this what it means to be a co-creator with Spirit? Talk about synchronicity, what unseen hand had been orchestrating this find?

However, I also knew to take things one step at a time. After nearly a quarter century in the real estate business, I knew that there are many obstacles to overcome before such a property can change hands, the first being whether the owner even wanted to sell it to me. The broker had already warned me that he was an opinionated, eccentric sort who could be wildly unpredictable in his moves.

Then there was the consideration of their original asking price, $22 million. That's a lot of money. But first things first: I'd meet the owner. If the ranch were meant to be mine, it would happen. Trust, detachment, clarity of intent—these were the qualities that I held to now.

Late in the afternoon in November, I drove to Big Sur and met the owner at the ranch. Dressed in overalls, looking like a farmer, Stan, 84 years old, physically fit and sharp as a whip, checked me out. Mincing no words, he let me know how he scorned developers and despised government intrusion. *Oh-oh, I was a developer,* I said to myself. He also told me how his family came to the area long ago in the late 1800s as homesteaders, attracted by the wildness of the land. Everything on the land they had built with their own hands.

"Right around the corner over there, my folks constructed their own house way back in 1919. You saw it. Still standing," he told me, proudly. "No highway back in those days—that didn't come till '39—so had to walk two miles just to get to the nearest town. Raised pigs, cows, and barley, that's two days over the mountain to take everything to market. Lived off the land, independent, and self-reliant, we were. Not like people nowadays, getting the government to do everything for them as they sit on their ass leeching off the rest of us. No wonder the whole country is turning soft with all their damn liberal subsidies."

We talked on for two hours, and all the time, I could sense him assessing me, wondering what kind of man I was. He had a good poker face; I could read little of his true intentions, but I sensed that in selling this property, he wasn't so much interested in money as he was in finding the right person to do right by the land.

"So, why you here?" (*That question again! First with all those Indians, and now this guy,* I said to myself.) "What're you going to do with all this property? Build condos?" he asked derisively.

"Hell no. I like it just the way it is, off the grid. I intend to be a steward of this property, keep its natural beauty away from developers and land subdividers. I no longer view the world in fragments. It's the whole that matters now. As a matter of fact, the first thing I'd do if I had the land," I told him with a flamboyant gesture, "is to cut the damn phone lines!"

In spite of himself, he let out one belch of a laugh, then quickly resumed his poker face. In that moment, I knew we had connected.

Feeling great after that first meeting, I met with him off and on, and negotiated with his broker, who told me that Stan was "pleased with me." After several months clarifying and agreeing to issues, we went into a long, nine-month escrow period. I needed that extra time, I explained to them, because I had a lot of work to do to find out as much as I could about the land, like getting it surveyed, assessing the septic tanks and the quality of water in the natural springs. It would cost me tens of thousands of dollars, but it was essential to get all my facts and stats straight, since, in that time, I would also need to find a partner.

Also, there were 40 tons of abandoned cars, metal working tools, old concrete, and rusty farm equipment (and a pile of bent nails three feet high!) built up over a 89-year period of homesteading that had to be gotten rid of in order to return the land to its pristine beauty.

Through the months, I would tell Stan more of my plans—fruit orchards, organic gardens, cleaning of the non-indigenous trees—and he would reveal colorful old stories of how it used to be during the Depression, and gradually, we gained a deep mutual respect for each other.

Meanwhile, I had the daunting task of finding a financial partner. I made calls, and instinctively, focused on Silicon Valley and Hollywood as the place for prospective investors with the financial clout for my purposes. Supplementing my calls, I placed straightforward ads in a business journal in Silicon Valley and in *Daily Variety* for show business people. Along with a few photos of the land, I had a few terse descriptions: *Red Tail Ranch*, Lopez Point, Big Sur; 1.5 miles of oceanfront, sweeping ocean and mountain views, three ranch estates, redwoods, oaks, springs, waterfalls…. off the grid.

After a few months, I received no serious offers and had a brief moment of doubt, "Can I really pull this off?" But immediately, I got back on center by reminding myself that my job was to "show up," do what I had to do, and let Spirit handle the rest. I had taken to working with a CD, *Create the Work You Love, the Art of Manifestation* by Rick

Jarow, Ph.D. It helped me to keep centered on my inner vision with clarity, courage, and drive, and let the outcome unfold as it will.

A month later, I got a call from someone who I knew casually from previous business dealings, and who was also a member in my Club.

"Looks like you've got an amazing piece of property. Tell me about it."

So I told him about the glories of the land, and my recent discoveries. It had been listed as 285 acres, but after my survey, we found that it was actually 385 acres, one hundred more than we first thought! What's more, after lawyers went over the Title Report, we found out it wasn't just one parcel, but actually *five* parcels, which gave us so much more freedom on how to work the land. Things were simply getting better and better.

I showed the potential partner the land, and after the first visit, he said, "I'll do it." Just like that! It fulfilled what he had been looking for: a special place to bring his family, a shrewd business deal, and the idea of leaving a legacy for our kids and grandchildren. We negotiated various points, and three months later, we closed the deal. Simple! A perfect partner.

Shortly thereafter, escrow closed without a hitch. I was the proud steward of Red Tail Ranch! Enthusiastically, I threw myself into all that needed to be done: complete remodeling of the existing house, including a new electrical system, plumbing with water from springs, increasing the water storage to four times its capacity, and of course, removing those forty tons of concrete and metal waste, bent nails and all.

We hired a full-time caretaker for the land. My partner and I began to restore, preserve, conserve, and revitalize the land—being stewards. I was elated, my dream of being an Earth Keeper was manifesting so simply. How grateful I felt toward my co-creating partner, Spirit. The magnificence of the outer world was reflecting all the deep changes in my inner world. Lizanne brought her special gifts to the major remodel of the dilapidated ranch house. She furnished the interiors with the perfect blend of comfort and elegance.

Stan and his brother were delighted watching how the land was shaping up. We had become quite friendly to the point of us casting a bronze plaque to honor their entire family for their pioneering spirit. This we embedded in a concrete wall on an auspicious spot on the property:

George and Esther Harlan and Their Sons
Eugene, Donald, and Stanley
Honored This Land from 1919 to 2007
God Bless This Land Forever in Their Memory

Inauguration Day

About a year and a half after I bought the land, in February, I had been working on a water-sharing arrangement with our neighbor, the Packards. Way up in the wilderness above the ranch, I investigated the upper watershed as I rode on my trusty All Terrain Vehicle (ATV). I loved these sturdy, 4-wheel-drive vehicles, about the size and weight of a couple of monster motorcycles, with their large wheels that allowed me to climb up and down steep inclines as they bounced over bumpy terrain.

After traveling a dirt mountain road up and up for about two miles, I found myself on a ridge 1,500 feet above the ranch house. What a view. It was a cool, overcast winter day, and the scent of the grass, still wet from the rains of the day before, was intoxicating. After a few minutes drinking it all in, I decided to head off the road down the ridge away from the ranch.

On this side, I could admire the raw beauty of the hillside. I slowed down to take it all in when the ATV began to slip sideways on the wet grass. Then, at its steep sideways angle, it started to shudder in strain. In a flash, I sobered up to reality—*The ATV is going to flip over!*

Instinctively, I leapt desperately into the air, barely clearing the ATV, and landed heavily onto the earth. Searing pain. I screamed! I had felt something snap my shinbone and tear ligaments and nerves just below my kneecap. Meanwhile, I heard the ATV whip through bushes, tumbling until it disappeared over a ledge. A moment of silence, then CRASH!

Disorientated, I realized my face was smashed into the earth with dirt crammed up my nostrils. With the full weight of my body, I had fallen onto the side of my head, twisting it at an angle that left me in excruciating pain…and with a broken collarbone. I tried to move, but found that my right leg felt like a limp piece of rubber. With the burning pain in my collarbone, I could not move my right arm. In short, I was practically paralyzed on my whole right side.

In spite of my agony, I forced myself to assess my predicament. *I'm on the other side of the ridge, off the beaten paths. How would anyone ever know I'm here?* There was less then three more hours of sunlight. The temperature, now in the mid 40s, would fast descend close to freezing at night. My leg and shoulder had already blown up like a balloon from the swelling. No cell phones in the ranch. Suddenly, I remembered that a few weeks before, a mountain lion had left a deer carcass not a quarter mile from the ranch house. In a flash of terror, I realized that this could really be the end—that I could very well die up here.

Immediately, I knew it was not the lion I should be concerned about; it was the potential meltdown of my psyche and determination to survive. Forcibly, I ordered myself to attune to Spirit. With all the profound training I had undergone over the past few years, I could not believe that I would be allowed to perish in the wilderness because of some "unfortunate" accident. *There are no mistakes.*

In an instant, another force seemed to take over. In an altered state, I knew only that I must make it to the top of the ridge. In no way would I lie here passively. Didn't I just declare that I am a man of destiny by being pro-active with my intents? The terrain that lay around me was filled with pointed rocks and thickets with little barbs; regardless, painfully, I started to squirm up the ridge on my left side.

The scratches from the rocks and barbs began to tear through my shirt and skin, drawing blood, which seeped through my shirt. These lacerations were becoming more painful than my broken bones. Rocking back and forth, inch by inch, I worked myself up towards the ridge. In a dreamy mood, I would suffer a moment of utter pain, but when it subsided, I would slip back into my altered state. After a laborious hour, I finally made it to the ridge and caught my breath. Looking over the Pacific, I knew I had another couple of hours left before sundown. It had rained in the morning and threatened more all day, but now rainclouds began to build.

Determined to get to the ranch and a phone, I began my descent down the hill by grasping the wet grass and slithering over the earth like a snake. Every so often, I would lose my balance and roll over a few times as my leg and shoulder exploded in pain. I screamed and struggled to regain my composure. The sun was lower, so it became a race between me reaching the ranch and the sun reaching the horizon.

After another hour and a half, I reached the dirt road that marked the top of the ranch. On the road, I tried to hop on one leg, but the shots of agony exhausted me after only one jump. I thought of dragging myself along the road, but with my body already bleeding from stones and barbs, it would be unbearable. I had to continue through the grass and thickets. Anyway, it would be a more direct route, I told myself. *Onward!* I demanded willfully.

As I made my way down, my spirits lifted briefly. I could barely see the ranch house about a mile away and a thousand feet below. A bird gently floated over me towards the house. "If I could fly, I'd be there in a few minutes," I told myself, "but alas, I'm only able to crawl, belly in the dirt, like a half-paralyzed snake." Accepting my fate, I forced myself to continue squirming down the hill in my race with the sun. Through the overcast sky, I could sense how the day was getting darker, so I focused on nothing but my mantra, "I am going to make it off this mountain."

After twenty minutes, I was able to crawl about a hundred feet below the road, and took a brief rest. I refused to give in to my pain and exhaustion. Suddenly, I heard the rumblings of a truck! I looked back up to the road and saw my neighbor, Bob, coming around the bend. He was the caretaker of the Packard ranch, and a living inspiration when it came to being a true steward of the land. One of the finest persons I had ever met, he was always willing to lend a helping hand, and here he was looking like a Santa with a Pendleton shirt, the jolliest St. Nick I had ever seen. Mustering all my strength, I yelled and yelled.

Finally, he heard the shouting, saw the half-mangled person clutching the grass. He came down the hill to size up the situation. Startled, he asked, "Adam? Is that you?"

"Bob, thank God," I said as I labored to catch my breath.

"What happened? What's broken?" he asked.

"My right leg and shoulder," I whispered, fighting off excruciating pain.

"Let's get you in the truck." With that, he climbed back up the hill and drove the truck as close as possible. Very gently, he picked me up to put me into the front seat, as I screamed in agony all the way.

Slowly, we began bouncing our way down the winding road back towards the house. Every bump exacerbated my torments.

"So lucky that I was driving along this way," he said. "I hadn't come this way for a few weeks, and rarely this late in the day."

"Thank God, Bob. I'm so grateful for you. I really fucked up," I blurted out.

"Let's not worry about that now, Adam," he said, consoling me.

My sense of shame and guilt was building up in me. How could I do such a stupid thing? Going down that steep incline on that ATV when I knew better. And, with no phone, no helmet, at the wrong time, with no one knowing. What arrogance to think that I'm above foolish risks.

When we got to the ranch house, Bob jumped out and got me some water and the phone. I had not had a drop for a long time and felt delirious. As I slumped in the front seat, I called Lizanne.

"Honey, I had an accident. I broke my leg and arm… But I'll be fine." I didn't want to make her worry more, because her mother had just passed away.

"Oh my God, I didn't hear from you, and have been calling and calling," she said frantically. "Where are you now?"

"Bob just saved me. We are at the house, and he's going to take me to the hospital," I said.

"I'm on my way," she said.

Bob and I began the two-hour drive up the winding road towards Monterey. At the emergency hospital, they operated on my leg and screwed it back together. The damage to the ACL and meniscus—the ligament and soft padding under the kneecap—was too much to repair all at once. The shoulder and right arm were repositioned and locked in place with a sling.

Lizanne arrived five hours later.

"I have never been so grateful to see anyone in my life," I told her, as tears rolled down my cheeks. "Actually, I am very lucky, so lucky to be alive." Lizanne wept. Her mother's recent passing plus this added drama was a bit too much for her to take. So, for the next three days, I rested at the hospital and began the slow road to recovery. At the end of that time, Lizanne drove me back to Malibu.

Insights

For the next three months, I was confined to the house to heal. Not a day went by that I did not delve into the deeper implications of this near-fatal experience. I truly could have died. I saw how my masculine arrogance was, yet again, overriding my feminine sensibilities. To ride that ATV off-road took me off-course, physically and psychologically. Wearing no helmet, running off into the wilderness alone with no communication with anyone about where I was going, was just plain arrogance. A bit of foresight could have easily prevented my painful ordeal.

Then I received a pleasant surprise. Alberto had come to visit. I had emailed him about my accident when he was in Australia, but on his way to the East Coast, he decided to detour so that he could pay me a visit and wish me well.

"Brother Alberto, thank you for coming!"

'It's great to be with you," he replied. "So, what's going on?"

"I thought that sometimes it's good to get lost in the wilderness, but I guess this time I took it too far!" I said sheepishly.

"I'll say!" he laughed. "Our journeys into the woods can sometimes get us lost with no way out."

"Yes, but I thought that a guide might *encourage* a student to get lost in order be found. It would retrain him to listen to intuition and not the ego."

"This may be true, but let's remember that when one goes into the wilderness, he must have a guide to begin with," he said. "Second, one's inner voice can often be drowned out by the loud voice of the ego."

"Yeah, that's true," I replied. "I was without guidance and fell prey to my ego who was declaring that I can do just as I please."

As we spoke, I recalled that right before I left the house, I had written a note about where I was going, even as my intuition was saying, "Don't go." I also had failed to call Bob to request permission to cross over to his land. I had seen him earlier going down the highway, and assumed that since he was not home anyway, why bother to call? Both intuition and ego were speaking loud and clear, but I had failed to choose wisely as to whom to follow.

"I would like to recommend a friend from my early days in Peru," Alberto said. "He's a master shaman named Randy. I think you should go see him when you recover."

"Great. I will." I replied.

Four months later, my braces were off, but I was still weak. Considering myself well on the mend, I took a five-day visit to Lake Tahoe to visit Alberto's friend, Randy. One memorable moment occurred on the last morning there.

I had woken that morning to a bright sunny day, and sat in his backyard, musing about "listening with my heart." I liked the idea and immediately began to tune in to the thousand birds that were singing away. Their music entered my ears, of course, but I *felt* them in my heart. After a few minutes, I lost myself in the world of their tweets and twerps. Then I heard a soft voice say to me, "Ask them to come to silence."

Without thinking, I obeyed the request and visualized radiating from my heart a gentle aura of…quietness. Before I knew it, the whole garden was still. No sounds. Silence. It was surreal. How could I have connected with a thousand birds and have them be quiet with me? One little baby chick, however, did not hear my intent, and continued to chirp away. *Ah, it's only a baby,* I told myself, *and will have plenty of time to learn to listen.*

From this experience, I realized that listening is not merely a reactionary sensation, but an art form, a practice that I now refer to as "listening to listen." It would prove important for me as I strove for greater mastery as an Earth Keeper where I would learn to attune to everything in nature from birds to stones to clouds to my fellow humans.

The gifts of that near-fatal day of my accident were beginning to mount: I gained insights on how to listen (and see) with my heart, it brought me face-to-face with my arrogance and hubris, and it increased my faith in the grace of Spirit that allowed me to survive in spite of my foibles.

On another level, I saw my accident as a form of *inauguration*. It was a cleaning up of old karma (arrogance, confusions) so that I'd be more clear and powerful for my role as an Earth Keeper on this land in Big Sur. It was also an initiation to maintain clarity and balance between the physical laws of Mother Nature and the transcendent laws of Spirit. Each world has its own laws, and I don't intend to get them confused ever again.

Back in Malibu, Lizanne and I settled into a new house. One afternoon in autumn, I took in the vista accented by the Santa Ana winds, a balmy breeze that lifted my spirits and promoted the deep knowing that "all's right with the world." A familiar voice interrupted my meditative state, someone from whom I had not heard from for six months.

"Congratulations. You have reclaimed your soul." It was Lila.

For a moment, I listened…from my heart. What she said was true, a gratifying comment that confirmed my own knowing. And yet, another part felt humbled; to "reclaim your soul" seemed to be a concept much bigger than me. *Here I go again, Ping-Ponging between extremes*, I said to myself. "So what's next?" I asked Lila, automatically, although I knew the answer.

"Just be. Just be the light of love that you are," she replied, silently.

Her confirmation made me fill with joy. Yes, all's right with the world. In this lifetime, I have it all. This time, however, unlike some of my previous lives, I will not throw it away.

An Audience with the King

The Red Tail Ranch had become my personal proving ground for my role as an Earth Keeper. The wisdom of the land was deeply held by plants and animals, and I often found myself having conversations with everything from the deer to the condor, from redwood trees to the *amphobis knuts* that live in the swimming hole near the house. On a walk recently, I found an entire snakeskin, a good omen for me to release my old skin to make room for the new. On another jaunt, I had discovered a lion's den with bones of a deer, and scratches on a nearby tree.

On the third anniversary to the day of closing escrow, I went on what had become a little ritual I do alone: a vigorous three- to five-mile hike through the property to connect with the land. Specifics on my calling as an Earth Keeper were solidifying through these walks and through my mesa with its stones (my "Board Meeting," I called it).

By now, I was hiking around the upper portion of the ranch. On a promontory, I could see way out into the Pacific where two whales were heading south to their warm winter home. A hawk flew by, and picking up my pace, I followed its direction through high grass up the hill and over the crest. Something made me slow down. I *sensed* something before I saw anything, and stopped. *Learning to see with my heart?* I conjectured. Gradually, not twenty feet away directly in front of me, I saw a face hidden among the tall grass, checking me out. We locked eyes. *A coyote?* I wondered.

So as not to disturb it, I kept my eyes locked on it as, slowly, I brought my binoculars up to my eyes. I focused and gasped. A moment of terror. Through the binoculars, I could clearly see that it was a mountain lion, the King. Inexplicably, my moment of fear dissolved into exhilaration. It had long been a dream of mine to run across such a magnificent creature. With eyes still locked, I noticed that his legs were crouched, ready to pounce. It had been stalking me for I don't know how long. My Ping Pong ball jumped to the other extreme as thoughts raced across my mind—*Run! That's stupid, it would only pounce on me. Climb the oak tree. More stupidity. It could climb the tree faster and better than me. Hold your ground and stand tall to show you're not afraid...*

Oddly, my fear changed into something strange. All this time that we were eye-to-eye, something had shifted so that I found myself saying silently to the lion, *You're so beautiful. Thank you for appearing before me. I love you.* We were soulfully connected. In love! All this time, the lion did not so much as twitch a whisker. Absolutely motionless on both our parts, we gazed at each for eternity, like lovers do. Of course I would never leave Lizanne for even a beauty like the lion.

After a long time, two or three minutes, I imagine, my *ego* kicks in, "Take his picture." Still eye-to-eye, I slowly reached down with my right hand for my camera. Suddenly, I sensed something different; he was rising, he was looking at me differently. Beyond thinking, I charged him, yelling loud, with arms raised. He sprang into the air—a full-grown, big lion—and bolted up the hill. Gaining twenty feet in one stride, he flew up the hill, and in a few seconds, disappeared into the redwoods.

For a moment, I was mesmerized at what just happened. Then, I was overjoyed. I knew that from then on, I would have no fear of him, that we had had "an understanding," that we had broken bread together. Walking on, I felt giddy with the gift of his appearance. Only recently, I had won new clarity regarding my masculine energy, and had half-jokingly said, "You can come out, now." Before I knew it, there he was, and in a most auspicious form, a king, no less.

When I got home, I was still buzzing from the experience and pored over books about animals, researched their symbolic meaning, and sought new levels of value in my encounter with the King. I felt that I had been anointed by him to fulfill my duty as an Earth Keeper.

I emailed Alberto about the incident, and received an email back.

"Fine medicine work. You are being called. Power is stalking you to serve big time."

On the Road of Destiny

Driving down the Pacific Coast Highway in Malibu during a bright day, Lizanne and I were looking forward to a great lunch at a favorite Italian restaurant of ours, one with a garden patio.

"What're you going to have for lunch?" Lizanne asked.

"Oh, a glass of champagne to toast you," I replied.

"Of course you are, but what are you going to eat?"

"Ahh, a big plate of seafood linguini with their special marinara sauce made from home-grown organic tomatoes."

"Yeah? Sounds delicious." Looking me over quick, she nodded to herself. "And I imagine you'd still look cute as a *fat* Earth Keeper," she quipped.

Involuntarily patting my belly, I groaned, "Thanks for the reminder, Miss Wisdom Keeper."

"You're very welcome, Mr. Earth Keeper... although you've never really told me what that really means."

"Oh, Lizanne, I finally got it, it's all been coming together. Imagine, we're a group of individuals and corporations buying up large tracts of pristine wilderness slated for development. We then ensure that it *doesn't* get developed! We're going to preserve its natural beauty as a great legacy for future generations."

"I like that," Lizanne said.

"Wait, I'm not done," I continued exuberantly. "Then, we set aside a small portion for development so that we can use the profits to restore, cultivate, and upkeep the land. Finally, we'd donate ten percent of those profits to build urban parks and organic food gardens in every town and city in the country. So imagine, you're sitting on a park bench, and you see a little kid come up proudly presenting his mother with zucchini, corn, and a juicy ripe tomato that he himself had grown. Wouldn't that just be great?"

"It would be, it really would be," Lizanne replied, as she leaned against me affectionately. "And you know what, I change my mind," she continued. "You *should* get that seafood linguini, and I even recommend an extra portion of that yummy tomato sauce."

With one arm on the wheel, and the other around Lizanne, I cruised the gentle curves of the Pacific Coast Highway, ever ready to show up at the next spot of my destiny, a steaming plate of seafood linguini.

QUESTIONS FOR DISCUSSION

Chapter 1:

1. "Whether you are a lion or gazelle, as soon as the sun rises, run like hell. Eat or be eaten!" Is this true if you want to succeed? If not, why not?

2. "Time is money." Do you agree?

3. What to you is "the American Dream" as it is generally understood? Do you aspire to this goal? If not, why not?

4. What is a psychic to you? Charlatans or seers? Are you answering from direct experience?

5. If Adam had "everything," (the house, the income, the Country Club membership) what's his problem? Why was he so conflicted?

Chapter 2:

6. What is a "wounded child" that the therapists mentioned? Why is it significant? Do you have one?

7. In the meeting with the therapist, what's the relation between feeling like a victim and taking responsibility for your own actions?

8. The key to Adam turning his life around had to do with a book that helped him to "look within." What does that mean to you?

9. Though Adam had felt distance and coldness from his mother, he never blamed her. Why?

Chapter 3:

10. In Adam's brother's bookshelf, one book seemed to jump out at him and helped change his life. Have you had such lucky accidents happen to you? Or do you explain them away because it's so irrational?

11. What is a "medicine walk"?

12. Adam kept hearing a "voice" that, reasonable or not, gave him profound advice and encouragement. What do you think is that voice? Is it "real"? Docs it matter?

13. What is the "Red Road" that Adam began studying?

14. What is the "Blue Road"?

Chapter 4:

15. The "voice" that Adam kept hearing seemed to steer him towards dreadful memories of death and pain. Why?

Chapter 5:

16. What is beyond the "Red Road" that Adam discovered?

17. Adam discovered that the only way to explore the the "Yellow Road" is to look within. What does that really mean? Have you ever done this?

18: Does death exist? What does death mean to you?

19. How did Adam's discovery of the "Yellow Road" affect his business?

20. In *A Course in Miracles*, Adam read, *The road to enlightenment requires forgiveness*. Why do you think that was so important to him? Who did he have to forgive?

21. What is a Vision Quest? How can it help you?

Chapter 6:

22. A cleansing ritual was practiced by Adam through "ritual burning." What does that mean? How does it work?

23. Adam's experience with his "ancestral father" came through meditative visions. Though highly unusual, what allowed Adam to accept his experiences, and what did he gain from them?

24. What is a Medicine Bag? How does it benefit its user?

25. Native Americans use the phrase "place of power." What does that signify?

Chapter 7:

26. Adam risked his life walking around Mitten in a blizzard. What was driving him on? How did his connection with the coyote help save him?

27. In Mitten, why did he suddenly put snow and mud slush on his face? Why did he yearn for a deeper connection to the earth?

28. After his jaunt around Mitten, he was filled with doubts. What doubts? Do you blame him? What eventually did he do to ease his mind?

29. Adam repeatedly whispers to himself that his job is not to reason why, but rather to merely "show up." What does that mean to you?

30. What is a "sweat lodge"?

31. After Chief G. went outside of the sweat lodge and retched with agonizing sounds, what did Adam realize that made him fill with gratitude for Chief G.?

Chapter 8:

32. In spite of all the anger, hatred, and vitriol that Gigi unleashed on Adam, he could still feel sadness and compassion for Gigi. What was his attitude that allowed him to do that?

33. Adam learned from *The Art of War* the principle of "invisibility." How did that help him?

34. Adam was asked by Lila, "How does it feel to reclaim yourself?" What does that mean?

35. How did Adam's strange Vision Quest affect Lizanne?

36. Adam loved the statement, "forgiving is for giving." What does that mean to you? What is more difficult and important than forgiving Gigi? Why is it so important to forgive yourself? What did Adam forgive of himself? Have you ever forgiven yourself?

37. What is "soul retrieval," which Adam underwent with his shaman friend, Jon?

38. What was Adam's "Children's Bill of Rights?" Do you agree with it?

39. How did Adam's shamanic perspective influence his business dealings, specifically the Student Housing Project? What do you think he would've done in the past?

40. What is the "Yellow Road"? What happened in Zion National Park that "initiated Adam into the Yellow Road"?

Chapter 9:

41. In the Native American tradition, what is "night stalking"?

42. What was the significance of Adam's past life as a homeless woman? How did it help him with this life?

43. How did Adam's past-life regression help him in this life? How can we accept such an idea as a past life if we can't "prove" it? What do you accept as real even though it can't be "proven"?

44. Which of Adam's past lives was the most fulfilling? In spite of paradise all around, he is troubled by what? What was the lesson for him in this life?

45. What does the Divine Feminine mean?

46. Why, as a kid, did Adam feel a "strange uneasiness" whenever he picked up a knife of any sort? How did it relate to his life as the son of an Indian Chief?

47. What ritual helped Adam forgive himself upon seeing the horrendous deeds he exercised as a Chief's son?

Chapter 10:

48. What is ayahuasca, and how can it help you?

49. In the trip to Peru, the shaman kept telling everyone to trust their feelings and intuition rather intellect. Why? Give examples of how Adam did this, of how he connected to the earth and physicality of Peru.

50. There was talk about everyone's "personal myth." What is it? What's yours?

51. Alberto talked about divorcing and then turning right around and marrying the same kind of woman. How do you see your own repeating patterns?

52. Alberto declares that "all initiations involve a death of sorts." Why should that be? Has this happened in your life?

53. What is the "Blue Road"? How did Adam get initiated into it?

54. Alberto declared a rare opportunity to connect with Mother Earth. The eagle, the jaguar, hummingbird, etc., each have resonance with some aspect of you. What's your take on each of these animals? What animals are special to you, and why?

55. Adam had an old thought of the jungle as a terrible place filled with predators. While in Peru, this whole idea changed. What happened? What was his new interpretation? Do you agree?

56. Name three insights Adam received because of his experience with ayahuasca.

57. To summarize for himself, Adam had great clarity of the "Four Roads." What are they, and how do you see them affecting your life?

Chapter 11:

58. What is the "Silver Road"? What's its distinction from the other Roads?

59. After his journey to Peru, Adam became much more "open-hearted." Give three examples. Has such a shift ever happened with you?

60. What is a "Life Map," and how can it help you?

61. When a large business venture went south because of the financial debacle, how did Adam accept his predicament? How would the "old Adam" have reacted?

62. Why did Adam and Lizanne go to the slums in Cambodia? Would you ever do anything like this?

63. What is a *Homo Luminous?*

64. What are the "Nine Initiation Rites"? Which one spoke loudest to Adam? Why?

65. One Christmas, Adam visited Gigi's family to see his kids. It turned out hellish, filled with rage, accusations, and threats. Knowing how Gigi can be, why did he go? What did he suffer? How did he react? What did he gain?

Chapter 12:

66. While trekking on Holy Mountain, Adam reflected on his four "personal angels." Who were they, and how did they each help in his transformation? Do you have personal "angels"? How do they help you?

67. In the initiations as Wisdom Keepers, Earth Keepers, and Star Keepers, one of them protects you from the great planetary changes that are upon us. It also turns you from *homo sapiens* into *Homo Luminous*. What does this mean to you? Do you believe it? On what basis do you make your opinion?

68. During the journey back down the Holy Mountain, Alberto told Adam, "Looks like you're no longer a half-baked human. You've been fully cooked." What happened that made him say that? How "cooked" are you?

69. According to Adam, what's the difference between fate and destiny?

70. Adam's first big venture as an Earth Keeper was his purchase of Red Tail Ranch in Big Sur. The land, partners, and money all seemed to fall in his lap, which Adam saw as a confirmation of his self-transformations. What does that mean? Have such "lucky accidents" ever happened to you? How so?

71. Adam had a terrible accident with an ATV and could have died. Though filled with pain and suffering, he saw the ordeal as an initiation to the land. Why did he say that? Have you had similar "baptisms by fire"?

72. After Adam's audience with "the King," Alberto told him, "Fine medicine work. You are being called. Power is stalking you to serve." What does that mean?

73. What is your destiny?

ABOUT THE AUTHOR

For the past 27 years ADAM C. HALL has brokered, acquired, developed, and redeveloped a broad range of real estate asset classes. He has extensive expertise in structured finance and has raised in excess of $1.5 billion in equity and debt from private and institutional sources alike. Adam is President and CEO of SCV Capital Partners, a private equity firm providing sustainable capital to new world ventures. As a leading impact investor, he is dedicated to the quadruple bottom line of Profits, People, Planet, and Peace. He is also the Managing Partner and Founder of EKA Legacy Partners, LLC—aka *The EarthKeeper Alliance*—a for-profit company that invests in large tracts of land. The company is dedicated to the *conservation, preservation,* and *restoration of the planet* with limited sustainable development and has received the highest five star GIIS rating and B Corp status as a socially and environmentally responsible company.

His passion for the environment has been recognized as bold and fearless. As an ecologist and "eartholgist," Adam entertains, educates, and enlightens with wisdom and knowledge. He is recognized as an accomplished speaker on ecology, environment, eMergent leadership, human innovation, and personal transformation. He is a board member of Earth Service Inc., a non-profit organization whose "Keep the Earth, Keep it Wild" campaign is focused on the greening of cities through the education of youth in urban gardens and investing in first stage companies promoting environmental entrepreneurship.

Adam is a father of three daughters and is a grandfather. He is a believer in lifelong learning, and enjoys reading, golfing, biking, skiing, hiking, yoga, and adventure travel. He is an avid student of *A Course in Miracles*, the Mayan Calendar, and the Tao Te Ching and Hua Hu Ching. He is a member of several environmental causes. He resides in Santa Barbara, California.

THE EARTHKEEPER WAY

A way of becoming, doing, and being on earth.

"The Earth is my Witness."
—Buddha

WITNESS: *a person whose existence or condition attests to or proves something. A living witness to generosity, a witness to the authenticity of being, attesting to the truth.*

KEEPER: *to maintain (some action), especially in accordance with specific requirements, a promise, to keep watch, to keep step, a keeper of humanity.*

"Earth . . . she calls us now to step out of being the insolent child.
Calls us to return to love and keep her."
—Lizanne Judge

EARTHONOMICS: *a holistic relationship between earth and material prosperity; a balanced exchange of goods and services that serves to preserve the earth; the interaction of humankind and the earth that aligns conservation with demand; a prosperous earth supports a wealthy humanity.*

"We can be green in both senses of the word."
—Adam C. Hall

Be the *witness*, become the *keeper*
of our humanity by practicing *earthonomics*

GAIA BLESSING

With you Great Mother Earth
We transform
With you GAIA, we now serve
With you Earth Mother
We now return to Divine Love

With you GAIA
We now become Light
With you Mother Earth
We are now One

With you GAIA
We now heal ourselves
With you Mother Earth
We now awaken again

Now, you too, Great Mother Earth
are healed

Heaven is where we stand
We now stand with you our
beloved Mother Earth

—Adam C. Hall
12.21.12
www.earthkeeper.us

JOIN US

We are all EarthKeepers!

The Book
www.earthkeeper.us
In-depth commentary
Share your feelings, experiences, and questions about *The EarthKeeper*

The Alliance
www.earthkeeperalliance.com
EarthKeeper Alliance is a for-profit investment fund, acquiring large tracts of well-located pristine land in the United States that is slated for development. We Undevelop, ensuring the property remains forever in its natural state while setting aside a small portion for sustainable development. We donate 10% of the profits to support the two initiatives of the EarthKeeper movement.

The Movement
www.EarthkeeperMovement.org
You are invited to join these initiatives:
Education of Youth in Inner City Gardens
and
One Piece of Trash a Day

Visit to receive a free e-video book
"21 Thought Leaders for the 21st Century"

Twitter: @EarthkeeperUS

Keep the earth—keep it wild!

QR CODES

The Book

The Alliance

The Movement

Other Offerings from Agape Media

Agape Media International (AMI) is dedicated to promoting artists and art forms that uplift the human spirit and inspiring individuals to contribute their gifts and talents to the creation of a world that works for everyone.

Books

Michael Bernard Beckwith | *TranscenDance Expanded* (Book & CD Set)

Cynthia Occelli | *Resurrecting Venus*

Dianne Burnett | *The Road to Reality*

Charles Holt | *Intuitive Rebel*

Carl Studna | *Click!—Choosing Love One Frame at a Time*

Michael Bernard Beckwith | *The Answer Is You*

Michael Bernard Beckwith | *40-Day Mind Fast Soul Feast*

Michael Bernard Beckwith | *Life Visioning*

Michael Bernard Beckwith | *Spiritual Liberation*

George & Sedena Cappannelli | *Do Not Go Quietly!—A Guide to Living Consciously and Aging Wisely for People Who Weren't Born Yesterday*

Lee McCormick, Kelly Sullivan Walden, Francis Rico & Gini Gentry | *Dreaming Heaven* (JourneyBook & DVD Set)

Adam C. Hall | *The EarthKeeper*

Ester Nicholson | *Soul Recovery*

Audio Programs by Michael Bernard Beckwith:

The Life Visioning Process

The Life Visioning Kit

The Rhythm of a Descended Master

Your Soul's Evolution

Living from the Overflow

DVDs

The Answer Is You

Spiritual Liberation, the Movie

Superwise Me!

Living in the Revelation

Music CDs

Music From The PBS Special - The Answer Is You feat. Will.I.Am, Siedah Garrett, Niki Haris, Rickie Byars Beckwith, Agape International Choir

Jami Lula & Spirit In The House | *There's A Healin' Goin' On*

Charles Holt | *I Am*

Charles Holt | *Rushing Over Me*

Rickie Byars Beckwith | *Supreme Inspiration*

Ester Nicholson | *Child Above The Sun*

Ben Dowling | The *Path of Peace*

Michael Bernard Beckwith | *TranscenDance*

Inspirational Oracle Cards

Layla Love | *She of God* Oracle Cards

Kelly Sullivan Walden | Dream Cards

Michael Bernard Beckwith | Life Lift-Off Cards

www.agapeme.com

For more information regarding
Agape International Spiritual Center
visit *www.agapelive.com*

Please Support These Outstanding Organizations

Sierra Club
Protecting Communities and Wild
Places
www.sierraclub.org

NRDC Natural Resources Defense
Council
The Earth Best Defense
www.nrdc.org

LOHAS Lifestyles of Health and
Sustainability
Healthy, People, Planet, Profits
www.lohas.com

Wiser Earth
Connecting Communities of Action
www.wiser.org

HeartMath
Creating a Deeper Richer Experience
of Life
www.hearthmath.com

Earth Island Institute
Leadership That Sustains the
Environment
www.earthisland.org

Trust for Public Land
Conserving Land for People
www.tpl.org

EarthWays Foundation
Rainforest Satiability
www.ECOfloresta.org

The Pachamama Alliance
Creating a Spiritual Filled Presence
on the Planet
www.pachamama.org

The Nature Conservancy
Protecting Nature, Preserving Life
www.nature.org

Earth Institute
Mobilizing Science Education and
Public Policy
www.earth.columbia.edu

Amazon Watch
Protecting Rainforest & Indigenous
People
www.amazonwatch.org

The Shift Network
Birthing Humanity
www.theshiftnetwork.com

Rain Forest Alliance
Ensuring Sustainable Livelihood
www.rainforestalliance.org

Global Green USA
Building a More Sustainable Future
www.globalgreen.org

LOA Tree
Live for a Better World
www.Loatree.com

WiserEarth

WiserEarth is a global village for sharing and kinship-building. Originally founded in 2002 by U.S. environmentalist Paul Hawken, WiserEarth's mission is to help advocates of social justice, indigenous rights, and environmental stewardship to discover one another, form partnerships, and magnify their impact through collaboration As of this writing, WiserEarth networks over 114,000 organizations and 75,000 members from every country except North Korea.

At its core, WiserEarth believes in the power of building alliances. As society becomes increasingly globalized, leveraging humanity's joint assets is the key to yielding positive social and environmental change. Collaborative efforts offer an incredible opportunity for us to harness our collective abilities, to share, connect and become more effective in addressing the complex, interrelated issues facing this generation and those to come. This is why WiserEarth's main project is Wiser.org, the online network that serves to connect grassroots leaders from around the world.

In order to create truly constructive dialogue, however, the men and women who tirelessly advocate for global health must meet face-to-face. Effective alliances rely on a foundation of trust forged through personal connection. That is why WiserEarth has scaled up its support to bring grassroots leaders together in local assemblies—called "WiserLocals"—around the world. WiserEarth has already witnessed over 100 WiserLocal gatherings, in nearly 20 countries, and these numbers continue to grow.

The folks at WiserEarth believe that by connecting local to global, by bridging online tools with offline collaboration, social and environmental change advocates can harness the power of collective intelligence, reduce duplication of effort, and fully realize their potential for global stewardship.

Check out WiserEarth and its projects at *www.Wiser.org*.

FACTS ABOUT
WISER.ORG
The Social Network for Sustainability

70,000 MEMBERS